Between Science and Literature

Between Science and Literature

AN INTRODUCTION
TO AUTOPOETICS

IRA LIVINGSTON

Foreword by
N. Katherine Hayles

UNIVERSITY OF ILLINOIS PRESS
Urbana and Chicago

© 2006 Ira Livingston
All rights reserved
Manufactured in the United States of America
♾ This book is printed on acid-free paper.
1 2 3 4 5 C P 5 4 3 2 1

Library of Congress Cataloging-in-Publication Data
Livingston, Ira, 1956–
Between science and literature: an introduction to autopoetics /
Ira Livingston; foreword by N. Katherine Hayles.
p.   cm.
Includes bibliographical references and index.
ISBN-13: 978-0-252-03008-6 (ISBN-13/cloth: alk. paper)
ISBN-10: 0-252-03008-7 (ISBN-10/cloth: alk. paper)
ISBN-13: 978-0-252-07254-3 (ISBN-13/paper: alk. paper)
ISBN-10: 0-252-07254-5 (ISBN-10/paper: alk. paper)
1. Literature—Philosophy. 2. Poetics. I. Title.
PN49.L538   2005
801—dc22   2005006664

As to those for whom to work hard, to begin and begin again, to attempt and to be mistaken, to go back and rework everything from top to bottom, and still find reason to hesitate from one step to the next—as to those, in short, for whom to work in the midst of uncertainty and apprehension is tantamount to failure, all I can say is that clearly we are not from the same planet.

—Michel Foucault, *The Use of Pleasure*

In a certain sense one cannot take too much care in handling philosophical mistakes, they contain so much truth.

—Ludwig Wittgenstein, *The Wittgenstein Reader*

Contents

Writing Between

N. KATHERINE HAYLES

Years ago I had the exhilarating—and frustrating—experience of coteaching an interdisciplinary seminar on reflexivity with a physicist and philosopher. The physicist led us through Gödel's incompleteness theorem to show how reflexivity entered into mathematics and physics; the philosopher guided us through Aristotle, Kant, Fichte, and others to trace the roots of reflexivity in the philosophical tradition; I added readings by Borges, Hofstadter, and Calvino. Yet in the end, the students appeared to be even more confused about what reflexivity was than when the seminar began; whether this can be counted as progress I leave to a Zen master to decide. In any event, despite our best efforts our stated goal of illuminating the expansive range and importance of reflexivity in a variety of fields certainly fell short of its mark.

I am all the more impressed, then, with Ira Livingston's achievement in *Between Science and Literature: An Introduction to Autopoetics.* Instructed by the lessons of Niklas Luhmann's systems theory, Deleuze and Guattari's rhizomatic *Thousand Plateaus,* Humberto Maturana's autopoiesis, and Foucault's epistemic analyses, he creates a powerful—dare I say seductive?—demonstration of reflexivity that argues for its seminal importance as the mode of performance characteristic of the postmodern era. Sensitive to the sweeping nature of such a claim, he is careful to avoid a "presentist" error that would locate reflexivity exclusively as a postmodernist phenomenon, illustrating its dynamics with a wide diversity of examples ranging from the "See Spot run" primers used to teach reading in the 1950s to Romantic poems and contemporary popular culture. The argument, rather, maintains that reflexivity in the contemporary era has become so interwoven with globalization, capitalist dynamics, scientific theories, verbal creations, and popular culture that it qualifies as the governing episteme of this period.

Writing with the easy confidence of someone who has thought deeply and well about his tutor texts, Livingston draws on many theorists without being overmastered by any. He is open to the lessons of many, but nearly everything he uses he also modifies at the same time. From Maturana, for example, he takes the idea of a system whose sole object is to reproduce itself, but he crucially modifies Maturana's autopoietic theory by insisting that all systems are continuously open to the environment and networked with other systems. From Luhmann he takes the important idea that a system copies into itself the system/environment distinction fundamental to its construction as a system, but he also modifies Luhmann by blurring the boundaries between system and environment, interpreting them through the rhizomatic dynamics of Deleuze and Guattari's "Body without Organs." He learns from Foucault but also insists that the circulation between physical materialities and discursive structures operates through continuous feedback loops that give physical realities a discursive dimension and systems of discourse physical effects. This part of his argument transforms into an analysis of the "science wars" as the reification of a false dichotomy between words and things. As he lucidly shows, words have performative effects that make them operate like things, while things have rhetorical dimensions that inescapably shape their significance and meaning. Above all, he sees systems bound together in a network through which flows of power and meaning circulate, each affecting the others and affected by them. Interfaces and boundaries, both within systems and between them, become the foci of special attention as sites where these flows become almost too evident—places, that is, where the dynamics that reveal these interconnections are "hidden in plain sight."

This book is more, however, than a discursive argument. It is also an experiment in rhetorical form and the performative possibilities of creating gaps and fissures (should we call them interfaces?) between discrete sections where connections are implied rather than explicated, left deliberately ambiguous so as to maximize the diverse ways in which readers can put the parts together. In a sense, the text exploits the radical polysemy of hypertext, though the exponential proliferation of possible pathways is achieved not through linking structures but through a certain cognitive indeterminacy and ambiguity about how the parts connect. Moving easily between homey examples, autobiographical narrative, and dense theoretical argumentation, *Between Science and Literature* performs what it argues for, the importance of "betweenness." Within its own body it performs the importance of performance, especially the flows between its parts and the sites where it astutely identifies and locates the flows within and between other bodies. It is, in other words, intensely reflexive about its desire to privilege reflexivity as the episteme in which we are now currently living.

No account of this book would be complete without recognizing the centrality of pleasure to its methodology and rhetorical strategies. Immediately apparent is the pleasure of engaging with writing this apparently relaxed and playful—effects usually achieved, of course, only through meticulous and painstaking attention to tone, rhetoric, and readerly response. From the first line the book draws us in with direct addresses to "you" the reader, with anecdotes drawn from the writer's past and present, with its everyday common sense and examples, with its confident yet modest tone. As the pages mount, the examples become more thoroughly analyzed, the argument more densely worked and reworked, leading to another kind of pleasure of working through challenging material and critically evaluating its claims. As the book draws to a close the tone becomes more political and polemical and the implications for politics and ethics more pointedly drawn, leading to yet another pleasure of engaging with passionate commitments strongly argued. The progression exemplifies what still remains the goal of all good literature, to please and to instruct—and to this we must surely now add, to perform and to connect through proliferating reflexive pathways.

Not everyone will agree with Livingston's arguments, conclusions, or even his methodologies. Nor does he imagine that they will. Part of the charm of this book is that it is not afraid to be wrong. Better to lay out a bold vision and make wide claims, this book seems to say, than to draw back into cautious reserve and timid modifications to accommodate critics—often an unfortunate strategy that ends up pleasing no one and losing the value of the initial insights. The insights here are in no danger of being lost, but they do take time and patience to realize fully. This is a book not only to read but also to reread, teasing out its multiple and far-reaching implications by traversing (some of) the multiple pathways it opens for us. And now, if I may take a page from the book that follows and indulge in direct address, dear reader, the rest is up to you.

Acknowledgments

Particular thanks to N. Katherine Hayles for her inspiration and her support of this book and to Joan Catapano, Steve Shaviro, and Susan Squier for their generous readings of the manuscript; to Samuel Delany for responding to my questions about the sources of "The Star Pit"; to Ed Cohen for many discussions (out of which came the term *antirealist naturalism*); to Carlos Simmerling and Hugh Sansom for the cover illustration and design; to Srikanth Mallavarapu for pointing me to Kuhn on Aristotle; and to Jay McRoy for recommending *Blood Music*. Special thanks to Paul Adams for starting the discussions among biologists and humanists (at SUNY–Stony Brook in 1997) that helped to inspire this book. For a variety of discrete advice, friendship, support, and inspiration along the way, thanks first of all to Cliff Siskin—and to Judith Butler, Bruno Clarke, Leonard Cohen, Nicolas Crook, George Cunningham, Judith Friedman, Judith Halberstam, Robert Harvey, Ann Kaplan, David Kazanjian, Dierdre Lynch, Peter Manning, Nick Mirzoeff, Josie Saldana, Jennifer Savran, Lang Walsh, Liam Walsh, and Kathleen Wilson—and to Alex Chasin and finally to Iona Man-Cheong, beyond all acknowledgments, for their love and courage.

Parts of chapters 13 and 14 are revised from my essay "Defrosting: Self/Poetry/Power/Science," which appeared in *Poetics/Politics,* edited by Amitava Kumar (New York: St. Martin's, 1999). Scattered parts of chapters 15 and 17 are revised from my essays "The No-Trump Bid on Romanticism and Gender," in *Romanticism and Gender,* edited by Anne Janowitz, *Essays and Studies* annual volume (Woodbridge, Suffolk, England: 1998), and "Indiscretions: Of Bodies, Genders, and Technologies," in *Processed Lives,* edited by Jennifer Terry and Melodie Calvert (London and New York: Routledge, 1997).

1

The Livingthinglikeness of Language

This book is an introduction to a constellation of ideas about self-reference and performativity. What these ideas have in common, to start with, is that they develop alternatives to the narrowly realist view of referential language. The focus on this common feature makes the book an introduction to the most important axis of literary and cultural theory throughout the past century. Along the way the reader will find various definitions of terms, examples and vignettes, images and catchphrases, exercises, and thought experiments that are intended to manufacture new intuitions about words *as* things.

But the axis of literary and cultural theory of the past century is turning, so this book also faces the future: as Allen Ginsberg said, "I'm putting my queer shoulder to the wheel." The work of this book is best described as the *groundwork* of creating and expanding the interzone between, on one hand, self-reference and performativity in literary and cultural theory and, on the other, related notions of autopoiesis and self-organizing systems in biology and other sciences and social sciences. What has made such an interzone possible is nothing less than an ongoing sea change in the relations among ways of knowing and engaging the world, in the *discursive ecology*. This book is a synthesis, an attempt to assess the basic conceptual and historical cruxes of this interzone and to push and pull them a little further. My general term for the interzone is *autopoetics,* that is, the study of "self-making" systems. The more specific term *autopoiesis* was first coined in 1972 by Chilean biologist Humberto Maturana to describe the biological "self-making" of living creatures (see chapter 13) and most famously adapted since then by German sociologist Niklas Luhmann, who describes the same process in social systems. My focus is on related processes in the realm of meaning, language, and culture. I have removed the *i* from *autopoiesis* in order to vernacularize the word but also to mark what I would like to remove from the concept (its reliance on specific, ideologically bound notions of the self, the I) and, by referencing *poetics* more pointedly, to mark the realms of culture and meaning I would like to include.

When I say that the work of this book is *groundwork,* what I mean is just about the opposite of laying down a stable foundation and a lot more like Wittgenstein's saying that "the whole of language must be thoroughly ploughed up" (277) and that it is philosophy's job to do so. This kind of groundwork goes through the workings of language, minutely turning and overturning as it goes, creating a more fertile ground in which new kinds of things can grow. "My propositions are elucidatory in this way," wrote Wittgenstein (shifting the metaphor): "he who understands me finally recognises them as senseless, when he has climbed out through them, on them, over them. (He must so to speak throw away the ladder, after he has climbed up on it.)" (31).

Theoretical biologist Stuart Kauffman once explained to an interviewer that his own early shift from philosophy into biology had been catalyzed by his realization that "if I had to choose, I would rather be Einstein than Wittgenstein" (cited in Waldrop 105). In other words, he preferred to make discoveries about the real things of hard science rather than the mere words and ideas of philosophy. But the title of Kauffman's subsequent book, *Investigations*—"blatantly borrowed," as he puts it (50), from Wittgenstein's *Philosophical Investigations*—signals another shift. Wittgenstein became exemplary for Kauffman in having followed his own advice and "thrown away the ladder" of his own more narrow early view of language ("logical atomism") in favor of a more dynamic engagement with the *livingthinglikeness* of language, the forms of language constituting something like "forms of life." Kauffman replays this shift in his own Wittgensteinization, or, rather, he got to a point where he no longer had to choose between Einstein and Wittgenstein and could *split the difference,* though it should also be noted that Einsteinian things and Wittgensteinian words were already moving into more of the same neighborhood anyway. The shift that keeps happening here is not Wittgenstein's or Kauffman's but part of the long-term sea change in ways of knowing the world, little waves on the surface of a big wave passing through all that we know.

The form of this book is part of its argument. It is made up of a series of linked essays, meaning that the chapters and subchapters echo and build on each other in such a way that they can be either read in sequence or browsed individually. In other words, they are semiautonomous, linked together not like a chain but more like chain mail—or, better yet, like a school of fish or a flock of birds. The multiple pieces operate according to a kind of holographic principle: each contains images of the others and of some partial version of the whole. So if you are reading this for the first time and you already understand it, you can stop reading now, since everything in the book has already been squashed into this preface, this paragraph. However, for example, those who have come to this paragraph having read other parts of the book (chapter 20 in particular) will have caught other resonances cleverly concealed here.

ASIDE

A Reader's Guide to Autopoiesis.   The early chapters of this book spin literary and discursive theory in an autopoetic direction, but the autopoiesis concept is not engaged as such until chapter 13, so those who want more of a sense of autopoiesis up front are invited to read chapter 13 first. To begin exploring further (*after* you have read this book, of course), I recommend starting with Luhmann's great nutshell version of autopoiesis as social theory, "The Autopoiesis of Social Systems" (*Essays* 1–20). Bruce Clarke's essay "Strong Constructivism" and Cary Wolfe's 1998 *Critical Environments* (especially pages 52–84) are both great introductions to Luhmannian autopoietic theory in action and in broader theoretical context (and, dear reader, please notice that these three recommendations add up to only sixty pages—but William Rasch's book *Niklas Luhmann's Modernity* would make a good addition). For an introduction to autopoiesis as a way of thinking about literary texts, David Roberts's essay "Self-Reference in Literature" (Baecker 27–45) and Joseph Tabbi's *Cognitive Fictions* (especially the introduction and first chapter) are good places to start. For a historicization of the notion of system that informs the development of the autopoiesis concept, I suggest Cliff Siskin's article "The Year of the System" or his book *Blaming the System,* and for situating systems theory generally in its recent discursive history and technological investments, N. Katherine Hayles's *How We Became Posthuman.* For an introduction to autopoietic biology, Humberto Maturana and Francisco Varela's 1973 essay "Autopoiesis: The Organization of the Living" (59-138) still works well.

2

Words and Things

This book takes off from a simple proposition: that language is kin to the world it inhabits; language *bears witness* to the world. Since I was trained as a literary theorist, I consider this mostly as a proposition and less as a truth, but the proposition itself suggests (in this case anyway) that there may be less difference between these two than you might think, so you can suit yourself.

What the proposition means, for a start, is that language cannot be understood as a God-given gift or a free human creation or a tool to be bent to human will, but only as an emergent and semiautonomous phenomenon, something more like galaxies, ecosystems, and bacteria. *Language* is shorthand here for a whole sprawling and heterogeneous network that can include everything from language considered in the abstract to individual utterances, functions and figures and patterns of speech (rhetoric), generic formations such as poems and science fiction, discourses and disciplines articulated with large-scale institutional structures (such as religion, literature, biology, and so on), and all that even more sprawling and ill-defined tangle called *culture.*

To start to get an idea of the kinship of nature and culture in this case, one could try to imagine what it would mean to have a *physics* or an *ecology of culture.* These are *metaphors,* since physics and ecology were developed with reference to different kinds of phenomena, but it is important to keep in mind that such differences among phenomena may be themselves neither natural nor eternal; they have been very selectively elaborated in modern language, discourse, and culture—and they are subject to ongoing rearrangement. Increasingly, in fact, there seem to be a number of concepts that move with relative ease—that fly under the radar—within and between the nature/culture divide otherwise so definitive for modern knowledge, concepts and paradigms such as *system, information, emergence, evolution, diversity, relativity, chaos, ecology, complexity;* these concepts perform *transcoding* operations among various realms of the knowledge network.

Although the traffic between the knowledge realms of nature and culture is as old as the realms themselves, modernity consigns much of the traffic to a black market. To take some easy examples, *science fiction* not only is illegitimate science but has also mostly been illegitimate literature as well; the use of metaphor, supposed to make good poetry, has mostly been thought to produce bad science. Though the traffic is changing (and that's what this book is about), it might be grandiose—at least at this time—to think that any constellation of transcoding concepts could be made to coalesce into a science or metascience of its own that could fully straddle the nature/culture divide. Likewise, the recent rise of science studies—a set of related fields that investigate the sciences as social and cultural phenomena—certainly does not mean that science studies has achieved the status of a science, much less that of a transcendent metascience, any more than Marxism was able to deliver a "nonideological study of ideology." Indeed, there is some question as to whether science studies is a stable discipline at all, especially since it has not achieved much of an institutional foothold. If no pretender to the throne of metascience is on the verge of being elevated, then perhaps science itself is being dragged down, back down into the mud-wrestling ring with other vulgar and popular knowledges? This seems to be what some scientists fear. Although disciplinary privilege may be in the process of being redistributed, I am much more interested in how the *kinds* of knowledge are changing than where they fit into an imaginary hierarchy, especially since the idea of a single hierarchy of knowledges seems as misguided as a hierarchy of living creatures. One might as well try to ascertain whether humans, plants, or viruses have been more successful.

The ecology of disciplines is changing as all of the webs of language, people, money, and technology get woven more tightly and widely. The coevolution and interdependence of disciplines are becoming more obvious, and all these changes in the web contribute in turn to changing the overall knowledge climate, shifting discursive niches and allowing for the emergence of new discursive creatures. Sometimes I would like to believe that these more mobile creatures—scurrying around the feet of the giant, sluggish disciplines—will inherit the earth, but I also know that they are not always as warm and fuzzy as the story would have it.

In many ways, too, the kinship of language and the world is an old and even an obsolete idea, part of a way of understanding that got left high and dry three centuries ago and has been repeatedly displaced since then. The story of how "the profound kinship of language with the world was . . . dissolved" is recounted in Foucault's *Order of Things* (43; as retitled from the French *Les mots et les choses*, literally *Words and Things*). But in another sense such a kinship is also new, even premature, part of a current reconfiguration of ways of knowing the world or, rather, a rewiring of our brains along with our worlds.

In this sense the paradigm seems mostly to serve ideologies of globalization and capitalist triumphalism that accompany an emerging world order that Michael Hardt and Antonio Negri call simply *Empire* (that is, *Empire* with a capital *E*, not modern imperialism but an altogether new global order of sovereignty). The idea of the kinship of language and the world in their mutual reconfigurations lends itself to a vaguely mystical New Age sense of connection and participation, to a kind of mock-Buddhist picture of a world of ongoing kaleidoscopic reconfigurations. This is most often (as I will discuss later) an aestheticizing and anesthetizing image of transnational capital in its swirling flows, its saturations and ongoing restructurings of all relations, but the *critical* potential of the paradigm has also begun to be tapped into.

So how does one go about separating the proposition from an ideology that seems to be so much in its grain, or is this even possible? Lenin faced such a problem as he considered how Marxists might make use of knowledge generated by mainstream economics, even though, "as a whole, the professors of economics are nothing but scientific salesman of the capitalist class." Acknowledging, nonetheless, that "you'll not make the slightest progress in the investigation of new economic phenomena unless you have recourse to the works of these 'salesman,'" Lenin challenged Marxists "to be able to master and adapt the achievements of these 'salesmen' . . . and to be able to *lop off their reactionary tendency*" (83; emphasis added). This challenge could well serve as a motto for this project, though history doesn't allow us to be so sanguine that reactionary tendencies can simply be "lopped off."

Even so, it may be that in another sense the idea of the kinship of words and things is *too radical* to be fully embraced either by scientists or by scholars of language and culture, at least insofar as it would require too much rethinking of their most fundamental working hypotheses. By the same token, though, it offers a way through the impasse between the sciences and their humanist critics in science studies. This impasse, sometimes known as the "science wars," got a whole lot uglier in 1996 when New York University physicist Alan Sokal managed to get a phony science studies article published in the humanities journal *Social Text.* Sokal claimed that the publication of his bogus article, which was full of extreme claims and bad science, showed that science studies was itself a bogus field with no real standards; the editors said they'd included his article in spite of its overstatements and theoretical naïveté (and in spite of Sokal's refusal to make revisions they'd requested) in their eagerness to encourage practicing scientists to join the discussion (especially, of course, if they seemed to be defectors to the humanist side). In any case, he wheeled in his gift and they accepted it, hollow and wooden as it was.

It is easy enough for each side to caricature the other. The cultural theorists in the humanities, one might say, like to show how science mistakes language for the world. In this account, scientific realism is like a kind of disavowed narcissism: having unwittingly fallen in love with its own reflection on the surface of things, science naively mistakes the thinly veiled projection of its own ideologies for universal and unmediated truth. This is what Marx meant (for example) when he said that Darwin had found "among beasts and plants his English society with its division of labor, competition . . . and the Malthusian struggle for existence" (157). More recent developments of this kind of critique of science are often lumped together under the term *constructionism,* which refers to the way scientific theory and practice are actively shaped and colored—constructed—by their social, ideological, and cultural contexts.

The sciences have lots of security and legitimacy but, by the same token, also a lot to lose (especially in times of downsizing and shifting paradigms), so their regal disdain for cultural theory sometimes gives way to hysterical and self-righteous fury. The world hangs in the balance, we are told. All the grand edifice of modernity painstakingly built since the Enlightenment is threatened, and any deviation from scientific realism is a backsliding step on a slippery slope to the morass of irrationality and barbarism that lies around us—and in us. This is how entrenched privilege, which always thinks the world revolves around it, argues when it feels threatened, understanding the slightest relativization of its power as total catastrophe. As another besieged monarch said, "Après nous, le déluge."

On the other hand, scientists tend to think that their cultural critics mistake the world for language. In this account, constructionism is a naive idealism that imagines material nature to be a kind of will-o'-the-wisp that offers no resistance to any interpretation whatsoever, a frictionless fiction. At the same time, though, constructionism is also caricatured as a hypersophisti-

cated theory that defies the most basic common sense (which is, not coincidentally, also a pretty good description of most of the important scientific
theories of the past century). To use Sokal's example, with its obvious rage
and violence: you can believe what you like about how gravity is a social and
cultural construct, but if I push you out a window, you'll still fall.

Interestingly, the same kind of argument works the other way around:
you can believe what you like about the objectivity of a scientific account
of things, but it will still be permeated with ideology. In other words, humanists can say to scientists about politics and language and culture what
scientists say to humanists about the physical world and the laws of nature:
in the words of an old TV commercial, "You're soaking in it!"

This symmetry points to what makes the impasse between scientists and
humanists so intractable: not the intensity with which the two parties disagree, but rather an unacknowledged and wrongheaded agreement between
them. They fight like cats tied together by their tails. What ties them together
is a common severing: both scientists and humanists tend to overstate the
independence of language from the world. Each begins by treating words
and things as separate and then offers to connect them, though in rather
different ways.

Science, one might say, offers to nail words to things. In this view, language
is fundamentally referential rather than creative, but there is a lot of slippage
between words and things. Ideally, words—or, more generally, categories
in language—should correspond perfectly to naturally occurring kinds of
things, that is, to what are often called the "joints of nature," places where
one kind of thing ends and another begins or where they are articulated together. Ideally, language is conceived as a space of pure, undistorted reference
to (or representation of) the world, rather like the controlled conditions of
a scientific experiment.

To say that language is referential—to anyone who studies language—is
about like saying "the sun rises" to an astronomer. You can get pretty far with
the idea of referential language—just as those who believed the earth was the
center of the universe were able to massage their paradigm for centuries to
make quite accurate astronomical predictions. One might even argue that an
inability to see beyond the referential dimension of language is an asset for
scientists, one that makes it easier to sustain belief in the scientific enterprise.
For many scientists, in fact, the term *self-referential* simply means *invalid,*
referring to a kind of self-reinforcing circular reasoning. But this kind of
rigidity works only up to a point. You can understand playing pool as pure
geometry, but if you want to know why some of your shots are going astray,

you'll have to start to understand the physics of the game: increasingly, to disavow all but the referential dimension of language will produce not only a very rudimentary understanding of language but a very constrained science as well. In fact, the increasing recognition and incorporation of ideas of self-reference and circularity into scientific paradigms is arguably one of the leading features of current shifts in knowledge.

You might say that Ferdinand de Saussure, the founder of structuralist linguistics, was the Copernicus of the study of language and culture, displacing *things* from the center of the language system. Saussure taught his students in the 1910s that the view of language as a referential nomenclature "stifles any inquiry into the true nature of linguistic structure" (16). Instead, Saussure taught that linguistic signs are arbitrary and language is a "self-contained whole" (10), a system of interrelational differences with no positive terms. In fact, the idea of the closure and autonomy of language goes back at least to the eighteenth century. For at least that long poets and novelists had been making related arguments about literature, namely, that their autonomy makes literary works subject to judgment only according to their own internal consistency and aesthetic complexity and not according to their verisimilitude.

This principle of autonomy has had many subsequent cultural incarnations, such as the "art for art's sake" of the movement known as aestheticism (in the 1890s) or the New Criticism movement of the 1950s and '60s. New Critics, for example, insisted on an essential literariness that distinguishes such works from all other productions of language and on the autonomy and integrity of individual works of literature as systems unto themselves. This insistence on distinctiveness tends to extend to an individual author's body of work, to genres, and to good literature as opposed to bad. This is not to say that New Criticism considered individual literary works (or genres or bodies of work) in a vacuum, but that it put autonomy first and relationality second.

The thing about autonomy, though, is that it's not ever autonomous. For example, it's easy to see (in hindsight, anyway) the broad outline of how New Criticism participated in a dominant ethos of 1950s North America with its postwar insistence on hard-edged order. In other words, New Criticism was not an autonomous or disinterested theory of literature but one that marched to the same drums as the emergent suburbs and sexualities of the 1950s. The point here is that the idea of autonomy and distinction is not only not autonomous; it's also not exclusively or primarily an *idea* but part of a real way of ordering the world.

In an even broader sense, self-organizing systems themselves are a defining feature of modernity. It has long been commonplace to define modernity as an increasing set of internal differentiations and specializations in society, economy, knowledge. This is not just an additive increase in complexity but to some extent the formation of something different in kind, involving new kinds of *separations and linkages* among systems and the subsystems that are themselves "autonomous, operatively closed component systems" (Luhmann, *Observations* 12): in this account, modernity *is* systematization. Independence and interdependence are two sides of the same coin here: subsystems become more interdependent and more autonomous at the same time. Such systematization is itself a kind of self-sustaining and fractal epidemic, generating divisions of labor as well as of knowledge and of land, heterogeneous complex entities ranging from cities to guilds and professions and corporations, modern nations themselves along with the so-called world system in which they participate. Globalization, we are often told, is the latest phase of this process.

If we grant this account of modernity as increasing self-organization, then the question arises as to how much the paradigm of self-contained and self-sustaining systems is a true description of the world (for example, of the universe as understood by physics and of the world of biology) versus how much it simply echoes and universalizes current economic and epistemological trends. Believe it or not, I will actually answer this question, but only after a detour. The detour, which really describes the path of all the essays in this book, has to begin by questioning the terms of the question, which set up an opposition between a referential theory (one that refers, more or less truthfully, to a world outside of itself) and a self-referential or performative one (that projects or enacts itself as a kind of self-fulfilling prophecy). But don't worry: this questioning of the terms of the question does not lead us further and further from an answer but closer, not further from action and ethics (and into more microscopic navel gazing) but into smarter action and ethics (and, maybe just as important, smarter inaction). The opposition of truth and performativity is not simply undecidable; it is a *false* opposition, even an *unscientific* one, and if you stick with performativity long enough you get back to a truth much more resonant and much less brittle than the one you left. For the moment, though, just by deferring the question of truth, one can still ask productively of a theory: What can it do and where can it go? What is it possible to think and to do with it, and what kinds of things or thoughts does it make more difficult or unintelligible?

The essays in this book are all openings and reopenings of these questions.

3

Thirds and Wings

If language is *of the world*, like galaxies and ecosystems, this means it *participates in what it represents*, though how privileged it may be either as a representative or as a participant remains to be seen. "Always part of the totality it represents" is how deconstructionist literary theorist Paul de Man characterized the operation of a symbol (191), at least as it had been conceived by the romantics in the late eighteenth century. De Man argued that the romantic doctrine of the symbol was a kind of philosophical bad faith, the retreat to a comforting wholism in order to avoid confronting the harsher realities of various kinds of alienation (most broadly, the alienation of "being in language") and of historical limits (most broadly, the predicament of "being in time"). Of course, even Coleridge recognized his own self-aggrandizement and bad faith in imagining the lines of his poetry to be like the strings of a harp caressed by a divine breeze and "all of animated nature" in turn to be nothing but "organic Harps diversely framed."

The critique of too easy wholism is still useful and necessary: the whole is not necessarily static or transcendent or determining or determinate or, perhaps most important, even singular. *The whole is part of the parts*—that is, it may participate in the system without any necessary privilege. But if deconstructionist theory threw out the baby of participation with the bathwater of totality, subsequent cultural studies theorists have worked to reimagine *participation without totality* and without absolutizing or rigidifying the separateness of language from the world (which can function as a comforting retreat in its own right).

The kinship of language and the world also compromises the doctrine known as realism. At the heart of realism is the belief in an ultimately definitive description of the world, a single "God's-eye view" toward which we should strive, even if we can only approach it. A more pluralist or "promiscuous" realism (as John Dupré describes it) proposes instead that "there are countless legitimate, objectively grounded ways of classifying objects in the world" (18). Though opening up realist dogma considerably, this kind of pluralism still seems to overstate the separation of language ("ways of classifying objects") from the world, only to overstate in turn its attachment ("grounding") to the world. All realisms, one might say, tend to rely at some level on a kind of *antinaturalism,* defined here as the belief in a radical or categorical discontinuity between language and nature. In the broader sense, such antinaturalism is a kind of exceptionalism about humanity, and in this sense it may derive from a Western religious tradition that situates humanity as categorically different from the fallen world it inhabits and can come to transcend. Naturalism, on the other hand, can stress instead a continuity of language and the world, or, to put it more accurately, naturalism insists only that the continuities and discontinuities between language and the world are not necessarily any more or less radical than those among other kinds of entities in the world. For those who like official-sounding names, the position being advanced here could be called *antirealist naturalism.*

Realism, as I have suggested, tends to efface or disavow the act of representation in order to pose as a transparent window or a perfectly reflecting mirror on the world; it downplays the medium in favor of the message. To start, one might say that antirealism (as I am using the term here) emphasizes instead the *refractivity* of language. The realist who dreams that the articulations of language could correspond perfectly to the "joints of nature"—dead words nailed to dead things—could only be a kind of *butcher,* of language and of nature. Instead, antirealism emphasizes language not as skeletal but as muscular, as performative, as able to make things happen precisely because it *straddles* the "joints" of things. But antirealist naturalism also makes a claim about the world, not just about language: it is a refractive and a muscular world, a world in which, finally, things don't correspond perfectly to other things *or to themselves.* Their noncorrespondence to themselves, one might say, comes from their being creatures of *relationships.* Even (or especially) the simplest or most elemental things—like gravity or quarks or what have you—are not *given* but have coevolved, have been produced and are sustained by—and are definable as—complex relationships, as most physicists and cosmologists will now tell you.

This leads to a paradox: it is precisely in its failure to represent the world perfectly, precisely in its refractivity, that language most resonates with the world. And this is where the *naturalism* comes in: such resonance is the mark of a real kinship.

It is not that language is either referential or self-referential but a *third* kind of thing. The world and language with it are not simple, jointed skeletons but muscular and moving things more like *wings*. Antirealist naturalism changes the scene from *words and things* to *thirds and wings*.

ASIDE

Withness, via Luhmann.   Cary Wolfe, describing Niklas Luhmann's account of language and communication in autopoietic social systems, offers a version of the "withness" paradigm, identifying the "constitutive blindness of all observations" (one might say all claims to *witness*) as "a blindness that does not separate or alienate us from the world but, paradoxically, guarantees our connection with it" (69). This is the case because, "for Luhmann, all observations are constructed atop a constitutive distinction that is paradoxical or tautological, and that the observing system which utilizes the distinction cannot acknowledge *as* paradoxical and at the same time engage in self-reproduction" (65–66). If all systems "are constituted by a necessary 'blind spot' that only *other* systems can see," then "the process of social reproduction depends on the 'unfolding,' the distribution and circulation, of these constitutive paradoxes (which would otherwise block systemic self-re-production) by a plurality of observing systems" (66); this formula extends the important insight of Marxist social theory and Lacanian psychoanalytic theory that social and psychic systems off-load their contradictions onto others. But if this is the case, how can a theory of language, as suggested here, propose to base itself on an *acknowledged* central paradox? Not by claiming a God's-eye view exempt from blind spots, but by complicating the monolithic distinctions (between blind-ness and insight and between self-reproduction and annihilation) characteristic of Luhmannian autopoiesis. I would say instead that such a theory can only *partially* operationalize the paradox that it acknowledges—for example, by continuing to use language as if it bore accurate witness to the world even while understanding that its witness is radically compromised by its withness. Likewise, such a theory can only *partially* reproduce itself, changing and mutating (and, one hopes, evolving) in the process. One problem with thinking in terms of systems whose mandate is to reproduce themselves (even if they mutate and evolve in the process) is that it tends to situate difference against a background of the same; this way of thinking has been a leading feature of modern knowledge production (as the next chapter explores). On the other hand, *resemblance* (or resonance or pattern) can be situ-ated against a background of sameness *and* difference.

Thinking in terms of *observation* cannot help bringing the old baggage of metaphors of vision, especially in positing distance between seer and seen (sometimes in order to claim some kind of objectivity) and by implying that what observers do is hang back and make representations (for instance, world pictures and maps) rather than, more fundamentally, engaging and being engaged by the world. The whole thrust of Luhmann's theorizing is to jettison this baggage, but even when the vision metaphor is used "under erasure" (that is, with implicit ironic quotation marks around it), success can be only partial.

The metaphor can be found pushing up against its limits in Wolfe's characterization of the way observers are "joined to the world and to each other by their constitutive but different blindspots" (70). In fact, a blind spot is located at a juncture Wolfe omits: it is the place where a patchworked organism is *joined to itself.* We are not just big eyeballs. Relativizing the vision metaphor a bit to take an already plural and non-self-identical self into account, one could say that the fruits of second-order observations can be tasted, smelled, or touched even when not seen, that withness is *borne,* embodied, and acted out even while fully denied.

4

The Order of Things
in a Nutshell

Epistemology is the study of knowledge; an *episteme* is a paradigm or a kind of logic—or more descriptively a kind of *ecology*—that governs various forms of knowledge at a specific time and place. Foucault's *Order of Things* traces shifts in the Western episteme since the seventeenth century, focusing on the interrelated histories of linguistics, biology, and economics. Of course, to call the interrelations among kinds of knowledge an *ecology* is to put an organicist spin on the story; at one time Foucault preferred to call what he was doing an *archaeology* of knowledge, though his metaphors in the O.T. tend to be more consistently *geological* (for example, in representing knowledges as deposits that displace and metamorphose previous strata). These metaphors help convey the sense of impersonal processes at work over very large scales of time and place. It may also be helpful to think of epistemic shifts in analogy with more clear-cut events: I like to use as such an analogy the "great vowel shift" in medieval English, in which the pronunciation of vowel sounds shifted, as if each were yoked in tandem, over the course of several centuries, leaving only traces of earlier pronunciations *fossilized* in English spelling. The point of this analogy is that nobody (and especially no governing body as such) *decided* to change vowel sounds; it was instead an *emergent* phenomenon. Nor did people seem to *hear* the sounds changing: the shift, we might say, was a historical phenomenon of too long a wavelength for human ears to hear and thus had to be *discovered* and reconstructed well after the fact. This analogy also helps show how we might remain entirely unaware of the most fundamental and sweeping changes in how we think, which happen across variously linked scales from the most minute to the most total—that is to say, they happen *fractally.*

Once upon a time (Foucault's account begins), in Europe during the Renaissance, knowledge was based on *resemblances.* Some famous examples of such a logic can be found in what has since been called *homeopathy* (the doctrine that cures work by virtue of resemblances between medicine and symptom) or in the Renaissance paradigm of the "Great Chain of Being" (the set of interlocking resemblances supposed to rule between microcosm and macrocosm, particularly the common hierarchical structures supposed to order the individual, the family, the commonwealth, and the cosmos). Where modernity would come to see the most fundamental differences, the Renaissance saw resemblances—for example, *between the sexes,* which were conceived as different not in kind but in degree: women were merely "cooler" and less perfect men, men turned inside out; ova were simply female sperm, and even menstruation was merely a special case of the many ways all bodies purge excesses of various fluids, which themselves were not fundamentally different but capable of transmuting into each other. Perhaps most fundamentally, modernity has displaced the resemblance between words and things, so for "we moderns" it is this resemblance that most characterizes the Renaissance in its difference from us—and notice that this differentiation of modernity from the Renaissance illustrates how much more definitive differences are than resemblances for modern knowledge!

For Renaissance knowledge, "the face of the world is covered with blazons" (Foucault, *Order* 27); nature is a book of these emblems to be read and interpreted, primarily according to the resonances or sympathies among things, where *sympathy* indicates a demonstrable kinship (that is, a kinship "on the face" of things, the real mark of a common *signature*), and signs signify by virtue of their actual resemblance to what they signify. For moderns and maybe even more for postmoderns, this epistemological regime tends to look like it treats both words and things *as words,* or as some hybrid between them that is closer to words than things—for example, as *hieroglyphs* to be deciphered. The kind of resemblance that seems to be returning or emerging in our time is more inclined to treat words and things *as things,* as suggested by an "ecology of discourse."

When a new episteme emerged in the early seventeenth century, knowledge based on resemblance was devalued: it was subsequently the *madman* who saw "nothing but resemblance and signs of resemblance everywhere" or at best the *poet* "who, beneath the named, constantly expected differences, rediscovers the buried kinships between things, their scattered resemblances" (49). Rather than informing all knowledge, similitude becomes a kind of foil, an "undifferentiated, shifting, unstable base on which knowledge can establish its relations, its measurements, and its identities" (68). It is instead "a solid grid of kinships that defines the general configuration of knowledge in the Classical age" (74). Whether the object of knowledge is the economy, living creatures, or language, it is defined by a classical knowledge whose mode is *representation* and whose icon is the *table*, which embodies the notion that

> all wealth is *coinable;* and it is by this means that it enters into *circulation*—in the same way that any natural being was *characterizable,* and could thereby find its place in a *taxonomy;* that any individual was *nameable* and could find its place in an *articulated language;* that any representation was *signifiable* and could find its place, in order to be known, in a *system of identities and differences.* (175; emphasis in original)

With the rise of the modern episteme in the late eighteenth century, classical knowledge was devalued in turn. The most characteristic dream of the classical episteme—that of an ideal language whose words and grammatical categories would perfectly and logically mirror the real categories and relationships of things in the world—came to be the province of cranks and madmen (while scientists, representing the most privileged kind of modern knowledge, remained invested in this dream *as a dream*). Modern knowledge invents *depth* and *density,* pushing the links and articulations among things to a place "outside representation, beyond its immediate visibility, in a sort of behind-the-scenes world even deeper and more dense than representation itself" (239). This "obscure verticality" dictates that "from now on things will be represented only from the depths of this density withdrawn into itself" (251). To take one example, whereas classical medicine sought to *taxonomize* diseases exhaustively in their intricate interrelationships, modern medicine *anatomizes,* seeking the hidden structures and origins of diseases in the depths of the body and the germs that attack it. Meaning in language must be sought in the depths as well: "Philology, as the analysis of what is said in the depths of discourse," became "the modern form of criticism" (298). It is as if the *width* of connections and tangled interrelationships that characterized classical words and things had been forcibly compressed so that all words/things became narrow and discrete but deep (as specialized knowledge is often said to be) and where the depths of an object or a self or a discipline are also the depths of its own history, the shapely trajectory of its own unique evolution and growth. This is part of the package deal modern knowledge offers (and in Foucault's account it is an offer you can't refuse): give up a wide world of interrelations (which come to seem unmanageably messy and sprawling anyway) but gain a depth and a discrete history and a self. *Give up the world,* say the devils and angels of modernity, *and gain a soul.*

The modern displacement of representation tends to devalue literature: "Literature becomes progressively more differentiated from the discourse of ideas, and encloses itself in a radical intransitivity," often coming to seem more fundamentally an escape from or "ludic denial" of mainstream values than the instrument of their circulation. Literature becomes *self-referential,* "merely a manifestation of a language which has no other law than that of affirming—in opposition to all other forms of discourse—its own precipitous existence; and so there is nothing for it to do but to curve back in a perpetual return upon itself; as if its discourse could have no other content but the expression of its own form" (300). Although self-referentiality as such was attributed primarily to literature, a similar closure affects other disciplinary objects, such as "living beings, objects of exchange, and words, when, abandoning representation, which had been their natural site hitherto, they withdraw into the depths of things and roll up upon themselves in accordance with the laws of life, production, and language" (313). Related organizing principles include *organicism* in biology and in literature (where *organic form* is one that emerges from the complex internal structures of the content rather than being imposed from outside) and *self-regulation* in such diverse sites as the institutional structures of professions and disciplines, machine design (the early steam engine's "governor" is a famous example), and the ideally self-regulating modern self itself.

How do such thoroughgoing changes in knowledge happen? Classical Marxism regarded knowledge (including ideology, theory, and philosophy) as part of a *superstructure* built on the foundation of a particular kind of economic *base* whose broad outlines (and whose changes) it echoes and elaborates. Foucault and others tended to treat knowledge as a semiautonomous realm in its own right or (in his later work) knowledges as parts of heterogeneous patchworks of ideas, practices, and institutions. Whichever model you prefer, imagine the whole assemblage being riven into realignment by some unspecified combination of slow tectonic shifts and sudden earthquakes. Some knowledges and ways of knowing will be abandoned, but most will be buttressed and retrofitted as long as possible (look over there, where priests and professors and politicians are holed up anxiously in their leaning towers!); some crumble altogether, but more often a wall or two collapses and perhaps the structure is cobbled together with another.

If it were possible to study the faults and stresses and anticipate the realignments well enough, would it be possible to find the epistemological equivalent of *the Nevada seaside,* some now disregarded way of thinking that will come to be repositioned as supremely valuable? Foucault was quite cautious—one might even say *coy*—when it came to forecasting such re-alignments: "Nothing can tell us in advance on which side the through road lies" (339). Predicting earthquakes is an unreliable business, but the lack of a transcendental vantage point is really not the problem, since after all (to paraphrase Blake), the mole and not the eagle is in touch with what's happening underground. Or to change the metaphor slightly, it is not *in spite of* our embeddedness in the web of forces that we study but *because* of it—because it pulls on us from various directions—that we can (like spiders) have some sense of what may be happening and where, even if "we can at the moment do no more than sense the possibility" (387) of large-scale epistemological change in the making.

Foucault's story of the emergence of the "human sciences"—and in particular of "man" and humanism as the object of study they constituted—ends with the suggestion that if the "fundamental arrangements of knowledge" were to "crumble, as the ground of Classical thought did, at the end of the eighteenth century, then one can certainly wager that man would be erased, like a face drawn in sand at the edge of a sea" (387). Again as in geology, we may be uncertain about exactly where and when big earthquakes will come, but we should at least respect the certainty that they *will* come. When it comes to academic disciplines, one might ask who is crazier, those who stake out land in Nevada for future seaside resorts or those who persist in buying bloated mansions on muddy slopes in Los Angeles?

For Foucault anyway, questions about major reconfigurations of knowledge "must be left in suspense, where they pose themselves, only with the knowledge that the possibility of posing them may well open the way to future thought" (386)—as if a geologist drilling for core samples might trigger an earthquake. Questions about knowledge and language can never be objective observations from safely outside the system in question, just as attempts to *change* knowledges must be *intra*ventions and infiltrations. Foucault's mode of doing this is typically to rehearse and rereherse what a given episteme dictates, actually *to speak in the voice of the episteme* in question with a kind of flattening dramatic irony that distances us from its pronouncements, to act as a kind of epistemic embalming fluid. Historicizing, in this model, is not so much the attempt to ascertain what happened as it is the attempt to *put behind us* the formation in question, to *make it history* in the colloquial sense of relegating it to the past, and especially to neutralize, to undermine, to euthanize a moribund regime of knowledge.

Hegel famously put it this way: "When philosophy paints its gray on gray, then has a form of life grown old, and with gray on gray it cannot be rejuvenated, but only known; the Owl of Minerva first takes flight with twilight closing in." This means that knowledge of what makes the current episteme tick would necessarily be marginalized, inadmissable. In fact (to develop the metaphor), owls do "spend the daytime in quiet, inconspicuous roosts"—rather like where we are now, dear reader, in this quiet and inconspicuous book, or so I want to say with a combination of humility and grandiosity. But Hegel's metaphor depends on a very limited kind of "serially monogamous" history in which one very different age or "form of life" completely succeeds another. Foucault's single-file parade of epistemes is similarly limited: although there is at least some plurality in layering (the new episteme is built on the ruins of the old), it is subordinated to a rigid hierarchy (in which one and only one episteme rules at any time). But what if more than one "form of life" is alive at any time, and what if they are more like species than individuals, not usually dying once and for all but mutating and coevolving? Philosophical knowledge might still be said to reside in the margins (the transitions and interstices between and among species), but the margins would at least be all over the place. Philosophy would no longer fly or stand, like a bird of prey, talons clutching the flesh of a dying age, but would ride, more or less a part of every transaction, like a ubiquitous virus. Like the angel in the film *Wings of Desire*, it would have to give up its transcendent perspective for a lowlier and more transient but more participative role.

ASIDE

Kuhn's Brilliant Mistake. Another famous version of a linear succession of frameworks is Thomas Kuhn's 1962 *The Structure of Scientific Revolutions*. Kuhn's frameworks are *paradigms* rather than epistemes, and they govern work in particular scientific fields rather than whole knowledge systems, but Kuhn and Foucault (at least when he wrote *The Order of Things*) both favored a "serial monogamy" of frameworks with rather abrupt change from one to another, along with a kind of perfect epistemological self-containment. This last feature is known in science studies as "internalism": treating science as if it cycles through its own changes for its own internal reasons, apart from the other histories in which it is embedded.

Kuhn's account of the history of science features long periods of stability in which ideas and experiments can be developed *within* a given paradigm—periods of "normal science," as he called it—punctuated by scientific revolutions in which the old paradigm is stretched to the breaking point and a new paradigm emerges.

Most people understand *paradigm* as a kind of crucial metaphor or central idea (for example, the old solar system model of the atom), but it can also be interpreted more broadly as a common ideology, or more materially as a shared set of institutional structures or procedures, or as a fuzzy set of all of the above, so long as it definitively organizes knowledge in the field in question. Kuhn shares with structuralism more broadly the tendency to emphasize a kind of snapshot account of structure so exclusively as to be incapable of accounting for time and history, making change seem by comparison chaotic, aberrant, or beside the point. Kuhn's exaggeration of the monolithic stability of paradigms melodramatizes the revolutionary sweep of their shift; this was the same song Foucault sang about epistemes (in other words, "the bigger they are, the harder they fall"). Most scholars seem now to agree that this is not a very good account of how things happen in science and that the fuzzy set of metaphors, practices, apparatuses, and institutions is yoked together in many ways but does not march in lockstep (see Galison). Philosopher Paul Feyerabend, who was especially grumpy about Kuhn and his followers, put it this way: "Whenever one tries to make his ideas more definite one finds that they are *false*. Was there ever a period of normal science in the history of thought? No—and I challenge anyone to prove to the contrary" (160).

I am more inclined to think that the failings and fudgings of *The Structure of Scientific Revolutions* (and of structuralism broadly) must be part of a package deal, the blind spots with which it had to pay for its insights about the contingency of scientific knowledge and the recognition that any given framework enables certain kinds of ideas at the expense of excluding others—Kuhn's own framework being no exception. After all, even for its most conservative and progressivist boosters, science itself is arguably a series of just such brilliant mistakes, since to be scientific at all an idea must be falsifiable and since arguably every past scientific idea or theory has been falsified or displaced or relativized every bit as much as we should hope (for the sake of progress) our current ideas will be. But the question of how Kuhn managed to be so smart and so dumb as to make his brilliant mistake and how he stuck to it (and how *it stuck*) is only more compelling the wronger he was. Kuhn himself identified (at least in retrospect) what amounts to a kind of "eureka" moment in his studies of Aristotle's physics, in the late 1940s—the paradigm shift from which his paradigm paradigm emerged. His question about Aristotle was roughly the same as ours about him: how could Aristotle have been so smart and so dumb? Kuhn thought he found the answer when he identified in the notions of *quality* and *position* what amounted to a governing principle (that is, a kind of protoparadigm) in Aristotle's thinking: "Position itself was, however, a quality in Aristotle's physics, and a body that changed its position therefore remained the same body only in the problematic sense that the child is the individual it becomes.

In a universe where qualities were primary, motion was necessarily a change-of-state rather than a state" (*Essential Tension* xi–xii).

Ideas that had seemed out of left field in Aristotle fell into place when Kuhn grasped the centrality of this notion, and in the process, he reports, "I did not become an Aristotelian physicist as a result, but I had to some extent learned to think like one" (xii). This kind of formula underlies the notion of progress in relation to the past: that we can come to understand other frameworks but not be bound by them, since our ability to shift frames makes our metaframeworks broader, higher, better. But to the contrary, it seems as if Kuhn *had indeed become an Aristotelian without knowing it,* at least insofar as what he identified as the central brilliant mistake of Aristotle's physics turns out to be pretty damn close to his own central brilliant mistake about paradigm shifts: the fetishization of position (that is, structure) as a primary quality makes motion or change seem revolutionary and all-encompassing. The uncanniness of this is captured by an old joke:

> Two Jews walk by a Christian church with a sign promising one thousand dollars to new converts. One wants to go in to see if he can collect the money by making an immediate, superficial conversion. In spite of his friend's objections, he goes in. His friend waits outside. One hour passes, then two, then three. Finally he emerges, and his friend asks (excitedly), "What happened—did you get the money?" and he responds (in a voice heavy with contempt): *"Is that all you people ever think about?"*

The joke suggests that a framework is a package deal and that you can't "get it" without being remade by it, without being subject to it and to its blindnesses along with its insights, its otherings and exclusions (in the case of the joke, its anti-Semitism). The joke is a salutary corrective to the presumption that one could occupy a privileged "metaframework" position, although it does manage to situate itself as "meta-anti-Semitic." But in the process it also makes frameworks all the more monolithic and conversion all the more revolutionary. To begin to suggest an alternative to the conversion model, it seems likelier that Kuhn was already seeing Aristotle through his own protoparadigmatic lenses to begin with, and that even more thoroughly in retrospect, after fully developing the paradigm paradigm, he saw his earlier study of Aristotle as more of a kind of conversion experience in terms of the "paradigm shift" paradigm. This account suggests that a framework is a kind of self-organizing system, a kind of whirlpool in linear time, not something that simply shifts from one to another at a given point but one that has to be ongoingly produced and reproduced and is both stable and unstable for this reason, like a spinning top. This also shows why the statically structuralist metaphor of the "framework" can get us only so far before it has to be pushed aside, like Wittgenstein's ladder.

In any case, historicizing at its best is driven not to try to blow up epistemes and start over but to salvage and use some of what the current or passing episteme has relegated to its margins. Theoretical questions are thus potentially transformative and *performative,* participating in shaping what they study. I will argue later that performativity itself can be thought of as an older kind of knowledge displaced by modernity's fixation on objectivity but now being salvaged from modernity's ruins, something like the figurines of their own gods that the Aztecs hid inside hollow Christian statuary that their conquerors forced them to make and to worship.

What is a performative question? To use a rather homely example, it is as if a sense of growing intimacy between two people getting to know each other were to lead one to ask the other, pointedly, "What is happening between us?" Though phrased as a request for information, the question participates fully in—and in fact *precipitates*—the object of its inquiry; the *meaning* of the question is *what it makes happen,* and who or what is *us* (friends? lovers? what?) hangs in the balance. It is clearly part of an experiment, a trial balloon, but neither the question nor any answer to it could possibly be disinterested, or, rather, it is clear that disinterestedness on the part of the questioner or respondent will also shape in very particular ways what is happening! It is important to notice that the question's participation does not *invalidate* the inquiry: on the contrary, that is what activates it at all, charging it with such interest. The philosopher of science Isabelle Stengers makes the case that it is precisely their *interest* that makes scientific questions work (83–84), where the *inter* in *interest* refers to the betweenness—the relationality—of the questioners and the things in question. One might say (dear reader!) that "what is happening between us" is *the* interesting question.

My book begins, in several senses, where Foucault left off *The Order of Things,* which is in any case the *Old* Testament of the Foucauldian faith. Foucault himself went on to revise the sense of the *episteme* as a closed set of interrelations—a plate tectonics of knowledge as hyperformalized as a kind of four-dimensional Rubik's Cube. In his later works Foucault continued to explore the interrelations of knowledge and power but less as abstract systems and more as *embodied* in practices and institutions and their particular histories and discourses. This shift in Foucault's work—from closed to open systems, one might say—characterizes a more general transition from structuralist to poststructuralist theory (see chapter 13 for an account of how autopoetic systems can be understood only as open *and* closed). In retrospect it seems now that it is the *airlessness* of the theoretical framework of the closed system itself (as much as it is the history presented therein) that gives the sense of impending change such utopian and apocalyptic sublimity—the sense that the angel that had stood guard at the tree of life is about to leave his post, as if the theorist were opening up a translucent rift in time through which he was able only to glimpse, pointing us toward a promised land that he could never hope to enter, a star beckoning us onward to a place where words (now relegated to *semantics*) and things (now situated in the realm of being or *ontology*) will rejoin: "In the firmament of our reflection there reigns a discourse—a perhaps inaccessible discourse—which would at the same time be an ontology and a semantics" (Foucault, *Order* 208).

More than three decades after *The Order of Things,* it is much easier to make the case that we have entered the promised land of the new episteme and, accordingly, much harder to sustain its utopian sublimity, especially given the way it is being sold to us by its many boosters and "scientific salesmen." Like the United States, the democratic promise of the episteme will have to be worked and tricked and wrung from it.

5

Artistic Interlude I:
The Sick Mind Continues to Infinity

It appears that certain aphasiacs, when shown various differently coloured skeins of wool on a table top, are consistently unable to arrange them in any coherent pattern. . . . Within this simple space in which things are normally arranged and given names, the aphasiac will create a multiplicity of tiny, fragmented regions in which nameless resemblances agglutinate things into unconnected islets; in one corner, they will place the lightest-coloured skeins, in another the red ones, somewhere else those that are softest in texture, in yet another place the longest, or those that have a tinge of purple or those that have been wound up into a ball. But no sooner have they been adumbrated than all these groupings dissolve again, for the field of identity that sustains them, however limited it may be, is still too wide not to be unstable; and so the sick mind continues to infinity, creating groups then dispersing them again, heaping up diverse similarities, destroying those that seem clearest, splitting up things that are identical, superimposing different criteria, frenziedly beginning all over again, becoming more and more disturbed, and teetering finally on the brink of anxiety.

—Michel Foucault, *The Order of Things*

Foucault milked the drama of "the sick mind" in implicit opposition to the supposedly stable and normal categories of language, science, and reason. Of course, it is more than a sick mind's fancy that things are capable of being categorized in all kinds of ways, capable of entering into a range of different and sometimes mutually irreconcilable kinds of relationships with other things. In fact, this capacity seems to be as fundamental to the things of physics and chemistry as it is to language, culture, and knowledge and to the webs of linkages and disjunctions between and among them. Clearly, though, different orderings of things do have different statuses in different contexts, even if this observation just raises the question of how many ways the orderings can themselves be ordered (without suggesting whether more or less stability can be manufactured at such a metalevel). You might think that the recognition that different orderings and metaorderings are possible would be especially obvious when examining a broad historical or cross-cultural range; in these cases we have come to expect (thanks a lot to structuralism) irreconcilable differences in how things are engaged, ordered, and valued. It is important to keep in mind, though, that even such differences between cultures and epistemes are mostly far from obvious and have proved to require very careful unearthing and, furthermore, that they are so volatile that engaging them cannot be as simple as producing a metacontext that contains them all: it turns out to be more like a process that changes everything. It is just as important to recognize (as poststructuralism has been better at doing) that a single ordering cannot maintain a seamless and uncontradictory hegemony even at a single historical moment or in a single culture or knowledge system, even if the fiction that it does so may be a very powerful one.

Where certain categorizations become hegemonic, others will be more or less unintelligible or devalued. Foucault argued that when *difference* became the ruling logic, *resemblance* became the province of mere poetry or even of "the sick mind." This became abundantly clear to me in a new way as I began rearranging my library, on a whim, to produce something like poetry or art merely by clustering books according to grammatical resemblances among their titles, as follows:

Chaos (Gleick)
Power (Dowding)
Nova (Delany)
Genome (Ridley)
Zipper (Friedel)
Dracula (Stoker)
Maitreya (Sarduy)
Hysteria (Johnson)
Neveryona (Delany)
Chaosmosis (Guattari)
Neuromancer (Gibson)
Homographesis (Edelman)
Capitalism (Saunders)
Pluralism (McLennan)
S/Z (Barthes)

NASA/Trek (Penley)
Poetics/Politics (Kumar)
Feminism/Postmodernism (Nicholson)
Culture/Metaculture (Mulhern)
Disorder and Order (P. Livingston)
Pride and Prejudice (Austen)
Romanticism and Consciousness (Bloom)
Nietzsche and Metaphor (Kofman)
Beamtimes and Lifetimes (Traweek)
Stars and Planets (Ekrutt)
Genes, Peoples, and Languages (Cavalli-Sforza)
Race, Class, and Gender . . . (Rothenberg)
Hustlers, Beats, and Others (Polsky)
Simians, Cyborgs, and Women (Haraway)
Money, Language, and Thought (Shell)
Romantics, Rebels, and Reactionaries (Butler)
Naturalism, Evolution, and Mind (Walsh)
Deceit, Desire, and the Novel (Girard)
Capitalism, the Family, and Personal Life (Zaretsky)
Troubadours, Trumpeters, Troubled Makers (Lee)
Romanticism, Nationalism, and the Revolt against Theory (Simpson)
Gossip, Grooming, and the Evolution of Language (Dunbar)
Cinema, Theory, and Political Responsibility in
    Contemporary Culture (McGee)

Positions (Derrida)
Labyrinths (Borges)
Mythologies (Yeats)
Awakenings (Sacks)
Illuminations (Rimbaud)
Investigations (Kauffman)
Disidentifications (Muñoz)
Anti-Semitic Stereotypes (Felsenstein)
Multi-Cultural Literacy (Simonson and Walker)
Middle English Lyrics (Luria and Hoffman)
Molecular Revolution (Guattari)
Monstrous Imagination (Huet)
Satanic Panic (Victor)
Silent Poetry (Mirzoeff)
Stranger Music (Cohen)

Literary Theory (Eagleton)
Natural Supernaturalism (Abrams)
Tennyson's Poetry (Tennyson)
Everybody's Autonomy (Spahr)
Hamilton's Blessing (Gordon)
Pandora's Hope (Latour)
Frankenstein's Children (Morus)
Queer Acts (Muñoz and Barrett)
Second Skins (Prosser)
Sapphic Slashers (Duggan)
Posthuman Bodies (Halberstam and Livingston)
Immigrant Acts (Lowe)
Primate Visions (Haraway)
Symbolic Economies (Goux)
Wuthering Heights (Brontë)
The Black Jacobins (James)
The Black Curtain (Woolrich)
The Persistent Desire (Nestle)
The Female Man (Russ)
The Romantic Ideology (McGann)
The Human Condition (Arendt)
The Postmodern Condition (Lyotard)
The Einstein Intersection (Delany)
The Unabomber Manifesto (Kaczynski)
The Literary Absolute (Lacoue-Labarthe and Nancy)
The Wittgenstein Reader (Wittgenstein)
The Lesbian Body (Wittig)
The Accursed Share (Bataille)
The Many-Headed Hydra (Linebaugh and Rediker)
The Complete English Poems (Donne)
The Nazi War on Cancer (Proctor)
The Norton Anthology of English Literature (Abrams)
Arrow of Chaos (I. Livingston)
City of Quartz (Davis)
Ecology of Fear (Davis)
Anatomy of Criticism (Frye)
Reproduction of Mothering (Chodorow)
Signs of Life (Sole and Goodwin)
Spirits of Fire (Rosso and Watkins)

Forms of Distance (Bei Dao)
Margins of Philosophy (Derrida)
Visions of Excess (Bataille)
People of the Book (Halbertal)
Epistemology of the Closet (Sedgwick)
The Feast of Love (Baxter)
The Well of Loneliness (Hall)
The Rhetoric of Romanticism (de Man)
The Troubadour of Knowledge (Serres)
The Subject of Semiotics (Silverman)
The History of Sexuality (Foucault)
The Philosophy of Biology (Hull and Ruse)
The Taming of Chance (Hacking)
The Botany of Desire (Pollan)
The Moment of Complexity (Taylor)
The Tales of Canterbury (Chaucer)
The Sextants of Beijing (Waley-Cohen)
The Order of Things (Foucault)
The Disorder of Things (Dupré)
The Evolution of Physics (Einstein and Infeld)
The Life of the Cosmos (Smolin)
The Birth of the Clinic (Foucault)
The Politics of the Family (Laing)
The Invention of Modern Science (Stengers)
The Practice of Everyday Life (de Certeau)
The Making of the English Working Class (Thompson)
The Simple Art of Murder (Chandler)
The Traditional Theory of Literature (R. Livingston)
The Elementary Structures of Kinship (Levi-Strauss)
The Presentation of Self in Everyday Life (Goffman)
The Four Fundamental Concepts of Psycho-Analysis (Lacan)
The Politics of Culture in the Shadow of Capital (Lowe and Lloyd)
War in the Age of Intelligent Machines (de Landa)
Gender and Sexuality in Twentieth-Century Chinese
  Literature and Society (Lu)
Women in the Eighteenth Century (Jones)
Keywords in Evolutionary Biology (Keller and Lloyd)
The Monster in the Machine (Hanafi)
Observations of Modernity (Luhmann)

Exercises in Style (Queneau)
Scaling in Biology (Brown and West)
Bastard Out of Carolina (Allison)
Aliens in America (Dean)

Reading through the rearranged titles reveals surprising consistencies (for example, the way *threeness* in titles seems to function as the sign of plurality in interrelation) and surprising inconsistencies (for instance, the ease with which couplings signify similarity or difference, the unease of the subordinations enacted by modifiers and possessives, the erratic orbit of *of*), along with variously promising ad hoc juxtapositions. The rearrangement magnifies crosscurrents and undertows in the otherwise regular flow of grammar and thus may induce a sense of the underlying turbulence of knowledge and language. I have to admit that just having the books on my shelves in this order feels like a kind of silent rebuke, a constant low-level disturbance, like having an epistemological ghost or alien in the room.

Since art can work with what is abjected by hegemonic categories, it is easy to make epistemological art by deploying grids and combinatories that play with similarity and difference. Here are just a few projects using everyday things around the house (Michel Foucault meets Martha Stewart):

* Make a grid of twelve-inch squares on your wall, with small nails at the intersections. Hang small objects of approximately the same size on the nails, each as different from each other as possible (for example, a book, a wine glass, a photograph, and so on).
* Assemble a group of very different objects and spray paint them all uniformly white.
* Affix labels to a cluster of objects, making the descriptions a mix of congruent and incongruent categories (such as "fork," "gift from Mother," "made of wood," and the like).
* Using strings, grid out a room into twelve-inch cubes and cut everything in the room along the grid lines (this will be a major technical challenge). Place the cut-out sections into clear Plexiglas cubes and stack them up slightly off-kilter.

6

An Introductory Vignette

Once upon a time, about a billion years ago (or so geologists say), near the middle of the North American continent, the earth split open and oozed out vast amounts of molten rock. As it cooled, the rock collapsed in on itself and formed a giant depression that would later fill up with the waters of Lake Superior. Millions of small air bubbles petrified in the cooling rock, riddling it with hollow vesicles. Rainwater percolated down and volcanic waters pulsed up through hairline fractures of the basalt. As dissolved minerals leached from the rock crystallized out of the water, they lined the interiors of the vesicles with thin layers, filling the vesicles to form nuggets of the semiprecious stone now known as Lake Superior agate. Because of the abundance of iron, mostly rusty reds tinge the translucent bands of chalcedony (a kind of quartz), often alternating with bands of white and crystal-clear. Long, slow erosion, followed by the advance and retreat of Ice Age glaciers, dislodged the agate nuggets from their basalt matrix, scattered them across the upper Midwest, and buried them again in the soil.

The fast, cold rivers that run into Lake Superior have cut deep gorges through the basalt that slopes steeply down to the lake. The rivers are stained the color of Coca-Cola by the dissolved iron, and the names of the rivers (Manitou, Baptism, Temperance, Knife, Gooseberry) speak of the lives and gods of the Native peoples and the white settlers who displaced them—the alternating bands of red and white that settled around the lake. The stalwart Protestants, whose God was a mighty fortress, called the concentrically banded rocks "fortification" agates. It was meant as a compliment. About a century of farming, quarrying, and road building exposed and scattered the agates again, and collectors have regathered them and rescattered their little bunches of agates around the globe.

To say that every agate tells the story of a billion years of earth and fire and water and humans in their various interactions is not really to distinguish them from anything else. After all, even the kitschiest piece of plastic junk is made of atoms forged in the hearts of exploding stars, come to life on earth in ancient forests, folded back into the ground and squeezed into oil before being pulled out, by earth's more recent stardust creatures, into their own convulsive history. As Leibniz put it (back in 1712), "Each simple substance has relations that express all the others, and is in consequence a perpetual living mirror of the universe" (24). Tzinacan, an Aztec priest in a short story by Jorge Luis Borges, puts it this way: "Even in human languages there is no proposition that does not imply the entire universe; to say *the tiger* is to say the tigers that begot it, the deer and turtles devoured by it, the grass on which the deer fed, the earth that was mother to the grass, the heaven that gave birth to the earth" (171). Borges's priest, imprisoned by Spanish conquistadores, finds in the patterned fur of a jaguar caged in an adjoining cell the ineffably perfect archetype of human language: the "God's Script," which speaks everything at once. To say I find in agates a northerner's version of what Tzinacan found in his jaguar is only to confirm what Borges seems to have anticipated, cannily (and uncannily) as ever: he placed his priest and jaguar in a round and compartmented fortress of stone.

It does seem to me that there is something especially elegant in the geology of agates, like an elemental game of rock-paper-scissors played out through all its permutations: liquid rock breaks through solid, air petrifies in rock, waters from earth and sky pulse through rock, rock dissolves in and separates from water, rock replaces air, water freezes into ice, ice grinds rock, rock separates from rock. The alternating bands of agates seem to make them fingerprints of these successive phases, reechoed in the subsequent waves of ice and of peoples in their collections and distributions of themselves and of agates. Even the atoms of which they are made—the atoms themselves aptly enough described as concentric nuggets of waves, or the larger layered nugget of our planet, or the solar system and the galaxy, concentric waves of nuggets—seem like fractal echoes of agates at different scales. The universe, one might say, is an agate of agates. As if to relieve so much self-similarity, every agate comprises not one pattern but many: depending on how erosion or human intervention has lathed or cross-sectioned an agate, the same features will appear in different configurations of plain surfaces, parallel lines, concentric cat's-eyes, or irregular serrations.

As it turns out, scientists have been hard at work getting to the bottom of these metaphors, or to put it another way, the fortuitous similarities between fundamentally different realms that characterize these metaphors are turning out to be not so fortuitous at all, but manifestations of processes that enable all the phenomena in question to be grouped into the same realm as self-organizing systems. After folding Borges's jaguar into my story about agates (based on what seems to be merely a clever poetic analogy between them), I am charmed to discover, via Philip Ball's *Self-Made Tapestry: Pattern Formation in Nature,* that the patterns of agates and jaguars seem to derive from versions of the same kind of "reaction-diffusion" process. Take a moment to register the wildness of this claim, given not just the differences between the sciences with primary jurisdiction over agate stripes and jaguar spots (that is, geology and evolutionary biology) but also the hegemony of an episteme of *difference* that relegates such apparently far-flung resemblances to the realm of metaphor. Ball tells how, in 1896, German chemist R. E. Liesegang showed that the crystallization of chemicals in a gelatinous medium could generate a pattern of regularly alternating rings. Liesegang saw a similarity with banded patterns in rocks; others went further to suggest that the rings might be "a simplified version of the stripes of tigers and zebras or the patterns on butterfly wings." A 1931 critic's comment that in such speculations "enthusiasm has been carried beyond the bounds of prudence" was typical of the mainstream response, and even Ball will venture only so far as to call the speculations a "lucky guess." In any case, for a start, "there is now good reason to suppose that many banded rock formations do indeed arise from cyclic precipitation" (62). Agate bands have smaller bands, which have even smaller bands (known as iris bands) invisible to the naked eye except by the iridescent shimmer they produce in some agates. The reaction-diffusion explanation has been most convincingly developed for the iris bands, but it seems that there must be "several hierarchical mechanisms for oscillatory patterning at play" (64). The fact that "this fractal quality is common to agates around the world" suggests a crystallization process that is (as the primary scientists put it) "universally complex" (Heaney 1564). This universal complexity leads to the jaguars, whose patterned spots (like those of leopards, their Old World cousins) may well derive from "a subset of reaction-diffusion processes called activator-inhibitor systems" (Ball 79). Such patterns were first theorized by Alan Turing in 1952 as "the chemical basis of morphogenesis," an article that began to be hailed as visionary in the 1970s, after two decades of neglect. Studies of Turing patterns have since suggested the likelihood that "the diverse range of pelt markings can be explained with the same basic mechanism," which depends on how the chemical that triggers cells to produce melanin (responsible for skin and hair pigmentation) is distributed during the first weeks of embryo formation (Ball 84). Patterns very close to leopard and jaguar spots have been reproduced in the lab in chemical solutions by "an activator–inhibitor scheme that involves two interacting chemical patterning mechanisms" (89). (And by the way, as its title indicates, physicist Janna Levin's *How the Universe Got Its Spots* relates pattern formation in leopards and jaguars to large-scale pattern-formation processes in the cosmos.)

Agates also speak to me in a more homely way, of my childhood in Minnesota, when I began collecting them. Some tell me more particular stories: this one I found in a gravel pit in Elk River, Minnesota; a retired welder (cranky old guy) with a homemade grinding rig in his basement polished it into a sphere for me. Later it came to sit on a bookcase in my apartment in San Francisco, and when I returned there a few hours after the big quake of 1989, the sphere had jumped from the shelf and rolled to the center of the floor. It was the only thing out of place in the room. I imagined the agate sphere wandering across the moving floor, confused by such high drama after its billion sedate years in the middle of the continent, almost too neat an allegory for my life at that moment.

As a kid, I guess I just got on a wavelength with agates. Their telltale colors and patterns make them leap out, to the trained eye, from the prevailing black basalts, darkly mottled granites, and dull shales. I catch a glimpse of the translucent red glow around the edges of an agate, like a hand held in front of the sun, and my own hand leaps to it. Looking for agates was a way of orienting myself to something in the world, something to do, a reason to take a walk along the edge of a road, treasure affirmed as such by the time and attention you devote to cultivating it, like love or life or work or money or identity or what have you. I have never bought or sold one, and I gave away to various friends, many of whom I have since lost, all the agates I ever found as a child. I still keep a boxful of some agates I have found since then, but I don't display them or even look at them much. I liked to find them, but I never cared about amassing a collection.

When I revisited Minnesota after moving away, I tried to hunt for agates in some of my favorite old gravel pits, but the owners, afraid of lawsuits, had all adopted a policy of chasing off agate pickers. Times had changed. Once, I showed my university ID and pretended to be a geologist. They gave me an hour in the pit, but the necessity of my little ruse had put the whole experience in another category, completely displacing the subtler charm of finding agates.

Eventually, I got a job in New York. The seacoast has never really spoken to me; it's not in my blood. The beaches of Long Island struck my eye with a stupefying sameness: all whites and beiges and pastels of plain quartzes and light-colored granites, uniformly rounded by the waves, like a vast crowd of nattering voices, and no one speaking to me. Not content even with so much sameness, the town where I lived had the beaches raked periodically with a giant machine, removing every rock larger than a golf ball. In these mostly white-flight suburbs of New York City, stretched out like the beaches along the north shore of Long Island, the dominance of whites and beiges and pastels seemed to define the people and their houses and clothing no less than the rocks on the beaches.

How was I supposed to orient myself? What was I supposed to look for on the beach? I made up categories as I went, playing with permutations of sameness and difference. One day I found myself assembling a little collection of round rocks in gradations of pink and red, another day clamshells in concentric size increments, as if I were trying to assemble an agate by gathering up various things among which its features had been scattered. One day I started finding spiral things (a dried tendril, a broken conch shell, a snail, a rusty bedspring). One day my friend and I collected the whitest rocks we could find and assembled them on the beach into a circular patch that shaded gradually, like the dots of a pointillist painting, into the surrounding whites and pastels. The idea was to make it just obvious enough to be noticed—like a test for color blindness—but subtle enough so that anyone who noticed it would have to wonder if it was a random, statistical occurrence or a deliberate installation. Another day I spelled out words using white rocks arranged into letters, again almost unnoticeable amid the not-very-different surrounding rocks. I noticed on one beach that the flattest stones, which the waves can carry farther than most, get deposited in a band about fifteen feet from the water's edge; a few feet farther up is a band of seaweed, shells, sponges, driftwood, and plastic junk. All our sorting and arranging is, after all, only an extension of what is already being done by the waves.

But this is not a story of nostalgia for bygone days when agates were agates. How could it be, when agates themselves are never merely themselves, and when the stories they tell are of ongoing waves of scatterings and gatherings—diasporas and ghettos—of complex reconfigurations, in which they participate but which seem to shape all words and things? There is a word for things that are never perfectly equivalent to themselves: we call them *signs*.

7

Sometimes a Cigar

Is there such a thing as things in themselves? We can at least circle around this question by thinking through one of the most famous pronouncements on the subject: Freud's supposed assertion that "sometimes a cigar is only a cigar."

To begin with, it should be noted that this is an especially dubious assertion from a man who kept smoking cigars even after he was diagnosed with the mouth cancer that would kill him and, finally, even after parts of his jaw had been cut away. Such devotion (not to mention such cancer) could have been inspired only by a cigar that was much *more* than a cigar. The dismissive assertion only seems more disingenuous in light of what Freud identified elsewhere as his drive to analyze his pleasures and his claim that "wherever I cannot do this . . . I am almost incapable of obtaining any pleasure. Some rationalistic, or perhaps analytic, turn of mind in me rebels against being moved by a thing without knowing why I am thus affected" ("Moses" 80– 81).

Still, as a former smoker, I can testify that addictions do seem to have an excessive singularity. What could ever hope to take the place of smoking, the elusive and ineffable smokingness of smoking (or the cigarness of cigars, if you prefer)? But what gives addictions their singularity is their *overdetermination* (to use Freud's term), that is, the number of things they take the place of—starting, no doubt, with the usual suspects, the defining fixations of the oral, anal, and genital phases of human development as Freud mapped it out (and cigars do seem to bear various resemblances to breasts, shit, and penises). As the explorer John Lloyd Stephens put it, one stormy night in the Yucatán in 1840: "Blessed be the man . . . who invented smoking, the soother and composer of a troubled spirit, allayer of angry passions, a comfort under the loss of breakfast, and to the roamer in desolate places, the solitary wayfarer through life, serving for 'wife, children, and friends'" (Von Hagen 158).

One really need not go so far afield to begin to unravel the paradoxes of Freud's assertion, since there is a glaring contradiction right at hand: what Freud's aphorism *says* contradicts what it *does,* since what it does is to refer to the cigar not just as a cigar but also as a philosophical and psychological example. To elaborate a little, what it does is to oppose the philosophical claim that seems to be advanced by Freudian psychoanalysis itself, namely, that every human activity is always rife with unconscious and symbolic meaning. One imagines Freud responding to cut off some interlocutor who has begun to analyze his cigar smoking; of course, he would not deny unconscious symbolism flat out (since to do so would be to disavow psychoanalysis) or even its priority in human affairs. He only asserts, apparently, that it can be temporarily ("sometimes") suspended. But this suspension of meaning is not something that simply happens: it is *something the statement itself attempts to enact.* In this sense, the statement seems to be mainly a polite way of saying, "Sometimes it's rude to analyze" or, more plainly, "Shut up and let me enjoy my cigar!" Or to put it another way: Freud's invention of psychoanalysis has been so successful that it has taken on a life of its own and has come back to haunt even his own most pedestrian pleasures; the statement reasserts psychoanalysis as a game whose rules its creator can make up as he goes along.

V. N. Volosinov began *Marxism and the Philosophy of Language* by distinguishing between an object qua object and an object qua sign: "A physical body equals itself, so to speak; it does not signify anything but wholly coincides with its particular, given nature." It is only "when the physical object is converted into a sign" that "such an object, to some degree, reflects and refracts another reality." But if the story I am telling has any bearing, there is a big problem with Volosinov's assertion, a problem that one can begin to identify by observing that the distinction between objects and signs itself *belongs to signs* but not to objects as so constituted. Volosinov hints at this himself: "A physical body equals itself, *so to speak*" (9). In other words, things-in-themselves are a convenient fiction, a way language distinguishes itself as intriguing and intelligent by caricaturing its Other as dumb and inert. But again, just ask any physicist: things are not inert; they do not coincide with themselves but emerge in complex webs of interrelation, outside of which they are inconceivable. In order to begin to redress this caricature (of smart words and dumb things), we need to engage both the materiality of language and the signlikeness of matter. (And by the way, it is fitting that *Volosinov* is not so simple to pin down, either: the name may be a pseudonym of Mikhail Bakhtin or of several authors working collaboratively.)

There is a would-be general science of signs—or at least a name for such a projected science—*semiotics,* first proposed in modern form in the late nineteenth and early twentieth centuries by American philosopher C. S. Peirce and independently by Ferdinand de Saussure. Peirce in particular wanted to extend the reach of semiotics to cover the entire universe, which he regarded as "perfused with signs, if it is not composed exclusively of signs" (cited in Noth 41), whereas Saussure was more concerned with establishing the independent status of language (in the more narrowly conceived sense) as a system-unto-itself. There are many reasons semiotics has neither coalesced into a discipline nor taken over the universe (though it has thrown off very bright sparks along the way); the shorthand version will have to suffice here: the modern chasm between words and things has remained too wide and deep. But this is the chasm that present epistemic shifts are closing, and if future disciplines can ever be built there, it will be over the wreckage of would-be Evel Knevels like semiotics as well as with the support of various flying buttresses from the "hard science" side (such as chaos and complexity theory, systems and information theory, and autopoiesis).

8

On Meaning

Occasionally, when I've been bored with a book I've been reading, I've flipped ahead through the pages and thought, there is nothing but *words* here!

What was I expecting?

Never mind that people have lived and died for what is written in books; at these moments, it is thoroughly dispiriting to reflect that the text to come—no matter how informative or meaningful—will only be, after all, more of the same, word following word, eyes scanning back and forth, back and forth, back and forth. The sky will not open. The world will not change.

This must be why Shakespeare has Macbeth, in a moment of hopeless fatalism, seem to describe living itself as the reading aloud of an already written text:

> Tomorrow, and tomorrow, and tomorrow
> Creeps in this petty pace from day to day,
> To the last syllable of recorded time . . .
>
> (5.3.19–21)

The repeated words "tomorrow, and tomorrow, and tomorrow" mark the repetitive sameness of reading, not only in the eyes scanning back and forth but also in the very marks on the page: the same thirty or so letters and punctuation marks, again and again, and mostly the same words, too, and in the very same grammatical patterns, repeated over and over with only petty permutations. This is *information:* a controlled mix of redundancy and predictability with novelty. Of course, it doesn't stop with language.

As Macbeth sees it, *days,* like words and syllables, follow one another with stultifying predictability. We might as well add *conversations, meals, dreams, sex acts, wars, generations, worlds, universes.* It doesn't *stop* with language, but maybe this steamrolling ennui *starts* with language, whose every single word seems to aspire to flatten all its referents to more of the same. This is the depressive view of language, the flip side of which would seem to be a yearning for apocalyptic escape. To one so deeply bored one wants to ask: how is it that you have inoculated yourself so effectively against thinking that nothing could move you?

On the other hand, one might emphasize difference and novelty. After all, every sentence in this book, with the exception of a few scattered quotations, will be unique to this book, and thus will be occurring here *for the first time in the history of the universe,* as far as we know. And this very same book, read by different people, will bear radically different fruits, and all the more so if it travels between cultures, in time and space. Even for a single reader, this book may well function at one moment to spark a long-lost memory or a new inspiration, at another a headache or a nap or just the blink of an eye. Far from being oppressively the same, arguably, a book is oppressively plural and different: its wake is too choppy and too fleeting; its meaning is too slipperily, swarmingly different at every moment even to handle, much less to master.

The meaning of a book *is* its wake, the little ripple of turbulence that often seems only to disappear (or may only *seem* to disappear) as it widens. Its meaning is how it is *in the loop,* how it is wired into the circuit of things, the circuit of making things and of making things happen, and humanity in turn is wired together and to the world through language (among other things). A book changes (though perhaps only slightly) the way we think and know, like a switchboard operator, reconfiguring synapses maybe even one at a time, and the wiring of the brain is wired to the circuitry that wires people together and to the world: "Puppet strings . . . are not tied to the supposed will of a puppeteer but to a multiplicity of nerve fibers, which form another puppet in other dimensions connected to the first" (Deleuze and Guattari 8). A book is a node in a network of nodes that are themselves networks. It is a variegated network with all kinds of gaps and disconnects and degrees of freedom wired into it, but it could not be a network at all if that were not the case (since if everything were connected perfectly to everything else, it would constitute an adamantine and eternally frozen crystal). There is no such thing as an independent thought: there is no thought that is not wired into the whole network, even if, as in dreams, the switch is turned off between thoughts and muscular actions—that is, all the more so if dreams are the safety valves for noise or excess that the system generates and must continue to dump or be compromised by.

ASIDE

Meaninglessness Is Not Possible. The famous example of a meaningless sentence invented by linguist Noam Chomsky—"Colorless green ideas sleep furiously"—has turned out to be famously meaningful. It seems to suggest that some ideas that are lively but relatively new and untried (green) and apparently invisible or easy to ignore or emotionally neutral (colorless) nonetheless must struggle desperately or violently (furiously) to remain unconscious (sleep). Of course, what Chomsky seemed to *mean* was that the sentence is meaningless if one rejects contradictions and metaphors as meaningless, and this is precisely the anxious disavowal that seems to underlie the blithe confidence of rationalist science; to disavow contradiction and metaphor is to "sleep furiously." Chomsky ends up illustrating, as did Goya in a famous engraving, that "the sleep of reason produces monsters." The sentence itself hatches into the meaningful monster the scientist disowned. Its meaning is in how it is thrown out and comes back to bite the scientist in the ass.

Peirce suggested that the thinglikeness of an idea can be appreciated in the "steadiness of the hypothesis that enables us to think about it" and thus the realization "that if our mental manipulation is delicate enough, the hypothesis will resist being changed" (89). If this friction is what makes for the labor of thinking, it is also what makes for its pleasure, its *frisson*. The friction derives not from dumb inertia but because all the synapses are wired in such a complex way with each other and with so much else. The philosopher Willard Quine argued that our hypothesized versions of the "laws of nature" are all rather arbitrary and changeable—or, rather, they would be so if many other hypotheses and calculations did not depend on them: the more in the loop they are (or the more in the more loops), the more difficult they are to reformulate; in business one would say that the *transition costs* are too high. Freud's word was *overdetermination:* multiple dream-thoughts converge to produce a single dream image capable of referencing all of them (thus, for example, the vampire who showed up in my dream had bushy eyebrows not just because vampires tend to have bushy eyebrows but also because my old professor Rene Girard had bushy eyebrows and so did the president of the college where my father taught—and also because of the *I* in *eyebrow* and the *ire* in *vampire* and the *Ira* in *Girard*). Memory tends to work like this too, like a safe deposit box that takes two different keys to open. Meaning is resonance, straddling, nodality, being in the middle.

The fact is, when I get bored and flip ahead through a book, I am not really oscillating wildly between existential despair and apocalyptic mania, I'm just looking for some pictures! I might even settle for a chart or graph, or even the intermittent interruption of otherwise unrelieved blocks of prose by bits of poems. I seem to require a kind of minimum heterogeneity. In other words, the difference between one word or sentence or paragraph and another—which is difference wholly *within* language, narrowly conceived—does not seem to make any difference to me at these moments, when words begin to fall on me like light rain and I search for some trace of difference *between* language and something else. This suggests one of the cruxes of the argument of this book: *meaning is the interaction of difference within and difference between,* the way they are wired together.

To recognize that thoughts are made of other thoughts and are raw material for new thoughts and that books are made of other books and are used in turn to make more books is merely depressive unless accompanied by the recognition that such self-organizing systems can be generated and sustained as nodes only in radically heterogeneous (that is, *lumpy*) networks and intersecting and incommensurable economies.

9

Fact and Fiction

Since the opposition between fact and fiction has come to seem such a given, it is surprising to find that the words *fact* and *fiction* both derive from Latin words that mean nearly the same thing—*to do* or *to make* (as does *poetry* from the Greek *poeien*). In English, *fiction* has always had the primary sense of something fashioned or feigned—though *fashion*, like *fact*, derives from the Latin *facere*, whereas *feign*, like *fiction*, comes from *fingere*. It took until the nineteenth century for the sense of fact as something actively done or made to be completely driven out by the sense of something that simply and passively *is*. Fiction too seems mostly to have fossilized into a genre, a stable kind of thing, a noun. In other words, the distinction between fact and fiction has itself come to seem like a fact. In fact, though, as even this thumbnail etymology shows, the distinction between fact and fiction is really a fiction, something people have manufactured.

In telling the story of how this state of affairs came to be, it would be misleading to repeat the old cliché that the ancients lived in an enchanted world, lacking our distinction between reality and fantasy—a childlike world we have since lost. For one thing, ancient languages are very capable of making similar distinctions using their own words. One might say instead that the distinction has branched out, wedging categories apart the way a tree root splits a sidewalk, or that some long-term continental drift in language has put oceans between once contiguous regions of discourse: "There rolls the deep where grew the tree," as Tennyson put it. As fact seems to have petrified into something that simply *is*, it has become more difficult, at least in ordinary language, to understand the world as an event, as something continuously made.

So how did the sibling rivalry between fact and fiction arise and devolve into such a crude and entrenched impasse (IS! Is NOT! IS! Is NOT!)? Well, it's a long story, culminating in the invention and polarization of *science* and *literature*—two more words that acquired their modern currency only in the nineteenth century. For example, scientific authority came to aspire to anonymous objectivity (for example, in the ideal of the repeatable experiment), whereas literature was fixed to subjectivity through the ideological figure of the author—a fixation Foucault identified as a way of containing "the great danger with which fiction threatens our world" ("Author" 118). Although this arrangement has been naturalized for so long as to seem common sense, it is in fact a reversal of much older traditions that attach *scientific authority to great authors* and *literary value to anonymity and repeatability* (especially when oral transmission and performance predominate over written texts). But the story is a soap opera, and these are only the first couple of episodes; stay tuned for more big plot twists.

As it is, so much of our world has seemed to be built on the distinction between fact and fiction that even imagining its being breached tends to take the form of an apocalyptic scenario. Jorge Luis Borges's 1940 short story "Tlön, Uqbar, Orbis Tertius" tells of a secret society that, for many generations, has been compiling an encyclopedia of Tlön, a fictional planet where even the physical world is subject to lively traffic between fact and fiction. When parts of the encyclopedia are discovered, the fascination with Tlön spreads like wildfire: "Almost immediately, reality began to yield. The truth is that it longed to yield" (17). Disciplines such as history begin to metamorphose into their Tlönian counterparts, and strange artifacts described in Tlön's archaeology begin to be found. The narrator—who has withdrawn into his own pre-Tlönian scholarly pursuits—gloomily predicts that within a hundred years or so, "the world will be Tlön" (18).

William Burroughs's short narrative "Apocalypse" (1990) starts with the premise that the god Pan was declared dead at the birth of Christ. Until then, Pan had induced "the sudden awareness that everything is alive and significant," and though he "lives on in the realm of imagination" he has been "neutralized, framed in music, entombed in books." Thus, when the collective realization that "nothing is true" begins to take hold, it leads to "a basic disruption of reality itself" in which "art leaves the frame and the word leaves the page." "One rent in the fabric is all it takes for pandemonium to sluice through": machines come alive, "graffiti through glass and steel like acid races across the sky in tornados of flaming colors," crowds panic as the earth breaks free of its orbit, and, finally, Pan "pulls down the sky" as the narrator chants, "Let . . . It . . . Come . . . Down."

The apocalypticism—or what we can now call, following Foucault and Burroughs, the *epistemological panic*—associated with breached boundaries between fact and fiction also informs a widespread strain of thinking about postmodernity (of which Borges and Burroughs are often taken as representative). We have been told that a leveling of distinctions between facts and images is leading us all down the road to irrationalism, relativism, amorality, and the loss of a consensual reality. Never mind that the breach is better characterized as the failure to sustain a modernist *fetish* about fact and a rationalist *ideology* that never were what they were cracked up to be, though they seem so to their adherents now that they have, in fact, cracked up. There is a very specific word—*romanticism*—for the *nostalgia for what never was*. In the late eighteenth and early nineteenth centuries, romanticism harkened back to a happy premodernity; two hundred or so years later, romanticism is just as likely to harken back to modernity itself: Remember those happy nuclear families? The comforting stability of sexual identity? The civility? The trust we had in our scientists and politicians? I don't!

Not surprisingly, science fiction is a genre in which questions of the borders between fact and fiction are commonly and obsessively thematized and theorized: what contradictions, costs, and consequences are attendant on maintaining such a border, and what are the costs or consequences of refusing to do so or of trying to do something else? Such theorizing amounts to nothing more or less than the work in question negotiating a role for itself in *policing* the border and in *trafficking* across it. In other words, self-reference is not only a navel-gazing metadiscourse in which the work in question meditates impotently on its own position but also a major part of how the work actually jockeys for discursive position and, in so doing, participates in reproducing and potentially changing the discursive ecology in which it operates. The two films I discuss below illustrate typically "modernist" and "postmodernist" jockeyings for position but both in ways that also gesture beyond the modern/postmodern distinction.

The 1997 comedy/action film *Men in Black* is based on the premise that alien beings from all across the universe live among us, passing as humans, and that the earth is constantly teetering on the brink of one cosmic crisis or another. A secret government agency is charged with managing the alien presence and with perpetuating the facade of an orderly planet inhabited only by terrestrial species—a real feat of information control. An ongoing joke in the film is that the agents turn to the most sensational of tabloids—such as the *Weekly World News*—for accurate information, whereas stolid sources like the *New York Times* are filled with what amount to cover stories. The joke seems to turn the tables on middle-class rationality and its contempt for tabloid-reading lowbrows, its sense of comfort with what it thinks it knows about the world, its confidence in the stability and orderliness of things.

The film also adds a nice twist to one of the oldest and most generically definitive devices in sci-fi and supernatural fiction, whereby the rationalists are helplessly befuddled in the face of what only those who reject scientific dogma can recognize. Hamlet's famous comment to his scholarly friend Horatio—"There is more in heaven and earth than is dreamt of by your philosophy"—still serves well as a motto for an abiding mistrust of all official versions of the world. But *Men in Black*'s twist is that official information control is ongoing and systematic—and *benign*. The profoundly alien is passed off as familiar, and fact is disguised as sensationalist fiction. Such damage control seems necessary to protect middle-class rationality, to foreclose mass hysteria. And this would seem to be a self-amplifying system: the more the sense of order and familiarity is shored up, the more it is likely to freak out upon confronting chaos and strangeness, thus the more it needs to be shored up. The film offers itself to us as a confidential aside, an ironic wink: we know the official version is a fiction, but a necessary fiction, for our own good.

This quietism contrasts starkly to the apparently revolutionary activism of the 1988 John Carpenter film *They Live*, an earlier film also based on the premise of aliens living on earth, passing as humans. The heroes of both films are a white man and a black man, and, curiously enough, special sunglasses play a key role in the plots of both films.

In *They Live*, the aliens have conspired with human elites to rule the world and exploit the human workers. Two workmen, one black and one white, find special sunglasses that enable them to recognize the aliens and to see the otherwise subliminal messages printed everywhere—exhortations to OBEY and CONSUME. In the climax of the film, the machine that projects the force field to cloak the aliens is finally destroyed by the two men, who die heroically in the process. A final series of vignettes shows people suddenly awakening from "false consciousness" as they see the now uncloaked aliens in their true ugliness and rise up to throw off their oppressors.

They Live is driven by the modernist premise that capitalist consumer society is the means of world domination by a devious and inhuman elite, and when this is revealed, the revolution will commence and the oppressors and their collaborators will be brought down. Like all science fiction, the film reconfigures identities and differences. Here, racial and ethnic difference is negated by heroic male bonding, and the otherness displaced by this negation is *added* to class difference, so that the significant difference is not between black and white or even between human and alien as such but between the workers and the elites keeping them down. Plenty of extra otherness is left over for women, too: the woman who appears to offer help turns out to be an alien agent, and the closing vignettes feature prominently a woman-on-top sex scene in which a recumbent man rises up in horror to throw off his partner when she is revealed to be a grotesque alien. The message is a familiar one: male-bonded working-class men are the only agents of truth and revolution; women are manipulative sirens.

The sunglasses neatly represent the film itself as it would like to be understood. Like its sunglasses, *They Live* offers to mediate the worldview of the spectator to undo the distorting mediation already in operation—the "false consciousness" of dominant ideology—and to reveal oppression as it really is. By emitting a force field that makes the aliens appear human, the projector stands nicely for the dominant ideology's erasure of class difference. Having done their work and enabled the projector to be destroyed, the sunglasses, like the film itself, are no longer needed: reality can now be seen as it is, without mediation.

However, unlike the cloaked aliens who can at least be revealed as such, the contradiction that defines the film is hidden *in plain sight:* social reality *cannot be revealed by realism* but only by science fiction. In other words, the "world as it really is" that the film offers to show us—one in which the ruling class is "literally" an alien species—is precisely the world as it really is *not,* not literally, anyway, but metaphorically. Metaphors both displace and condense what they stand for: the representation of class difference as species difference does more than simply transpose or displace one kind of difference onto another; it also works to condense it, to make it more discrete, more representable, more visualizable in the first place. One might go on to ask whether representing the complex process of radical consciousness raising as something so succinct as putting on a pair of sunglasses—or as watching a single film—offers not a metaphor to be realized but a metaphor *instead* of a reality, a kind of inoculation with the dead virus of activism.

In fact, this question is nicely thematized in a 1999 episode of the much more elaborately paranoid *X Files,* in which agents Mulder and Scully are captured and are about to be digested by a giant underground fungus that, in order to lull its victims into passivity, induces in them the dream that their everyday lives are continuing, a nice figure for any dominant ideology (and also very close to the premise of the 1999-2003 *Matrix* film series). Scully figures out that this must be the case, and this realization enables the two of them to struggle up from underground and gain their freedom. But wait: it is only when they realize that their struggle to freedom was *too easy*—that it was *itself* a lulling dream induced by the fungus—that they can truly begin the struggle that leads to their rescue. Again, though, it is hard to say whether this extra twist offers a loophole big enough to wiggle out of ideology and into freedom (not bloody likely, eh?) or whether it just leads to a higher-class prison, since as Paul de Man once put it, "To know inauthenticity is not the same as to be authentic" (214). And de Man knew plenty about inauthenticity, since at the time he was a literary theorist at Yale (higher-class prison indeed) with a secret past as a Nazi-collaborationist journalist. In any case, such typically vexed postmodern complexity is definitive for the *X Files* main characters, government agents whose zeal to find and reveal the truth about paranormal events is continually co-opted by their employers, who are interested in covering it up. Thus, workers in the culture industry thematize their own dilemma.

This liminal "insider/outsider" status is also definitive for the agents of *Men in Black.* The "They" of *They Live,* the professional and managerial class represented as aliens in the Reagan-era film, are the "Us" of the later film, the men in black of *Men in Black,* but now it's "hip to be square." The new recruit (Will Smith) agrees to "sever all human contact" in order to join the agency, and just as he puts on the conspicuously anonymous black suit that will be his uniform from that day forward, the voice-over informs us that the agency is "above the system; over it; beyond it. We're 'they'; we're 'them'; we are the men in black."

In the postmodern world-picture offered by the film—the world of cosmic diaspora and transgalactic capital—difference must be not eradicated but regulated, as it offers both opportunity and danger. The men in black are the ones who can engage with aplomb otherwise mind-boggling difference; the agency "licenses, monitors, and polices" all alien activity on the planet. They ensure that the Other passes as the Self; they maintain the fiction of a shared identity, a sovereign nation, and a consensual rationality—a job all the more important, it seems, since it has become clear that identity, sovereignty, consensus, and reason are available *only* as fictions. These secret agents are so hyperprofessional, so supremely *cool* and competent (in the face of freaked-out people, rampaging and malevolent aliens, imminent Armageddon, and the like), that they make the James Bonds of old look positively hysterical.

ASIDE

Coolness. Two boys, about five and six years old, were sitting next to me on the subway. They were taking turns snapping their fingers and clapping and waving their hands inches from each other's face, trying not to blink. I realized that they were training each other to be *men,* with the implication that the ideal man is so phlegmatic as to be almost totally unresponsive. I noticed a young woman sitting across from me, also observing the boys. Her arms were folded across her chest, and she looked hurt and angry.

Such *coolness* is finally what the film is selling, *literally. Men in Black's* special sunglasses are worn by the agents to block the effects of the "Neuralyzer"—a flash device they use to erase the memory of people who have seen aliens and to make them receptive to a hypnotically implanted "screen memory." The Neuralyzer and sunglasses are imported alien technologies, along with Velcro and microwave ovens, the patents on which generate the agency's funding. In actuality, of course, the film tie-in was used to market the sunglasses and watches worn by the agents.

In making the agents immune to their own brainwashing, the sunglasses enable them to spread their cover stories without themselves forgetting the truth; in other words, they represent a *technology of irony* with which, apparently, all ideologues must be equipped. The thoroughgoingness of this irony, and with it the film itself, is further represented by the film's tabloids, since they are where the truth is hidden most conspicuously in plain sight, *generically,* as a kind of sensational fiction, as in the film itself. *They Live* had offered to reveal transparent, unmediated truth as such, only to show more nakedly its metaphorical and generically mediated—that is, science fictional—premise. *Men in Black,* we might say, suggests instead one of the first principles of antirealism: that whatever represents itself as a transparent window onto the truth—as realism—is thereby suspect, inherently untrustworthy, unrealistic.

Although the film clearly plays on anxieties about immigration and diplomacy in a global economy (with *intergalactic* substituted for *global*), it tries to refuse the simplest reading of its extraterrestrials as science-fictionalized immigrants. In the opening sequence, a dumb local sheriff begins harassing a busload of Mexicans being brought illegally across the border, but when the men in black show up, they pointedly release the immigrants, seeing correctly that the only real danger is the single extraterrestrial merely *passing* as an undocumented immigrant.

After the opening sequence of the film, a tired older white agent retires. Agent K (Tommy Lee Jones) then recruits and trains J (Will Smith, a younger black man), and at the end of the film K retires in turn, returning to enjoy private life and his long-lost love (after the obligatory memory wipe). The film's final scene shows J with *his* new recruit, a young (and suitably hyperprofessional) white woman with whom he had been flirting. The implication is clear: unlike his predecessor, J will be able to mix love and work in a profession now admitting women. Remarkably, then, for a big-budget Hollywood film, *Men in Black* manages to suggest early retirement as the best option for two older white men, and appreciatively but without even making an issue of it, to replace them with a younger black man and the white woman who is his love interest. The catch, of course—and it is a pretty big one—is that the new agents are assimilating perfectly into the hetero-WASP-guy impassiveness that characterizes professionalism in the film, thus conforming to the imperative to assimilate that they enforce, in turn, on all aliens. The message is clear: identity must be sacrificed to be an insider; to enjoy the privileges of real citizenship, one must become an unmarked and transcendental subject.

Both films thematize their own contradictory status as political and epistemological acts. But if they both end up passing as generically appropriate science fiction, and if in so doing they reproduce the fact/fiction border more or less intact, as they found it, what's the point? To this depressive question one might pose another: who says the fact/fiction border is intact? In order to be actuated as the possibly "miraculous weapons" they might be (that was Aimé Césaire's phrase for revolutionary artworks), science fiction texts in particular must be read against the grain, as the men in black read the tabloids—not as true facts but at least as potentially valid theory.

10

How Bad Facts
Make Good Theories

It is a truism that a "higher truth" than the merely factual is evoked in literature. What this usually means is that by not getting bogged down in the facts (understood as particular historical details), a work of fiction or poetry is better able to paint a "big picture" of how the world works and what kind of world it is; it misses the trees in order to see the forest. Mary Shelley's *Frankenstein,* for example, is prefaced with the typically romantic claim that her story, "however impossible as a physical fact, affords a point of view to the imagination for the delineating of human passions more comprehensive and commanding than any which the ordinary relations of existing events allows" (6). The claim is a typically romantic *power move* in staking out for itself an almost transcendental or panoptic viewpoint with "commanding" oversight over the merely "ordinary"; such a claim resonates fully with an ideology that sets mental and managerial power over physical labor. To the hierarchizing function of such metaphysical "higher truth" claims we can oppose a related but more horizontal claim focused on *kinds* of knowledge rather than *degrees:* that literature has been privileged to think through the self-referentiality banished from science and that science fiction's hybrid and marginal location gives it a special privilege to rethink epistemological questions even as this privilege seems to come with the apparently high price of a loss of legitimacy. Ideologies function to push out onto their subordinates the contradictions that would otherwise compromise them (that is, so as to seem themselves seamless and internally consistent). To bear these contradictions is not automatically to know them, and knowing them is not the same as reactivating them, which may be a question not of throwing them off but of learning how to use them to push back. This kind of partial leverage is what we try to gain by reading science fiction (in the past section), tabloid journalism, and even madness (in this section) as theory and philosophy. I leave mostly until chapter 18 the broader question of what kinds of knowledge may be particularly available to those who straddle identities or who are hybrids or some not-quite-legitimate combination of insider and outsider.

When I've made tabloids like the *Weekly World News* the object of literary analysis in the classroom, many of my students have been eager to distinguish themselves from what they characterize as gullible masses: people who—like children or primitives who cannot tell fact from fiction—actually *believe* such nonsense. It is all very well, some have said to me, for an ivory-tower philosopher to indulge in theoretical speculations about the value and epistemological status of the tabloid world, but the merely gullible mass of tabloid readers is not inclined to any such meditations. And yes, I would reply (and to my dear readers, too), the work I do for you, and try to teach you to do, is in thinking through and trying to articulate the epistemological status of texts. This a difficult job, by the way, and all the more so because every reader constantly, delicately, and almost automatically negotiates epistemological questions without thinking much about them, if only to set truth questions aside. Dividing things into fact and fiction need not be the focus of every reading, and I would guess that most tabloid readers do not simply either believe or disbelieve the stories they read.

I admit that I am disinclined to believe (for example) the various articles I have seen that claim extraterrestrial aliens control U.S. presidential elections, but the story does seem to get at some important flavor or tenor—something politically crucial—having to do with forces that seem to be beyond individual and even collective control, that seem to have a life of their own. I am disturbed by the tabloid picture of a world often built on racist and xenophobic principles, a world also in which a few are endowed with prodigious powers, leaving for the rest of us a sense of helpless fatalism or quick fixes. But I see such a world in the *New York Times*, too! The sense of alienation—the sense that one does not participate in power—is characteristic of modernity.

Anthropologists used to characterize "primitive" cultures by their sense of "mystical participation": the sense of human kinship with nature (for example, as symbolized by animal totems with which clans or individuals identify) and even the sense that natural processes (such as daily and seasonal cycles) depend on the performance of certain rituals, the omission of which would jeopardize the universe. To moderns, this tends to look like a kind of delusion of grandeur, like the egotism of isolated tribes who have no other name for themselves but "the people," or the premodern assumption that the earth is the center of the cosmos.

In this account, the displacement of the earth from the center of the universe by Copernicus is the paradigmatic paradigm shift. Scientific rationality brings a humility that makes the primitive's abasement to his god look like the most presumptuous arrogance: as if there were a god who cared for human prayers, or as if the universe had "chosen people" or nature was any respecter of persons! But notice, too, that what comes to be called "science" is, at the same time, often associated not with humility but with the most Promethean hubris—with playing God, in fact. In modern horror films, science often produces monsters by meddling with forces beyond its control, though it is most often science that vanquishes the monsters in turn.

Modernity, as I have mentioned, is commonly construed as a complication, diversification, and semiautonomization of the structures of knowledge and power; science is, of course, one of the semiautonomous institutions in this modern mix. This autonomy had to be won; it had to be leveraged from the inside: in Steven Shapin and Simon Schaffer's account, for example, Boyle's air pump was simultaneously a device to produce a partial vacuum and, in the process, a means to wrest away some power and authority from the aristocracy (for a nutshell account, see Latour, "Ethnography").

Is it possible that modern epistemology, which humbles and decenters humans before *nature,* follows from the extent (both quantitatively and qualitatively) to which modern *society and culture* as a totality exceed the power and knowledge of individuals or groups within it, the extent to which the totality is *delinked* or autonomized? Science and technology do seem to reproduce and intensify such a world, as indeed do all forms of specialized knowledge and elite power. From Dr. Frankenstein to Dr. Strangelove and beyond, the story of science and technology "out of control" or "taking on a life of its own" validates its own epistemology while producing the characteristic structure of feeling (acute in postmodernity but much older) that construes culture *as* nature and as a kind of juggernaut beyond human control.

There are many more or less illegitimate epistemological resistances to such a world. For example, the pseudoscience of astrology seems to have ensured a niche for itself by affirming the very thing that science seems to negate: the ongoing participation of personality and daily life in the order of the cosmos at large. Like the sciences of genetics and psychology, astrology holds out the promise of revealing fundamental principles of human predispositions, personality types, and their dynamic permutations. But whereas genetics and psychology have been driven to categorize differences mostly in terms of normalcy and deviance—and to understand their own roles in terms of intervention and control or cure—astrology is mostly predicated on identifying *benign* differences that can be strategically negotiated but are essentially intractable and certainly not subject to "cure."

This amounts to much more than just saying astrology thrives by catering to desires science does not address—the desire for cosmic participation, the desire to be recognized as different without being pathologized. To leave it at that would only underwrite the familiar account of science as offering brutal facts, while everything else offers feel-good fictions. There is a baby in the astrological bathwater, a theory of connectedness and benign difference and of the wrongheadedness of the rage to intervene and control. Arguably, these virtues of astrology are increasingly being recognized in science; at least popular narratives of current paradigm shifts in science tend to represent science as incorporating or synthesizing its Others (see chapter 19).

Beyond tabloids and astrology, the most illegitimate theorizing crosses over into insanity. Freud was not the first to mine madness for the cultural and social knowledge buried there but the first to systematize that operation; arguably, the degeneration of psychoanalysis into a private, meliorative procedure rather than a way of producing cultural knowledge (of pushing back on the contradictions) has worked pretty effectively as a way of reburying such insights (see Weinstein). Freud was particularly struck by the idea that the mad may live out the epistemological contradictions that psychoanalysis attempts to leverage when he came to read Dr. Schreber's account of his paranoid delusions. Freud was struck by how much Schreber's delusions (of divine rays and so forth) seemed to be precise *literalizations* of the psychological processes and structures that his own psychoanalytic theories had described; the parallels were so close that Freud felt obliged to remind the reader, "I had developed my theory of paranoia before I became acquainted with the contents of Schreber's book" ("Paranoia" 182).

I felt much the same way when I read Richard Kopperdahl's account ("Crazy in New York") of how a curious obsession developed into madness. When shooting pool, Kopperdahl became obsessed with what is called body English, where after taking a shot, a player will jerk and twist his body as if magically to communicate some motion to the ball, to make it spin more in the desired direction. Reasoning generously that people would not so commonly expend so much energy on body English unless it had some real usefulness, Kopperdahl asked himself whether there might not be some context in which body English would really work. This question generated the "eureka" moment that was to be Kopperdahl's decisive step toward madness: body English would work *underwater,* where a twisting motion would generate eddies that could *really* affect objects just out of reach. Humans must have lived for eons as aquatic creatures—during the time of the biblical Flood—and body English must be a behavioral remnant of what was once an effective practice. From here, Kopperdahl somehow decided that he could *still* breathe underwater. This led to some dangerous experiments and, soon after, to the locked ward at Bellevue.

There is an elegant and compelling logic to Kopperdahl's obsession. Pool and billiards have been—since their rise to popularity among European elites in the rationalist eighteenth century—the classic examples of linear, mechanistic cause and effect (object A strikes object B, which in turn strikes object C, and so on). One's ability to influence the course of events is limited to a single stroke, a momentary touch of the cue stick on the cue ball; after that, one can only stand back and watch the result, which is supposed to follow in a mechanical and completely deterministic way from the single touch that set the ball in motion. In this model, the player resembles an absentee god who sets a clockwork universe in motion and then withdraws, a narrative that opposes older accounts of a world in which God or gods participate continuously and remain accessible to human interaction.

The dominant model proposes geometry as sufficient to account for what happens in pool; its "geometricity" is what gives the game its abstract cleanness, what recommends it as a model to begin with. Indeed, with its spherical balls and flat, level surface, the game seems to have been engineered to be as close as possible to a linear and mechanistic idealization of the world. It is true that you can become a mediocre pool player by mastering the geometry of the game, which accounts for a lot of what happens. But the effects of friction—the continuous feedback loop between the ball and its environment (table surface, rails, other balls)—are what push the game into the realm of physics and nonlinearity, and English takes advantage of this. Topspin causes the cue ball to follow the object ball after striking it; bottom English ("draw") will cause the cue to stop dead or recoil after striking the object ball; left and right English spin the cue ball off its otherwise straight course. The effect of spin can also be changed by adjusting the speed of the ball or by hitting it off a rail; in some cases spin can also be effectively transferred from the cue ball to the object ball. The further from the original stroke, the more nonlinearities are amplified: as anyone who has played pool knows, shots in which A hits B, B hits C, and C hits D are monstrously difficult because the margin for error gets smaller and smaller, rapidly exceeding human visual acuity, computational ability, and hand–eye coordination—and reaching the point where even perfect accuracy in these could not override the effects of tiny irregularities in the playing surface, cue tip, and more. The more balls involved, the more difficult or impossible it becomes to predict where each will end up: this is why even the best players cannot with any consistency hit a particular ball into a particular pocket on the break shot, which involves all fifteen balls. It is easy to see that the linear, determinist model of the game had to have been developed from *billiards,* played with only two object balls, rather than pool, with fifteen.

The use of English pushes the game more into the realm of nonlinearity, but it is also a big part of what distinguishes a good player from a mediocre one—or as another writer put it, in a game between a Newtonian and a non-Newtonian player, "The only deterministic, Newtonian event observable would be the arithmetic reduction in the thickness of [the Newtonian's] wallet" (Smith 12). Kopperdahl explains that "English, the heart and soul of pool, gives the game a nearly magical quality" and that body English is "the most magical English of all." Given the dominant geometric, idealized, linear, determinist account of pool, it is easy to see how English gets situated as unreason—even in the positive sense of "heart and soul"—and, finally, as magic.

Remarkably, Kopperdahl's crazy scenario of human evolution very precisely reproduces the anthropologist's story: once upon a time, humans participated mystically in the world; we seemed to be connected in some subtle way with the things of the world (as the player who uses body English seems to identify with the ball) and to be able to influence them, ritually, through this connection. In this sense, body English is really a symptom, a "return of the repressed," as if the body continued to enact what had in fact been mostly purged by the rules of the game (the possibility of ongoing participation) and further erased by the linear, deterministic account of how the balls themselves behave. If body English is efficacious insofar as it preserves at least the memory of what the determinist account has not been able to eradicate, it is also counterproductive in allowing nonlinearity to be reduced to a convulsive afterthought. If the player could reintegrate nonlinearity into his model of the game, if his strokes were fully informed in the first place by such a model and not the impoverished linear one, perhaps he would forego the ritual tic of body English. But this scenario seems too optimistic given that it is not only the *model of the game* but *the game itself* that has worked systematically to exclude nonlinearity. We can at least say that something in us instinctively recoils—literally and symbolically—from a linearly deterministic world in which our ongoing participation has no part.

For all its metaphorical truth, though, Kopperdahl's mad theory goes wrong by reductively literalizing in several ways. It makes a particular game bear the whole burden of representing the world, and it reduces the complex history of changing ways of living in the world to a simple fact ("humans once lived in water"), just as it reduces the sense of ongoing participation in the world—in spite of an "official version" that excludes it—to a simple fact ("I can still breathe underwater"). It even reads the Bible not as myth or metaphor but as a distorted account of historical fact—an account one need not *interpret* but can simply *decode* with the proper key (the biblical Flood must refer to the fact of a previous aquatic age). Maybe part of what drove Kopperdahl mad was that he too thoroughly fetishized the rationalist, realist, reductionist, referentialist account in the first place, overvaluing facts as such and devaluing and disavowing metaphor, but these are also the ways he most resembles the classical caricature of a scientist! "The peculiarity of the schizophrenic," as Gregory Bateson puts it, is precisely the misrecognition that cultural critics attribute to the scientist: "not that he uses metaphors, but that he uses *unlabeled* metaphors" (205).

There is one more looping stitch that knits metaphor, madness, theory, and science together in this account. Given the scientificity of his madness and the madness of his scientificity, it may come as no surprise that, apparently unknown to Kopperdahl (he does not mention it, in any case), as he began his descent into madness, some scientists of evolution were seriously considering a theory that humans evolved from an ape species that had been driven into the water by flooding and eons later returned to land. As in Kopperdahl's account, the primary scientific evidence for the theory is the contemporary presence of human features (body English not among them, however) that can be neatly explained as adaptations to aquatic life in the distant past! First proposed in 1960, the theory was developed by Elaine Morgan in *The Aquatic Ape* (1982), and the debate it started has been simmering—though very much on a scientific back burner—since then; the opposing positions were gathered in the 1991 volume edited by Machteld Roede and others, *The Aquatic Ape: Fact or Fiction?*

11

Self-Reference I

Linguist Roman Jakobson identified *self-reference* as the predominant linguistic function of poetry; he called it *poeticity*. The term refers to the way poetry tends to call attention to itself as an artifact of language—for example, by rhyme or meter or special diction—so as to make *what* is being said secondary to *how* it is being said. As such, poetry is opposed to referential discourse, which tends to efface its own artifice, the better to represent itself as a transparent window onto the world—a ploy also known as *realism*. An extreme form of self-reference may be where "the medium *is* the message," but Jakobson's point was that all discourses and statements perform referential, self-referential, and other functions and that each function is crucial even where subordinated to others.

Beyond the formal patterning of poems by devices such as rhyme and meter, poetic self-reference edges into kinds of metadiscourse in which text takes itself as one of its themes. Such thematization is sometimes accomplished by familiar devices such as plays within plays or through less explicitly reflexive images, as in the many romantic poems in which poets and poetry are represented by images of singing birds, wind-caressed harps, or babbling brooks.

These self-references can produce multiple and contradictory effects. They can call the realism of the text into question, inviting readers to recognize the act of representation as a thing in itself, bearing only an uncertain relation to what it represents. But this recognition need not simply undermine the reader's trust in the verisimilitude of the text, or in so doing may drive the reader to find some higher ground, some truth or truism inescapable even in fantasy. By producing parallels, permutations, and oppositions between the text and the way it represents itself, self-reference often tries to level the difference between signifier and signified, to enhance its "ring of truth." For example, in poems where poetry is represented as birdsong, the effect may be to pitch the text as beautiful, natural, and unforced.

Self-reference echoes the split between text and world in the text itself, or as Luhmann put it, "The system copies the difference between system and environment into itself and uses it as a premise of its own operations" (*Observations* 110). There is a nest of related paradoxes here. How could the system copy the difference between itself and its environment to use as a premise of its own operations if this difference is what brings it into being in the first place or, rather, what *it brings into being*? Doesn't the system have to be operative to perform the act of copying supposed to *premise* its operations? The most basic answer to these questions (which will be explored further in chapter 13) is that a self-referential system simply *is* and *operates as* such a nest of paradoxes.

Self-reference is not merely a literary or rhetorical trick, manipulated by clever authors and revealed by clever critics. It is the stuff of everyday linguistic interactions; perhaps at some level it is a part of all interactions. Before going on to consider this pervasiveness, I want to establish some basic terms and to flesh out the workings of self-reference by considering several very short texts. But before engaging these texts relatively minutely, let me also make one thing perfectly clear (as Richard Nixon used to say). I don't want to claim (as the romantics often wanted to do) that self-referential literary texts are essentially *little organisms* but that because literary self-referentialism was heightened as it evolved with and against scientific referentialism, such texts are a good place to begin to investigate the various operations of self-reference. Especially now that science has begun to reincorporate the self-reference paradigm, the ways these texts *bear witness* to a changing discursive ecology are particularly important, and inquiry should work to open and keep open the questions of what kinds of knowledge can be gained by studying texts and of how the most minute kinds of textual self-reference will turn out to be related to self-reference in language and culture more broadly and in social and natural systems.

A first and very famous example is Ezra Pound's two-line poem from 1926, "On a Station in the Metro":

The apparition of these faces in the crowd;
Petals on a wet, black bough.

The poem is famous for its compellingly brief parallel between two otherwise very different images. The rush-hour crowd in the Paris subway (the Metro) seems to be an entirely artificial phenomenon, shaped by modern technology and architecture and by the mechanical rhythms of train schedules and the urban workday. On the other hand, one imagines that fallen petals stick spontaneously to a wet branch by a chance conjunction of the wild, natural forces of rain, wind, and organic growth. A visual similarity arises, between these otherwise very different phenomena, because the crowd stretches out along the platform as if along a branch and because—apparently—the faces stand out ghostly pale against the background of dark clothing and the low light of the tunnel (*apparition* connoting both simple *appearance* and *ghost*). Notice that both station and bough constitute a single segment of a larger branching network—subway system and tree—of which each is a part.

The resemblance is supposed to be a pleasant surprise. Subways usually typify all that is ugly, mundane, and unpoetic about Western modernity, whereas petals and bare branches are associated with the timelessly beautiful realms of nature and art; perhaps they suggest the elegant aesthetics of a Japanese woodblock print. Of course, these expectations and habitual associations have been shaped by art itself, including modern poetry, and this is one way the poem refers to itself as a modern poem: it plays with the opposition between the poetic and the antipoetic, an opposition it creates. But this does not quite capture the sophistication of the ploy: modern poetry has taught us to expect it to show us beauty where we don't expect it, to *make* things poetic; this is its claim to fame. "On a Station in the Metro" is a quintessentially modern poem because it works a simultaneous opposition and identity between what is poetic and unpoetic.

Most generally, one might say about poetry or other self-referential systems that they are elaborations of the difference between themselves and what is not themselves. Another way, then, that texts are self-referential is through *intertextuality*: all texts refer to other texts, gaining their meaning by performing various permutations on other texts. While the poem is pointing to things in the world—while it is saying all of the other things it says—what it is also doing is saying that "this is a poem and not (for example) a scientific treatise" and that "this is *this* poem and not *another* poem." (Note that it could also try to say "this is a poem *and* a scientific treatise," but that would be a difficult pitch to make. I am trying to do it here. Is it working? Will you buy this bridge from me?) In other words (and as Foucault pointed out), statements are meaningful as they differ from, or perform permutations on, other statements and categories of statements. Another way of saying this is that statements are meaningful according to what they *don't* say.

An obvious intertext for Pound's poem is Percy Shelley's 1819 "Ode to the West Wind," which begins as follows:

O wild West Wind, thou breath of Autumn's being,
Thou, from whose unseen presence the leaves dead
Are driven, like ghosts from an enchanter fleeing,

Yellow, black, and pale, and hectic red,
Pestilence-stricken multitudes: O Thou,
Who chariotest to their dark wintry bed

The winged seeds, where they lie cold and low,
Each like a corpse within its grave . . .

(221)

Notice that Pound's images rework some of the main elements of Shelley's, repeating the parallel between windblown foliage and driven crowds, focusing again on their ghostliness and on their transportation underground. Shelley, in turn, had reworked "the traditional epic simile found in Homer, Virgil, Dante and Milton, in which souls of the dead are compared to fallen leaves driven by the wind" (Shelley 221). Here we might (but let's not!) enter the territory of a very narrow kind of literary history ("Images of Windblown Foliage in the Western Poetic Tradition") that goes along with "the dominance of pale faces"—Pound, Shelley, Milton, Dante, Virgil, Homer—stretched out along the bough of Literature. Here self-reference enables us to construe literature in the narrowest and most exclusionary way, though by the same token (and in case you missed it, that was a bad subway joke) we are enabled to catch this construction in the act. One clue here is the way Pound's image *whitens* the inclusive racial spectrum of all humanity posited by Shelley's image of "yellow, black, and pale, and hectic red."

There is also a more intimate kind of self-reference in Pound's poem. The series of faces stretched out through the crowd and the petals along the bough also resemble *the letters and words of the poem,* stretched out as they are along the horizontal, long- and-narrow shape of its two lines. One might say that the black letters against the white page form a kind of photographic negative of the pale faces and petals against their dark backgrounds. These observations may also remind us that the poem, too—like the station and the bough—is a single segment of an interconnected, branching network of poetry, literature, language.

This self-reference is specific to *this* poem in its actual physical appearance. The resemblance between the poem and its two images would have been unnoticeable if the poem had been written in a more usual, squarish stanza. It seems, then, that this self-referential resonance may be enhanced when the poem is seen on the page as well as heard; in other words, the poem also posits itself as a particular written artifact.

The specific resemblance between the poem and its images makes a very striking point. Language is usually arbitrary in reference to what it represents: there is no necessary relation whatsoever between the specific physicality of the words and what they signify; that is, the sounds and shapes of the French term *metro* (or the American *subway* or the British *underground*) bear no specific relation to the sounds and shapes of actual subways. But the poem takes this arbitrariness, this nonrelation, and makes it into a likeness.

Is this a fortuitous likeness or a real kinship? The poem's images give us terms to think about this question; they *thematize* the question. We can develop the terms by interrogating the images. Have the petals stuck to the bough because the wind and rain have blown them there, randomly, from some flower somewhere else, or are they parts of flowers actually growing from the branch? It seems more likely that this might be a flowering tree and that the petals of its own flowers have been blown back onto its branches. In any case, we can ask the same questions about the petals in relation to the bough that we can ask about the petalled bough in relation to the subway crowd and the poem in relation to both of them: are these things from different realms that have entered into some ephemeral conjunction, or has part of a larger network connected back onto itself in the combinatory cycle of some universal ecology? How hetero- and homogeneous and how closed and open are the networks in relation to each other and to themselves? Are things and words—nature and culture—siblings or strange bedfellows? The work of the poem is to open such questions, and its success and its ongoing capacity to interest us lie not in the extent to which it is able to resolve them but in holding them open. Where the strands cross, the poem presses its finger, leaving the knot to be tied by its readers.

Here it might be helpful to think of an analogue to the poem. Godfrey Reggio's 1983 film *Koyannisqatsi* juxtaposes time-lapse scenes of natural processes such as cloud formation with urban and technological patterns such as auto and pedestrian traffic to suggest both that modern life is dangerously "out of balance" with nature (the translation of the film's title) and, simultaneously, that it continues to belong to a larger ecology of flows and patterns.

Insofar as self-reference suggests a real kinship of some kind between the text and its referent, it moves from proposing mere metaphors to asserting itself as a Symbol (capitalized here to indicate the special sense of the term as developed in romanticism). A metaphor suggests a parallel between two unrelated realms; a Symbol purports to *participate* in what it represents, as here in the suggestion that poetry and language may belong, like flowering trees and subways, to an ecology of circulating similarities and differences—a network of networks that is the dynamic interrelation of them all. As I suggested before, the trick is to affirm the participation while continuing to hold at bay the suggestion of a singular totality.

Another famous two-line text, which for a generation of readers has come to stand for the process of being taught to read, will help develop the concept of *performative* self-reference:

See Spot run.
Run, Spot, run.

The first line implies a scene of two people and a dog named Spot; one of the viewers directs the attention of the other to the dog and tells the other to watch it run. In the second line, one or both of the viewers exhort the dog to keep running. The self-referential twist of these lines is that the fictional scene *corresponds to the real scene of reading,* in which a teacher directs the attention of a pupil to follow the running sequence of letters and words on the page. Because the second line is made up of words already familiar from the first, the process is speeded up and made almost automatic, which is of course the object of the lesson: to make reading "second nature." This automation is already suggested by the image: of course, letters and words are stationary; they don't really "run" across the page. The only running spot is the moving focus of the pupil's pupils. By attributing movement to the text itself, the work of reading as performed by the reader's eyes is effaced; the reader is not even exhorted to "watch" but merely to "see," as if one passively follows a text and exhorts it to do what it is already doing, on its own.

So the text operates to focus the attention, to turn it into a "spot" and train it to run back and forth: it tries to make us into reading machines in a way that seems to justify Donna Haraway's observation that "our machines are disturbingly lively, and we ourselves frighteningly inert" (152). In so doing, the text enacts a disciplinary ideology that, with the Dick and Jane series, reached its hegemonic peak in the 1950s United States, when 80 percent of first graders were learning to read with Dick and Jane—and spending up to 40 percent of each school day doing so (Kismaric and Heiferman 21, 78). Of course, to assess fully the historical/ideological and cultural/linguistic specificity of this way of teaching reading would involve looking at how reading has been taught in other languages and cultures and at other times.

The strategic integrity and specificity of the disciplinary operation of the text can be suggested by a counterexample: imagine replacing "Run, Spot, run" with "Stop, Spot, stop!" Here a curious contradiction is produced because *the eye* is meant to keep running even though *Spot* is commanded to stop. Even more distracting, the obviousness of the rearrangement of the same four letters into two different words *(s, t, o, p* and *s, p, o, t)* heightens the turbulence in the otherwise smooth, linear stream of the text; it slows the reader down to consider the artifacticity of words; it is, in other words, *too poetic.*

The parallel between the actual scene of reading and the fictional scene in the text is a little too precise to be merely something read into the text, after the fact, by a clever interpretation. The sense that one may be overreading is often put in terms of the writer's intention: did the writers of "See Spot run" *really* set out to find subject matter that could also be an image of the reading process itself? Well, they might well have, but they needn't have gone out of their way to do so, since when one immerses oneself in a task (such as teaching people to read), one allows oneself to be directed by its logic and allows its terms to be the terms of engagement; *self-reference pulls intentionality into its own orbit.* This is not to say that every single image in the Dick and Jane series will be such a striking image of the reading process itself, only that such images will be selected much more strongly in such a context and will assume more resonance and importance. Such a selection is illustrated by the retroactive process whereby readers have taken this particular two-line excerpt to stand for the whole series and for the process of learning to read. In fact, I have not been able to locate the precise lines as such in the series at all; the little two-line poem seems to be a conflation of various related lines, a collective misremembering that has stuck because it distills the dynamics of the series so nicely.

One might well say that the text is not really *about* two people watching a dog. It refers to them only as an image of itself, only as an expedient means to an end. But the means and end are the same: one reads in order to learn to read. This is why the text also is not *about* learning to read (the way a scholarly article on literacy training would be); it is not really *about* anything, and this is why it's not sufficient to call it self-referential. Its primary function is not to refer to something but to make something happen, and it *is* a primary part of the something it makes happen. It is *performative.*

Performative is philosopher J. L. Austin's term for a way of "doing things with words": a kind of utterance in which the words themselves constitute the action. Common performatives are "Thank you" or "I apologize" or "I christen this ship the *Queen Mary.*" What does poetry perform? A love poem can perform love (the labor lavished on the artifact providing its own evidence) and power (as in the old ploy of immortalizing the beloved)—and, according to a recent U.S. Navy code, "unwanted poetry" can even constitute, in itself, sexual harassment. African American traditional and popular forms such as "signifying" or "the dozens"—no less than the high oratory of political speeches—are performative rituals of identity production and exclusion, just as certain kinds of cultural competence or literacy can be performed by the "right" kind of writing or reading (or writing about) poetry.

Just as with Jakobson's conception of self-reference, it is important to understand the performative as a dimension of all statements, even where this dimension seems to be subordinated. A statement like "The sky is blue" is in an exemplary way *not* performative, at least insofar as my saying it does not make it so (you can go to the window and check), but if the speaker of another language has just asked me to define *blue,* then my saying so *does* make it so insofar as it constitutes a performative act of definition, even if I have lied and the sky is really gray: disinformation is performative, too. But even in other contexts my saying "The sky is blue" will perform some kind of assertion of authority, meteorological or linguistic or both, attempting to position me in relation to an interlocutor and to language, though this performative function may be obscured by the referential dimension of the statement.

ASIDE

Languaging the Universe. But (asks a reader) although my saying "The sky is blue" can influence my interlocutor, can it ever have any purchase on *the sky?* Even disregarding the question of how much the quality of blueness may reside in the sky or the beholder (a serious scientific question, by the way), we should remember at least that the sky was created and is sustained by the exhalations of earthly creatures (and if you don't believe me, just try to find blue skies on Uranus). Insofar as our perceptions of and statements about the sky can influence our own ecological behavior, they can certainly have some effect on the sky's color! Of course, the effect of any single statement will be negligible, but statements participate in discursive ecologies that are really (I mean *in actuality*) entities fully involved (*players,* we could say) in the physical universe. Changes in their intrarelationality may change their interrelationality as well.

But (asks the same wise guy) can any discursive ecology or any human action make a difference in the structure of the universe? Of course, I don't have a crystal ball, but isn't a universe with life in it a different universe than a lifeless one, or is life just an optional accessory? And if the organization of human brains (as we are sometimes told) is in some senses more complex than the universe in/out of which they emerged, doesn't that make it a different universe? And does language then make for a different universe? If not, is it because life and language are in some sense part of the structure in the first place, that is, because it's that *kind* of universe?

But (asks the reader again, who is beginning to get annoying), in any case, aren't living things *latecomers,* unable to alter the fundamental relationships (forces, particles, and so on) out of which they emerge? Or as God asked Job, where were you when I made the universe, Mr. Know-It-All? Well, it seems to me that we're still making it, but if you insist that it is a kind of cake with things at the bottom and a mere frosting of words on the top, I will just keep reminding you that there's frosting between the layers as well (or, to get cute about it, that the distinction between ontology and semantics belongs to semantics). Or finally, just to be petulant in return, if words don't matter to quarks and gravity (that is, if quarks and gravity could get along just as well without words), then maybe quarks and gravity don't matter to words either: one could imagine, anyway, that language could evolve in a sufficiently complex universe with *different* particles and forces altogether. In fact, *these very words* have metamorphosed from being made of chemical reactions (in my brain) to dancing light (on my computer screen) to sluggish ink (on this page) without missing a beat: they kept marching on, to their different drummer, in exactly the same order, never registering even the slightest concern.

A performative statement cannot be evaluated according to its truth or falsity: if I say "I apologize," you can question my sincerity, but I can protest that my statement did, in itself, constitute an apology—arguably even more so if I *didn't* mean it, since then it would be more of a testament to your power to wring an apology from me. Austin proposes that performative statements be evaluated according to what he calls their *happiness:* for a performance to be *happy* it must work within its idiom; the speaker must have the proper performative authority. I can performatively "claim this land in the name of Queen Isabella," but only a set of relations extrinsic to the statement (how I am positioned as a historical agent) can say whether the statement is a *happy* one and for whom, whether I am celebrated or hated or taken away in a straitjacket. But this account seems prejudicially to polarize text and context (what is intrinsic and extrinsic to the statement itself), because among what statements work to perform, to constitute, to negotiate and renegotiate, are the very terms of their idiom and authority. Perhaps the extent—always partial and relational—to which statements can achieve such power is the extent to which they can be called poetic (in the sense of their *poiesis,* their power to shape and make the system of which they are a part).

And what is the *extent* of poetry? How local, how momentary, are the powers of art? Literary theorist Mikhail Bakhtin related the novel to the tradition of Carnival, in which, for a specified time, all power relations are turned ritually upside down (beggars dress as kings, aristocrats as highwaymen, men as women, and so on); art can be a kind of portable carnival, a way of letting off steam, a ritually contained safety valve. How much does this safety valve protect the status quo, and how much does it threaten to subvert it? How *leaky* is the valve? Perhaps it is not the ritual but what leaks from it that can be called poetic.

One final two-line text—a question and answer from a television news segment—will develop some of the nuances of self-reference and performativity. Sometime back in late 1995, I watched the local New York CBS News anchorman getting a preview of the upcoming national news from network anchor Dan Rather. He asked Rather if the just-announced convictions of then president Clinton's old cronies (in the Arkansas land-speculation scam known as Whitewater) would damage Clinton's 1996 reelection campaign. Rather responded, gravely, that the convictions were *very damaging indeed.*

There are several ways of understanding Rather's response. Though uttered as a simple fact, it seems to be more of a prediction, perhaps based on expertise gleaned from similar circumstances. Or is it more like a would-be self-fulfilling prophecy, a disguised way of telling people what to think? After all, the damage to Clinton's reelection does not follow automatically from the verdict but is based on how the verdict is communicated to and interpreted for and by voters, and Rather's statement does not stand outside this process but participates in it. We could break down the interchange as follows: the local anchorman presumes to stand in for the viewers—the "people"—who ask, "How should we respond?" to which Rather replies, in effect, "You will be gravely concerned, as I am." But this is still a bit simplistic. The question is really more like, "What will *others* think?" and the answer—that *they* will be gravely concerned—implies that *you* should be upset also. In other words, even if you are not upset, enough *other* people will be upset so that, like it or not, you will have to reckon with the repercussions: it begins to seem like a *fact,* beyond one's control. If enough people are upset, perhaps Clinton himself will be "upset" in the election, so perhaps you must reconsider your position or vote. The concern is manufactured by being projected onto others and then introjected.

ASIDE

Othering. I remember an even more elegant example of projection-introjection from a previous presidential primary campaign. Evidence of candidate Gary Hart's extramarital affairs had just been revealed, and one television news program took a poll to determine whether the revelations about Hart would cause people to consider changing their votes; about three-fourths at that time said no. However, when asked if they thought the revelations would cause *others* to change their votes, the same margin said *yes*. Whatever exact percentage answered no and then yes, one can only guess that they were concerned to represent themselves as "not prudish" or as able to separate the candidate's "personal life" from his policies in a hard-nosed and rational way, while not extending this credit to others. Similarly, when asked how much of their trash they recycle, people report a percentage that turns out to be much higher than their actual practice, as researchers have discovered from empirical study—that is, from sifting through garbage (the archetype of empirical research!). But when asked how much they think *their neighbors* recycle, they tend to give a much lower percentage, one that tends to represent *their own* practice so accurately that researchers have learned that they can count on people's estimates of their neighbors to represent themselves.

There was no discussion about whether or how the conviction implicated the Clintons—and in fact the judge had gone out of his way to assert that it did not—but only about how it would be *perceived*. Like some paradox of postmodern physics, there is *spin* but no particle. This kind of closed catalytic reaction—in which the investigation generates a cover-up, which becomes the subject of the investigation, and so on—characterized the Whitewater investigation throughout; indeed, it seems to be a defining feature of the postmodern media event in general.

There is a third, related, way of understanding it: that Rather's response is a self-referential statement whose main import is, "This is a BIG story!" Of course, newsmen cannot simply scream repeatedly, "This is a big story! This is a big story!"—nor can they say aloud, "I want you to be very concerned about this because your concern makes it a big story and makes me the privileged mediator of the imaginary world in which you live." For the ploy to have a chance to work, the self-referential and performative dimensions of the utterance must be fully subordinated and even disavowed (which means that their disavowal must also be disavowed). But notice that one may even see through the statement without completely undermining its efficacy if one simply believes that *others are not so astute;* that is, "I see that the statement aims to *produce* the concern it purports merely to *describe,* but others, who are more gullible, will actually believe that the widespread concern exists and will be concerned accordingly, and thus I must also be concerned."

It is important to recognize that there are no *others* except as invented by the structure of the statement, though with potentially real consequences. Are these others perhaps the fabled *silent majority?* Well, first of all, they are the subjects of reporting whom the reporter purports to stand *outside of*—as an anthropologist stands outside his subjects. If this view is disparaging, and it is, there is another more flattering but no less self-serving one: Hillary Clinton, when asked a version of the same question ("Will Whitewater damage Bill Clinton's chances for reelection?"), responded to the effect that the American people are smart enough to recognize that attempts to tarnish the Clintons are politically motivated.

What relation between self-reference and performativity is suggested by these examples? The performativity of the statement—its ability to *enact* the damage to Clinton to which it refers or even to achieve its implicit purpose of inflating itself as a story—*depends on its self-referentiality being subordinated.* This is also the case with "See Spot run": to notice its self-reference is a distraction from the linear, straight-ahead mandate it seeks to impress on its reader—though probably not such a fatal distraction. This shows some of the difference between how these texts are positioned: to see their self-reference is perhaps to appreciate them more as poetry but thereby tends to detract from them as pedagogy or news.

12

Self-Reference II

      This section develops another couple of important dimensions of self-reference via the consideration of three literary texts—from 1853, 1936, and 1970—that refer to themselves, circuitously, as economic transactions. These texts differ from the ones we have just considered, at least insofar as a text is not a running dog or a subway station, whereas it often does (as in these cases) form part of an economic transaction. Such self-reference opens the question of to what extent the text's economic role may subsume or saturate whatever other dimensions in which it may operate (that is, the other ways in which it can mean something). This question is crucial (it is the *hinge*) for assessing the contradictory ways that art defines itself with and against other art (for example, as high art works to distinguish itself from low) at the same time that it defines itself with and against the marketplace (where more distinction from other commodities has tended to increase its value as cultural capital—and often, therefore, its commodity value as well). I have chosen three texts, in a relatively long-term chronological series, so as to begin to explore (in very broad outline, anyway) the changing constellation of these historical, economic, and cultural relationships.

    Exploring this question enables us to attend to another kind of question or metaquestion along the way, about the operation of self-reference. It turns out that the point at which the text closes back on itself is also where it connects with everything that sustains it, a kind of *navel* (which is what makes navel-gazing texts into lenses onto themselves and the world). At the very least, this should remind us that texts (like other living things) can be born and stay alive and continue to produce and reproduce themselves only by remaining *unborn,* that is, by remaining hooked into an ecology, in the womb of a world of other texts and transactions with other things and living things. (And again, this is not to say that texts are living things but that their livingthing-likeness—their resemblance to and difference from living things—marks them as siblings.) If you read a literary text closely (as the New Critics taught), you see the intricacies of its self-enclosed literarity and textuality, but if you read even more closely, it opens back onto the world again.

Matthew Arnold's 1853 poem "The Scholar Gypsy" is a meditation on an Oxford student who drops out of the modern world to join the Gypsies and learn their magic arts. In the poem's final section, the narrator addresses the scholar Gypsy, warning him to avoid being corrupted by his contacts with modernity. In the course of this warning, he compares the scholar Gypsy to ancient Iberian traders, "shy traffickers" who had worked out a way of conducting trade without any face-to-face interactions with their trading partners (the more modern and gregarious Greeks): the Iberians would leave their "corded bales" on beaches and withdraw; buyers would leave money on the bales and withdraw; if payment was sufficient, the Iberians would take it and leave the bales for their buyers. This image ends the poem.

It is clear that the poem as a whole is a reflection on the status of poets in a modern world; Arnold describes the "magic arts" of the Gypsies in terms that could just as well refer to poetry. The "shy traffickers" of the final image also strikingly resemble writers, whose work is mostly solitary and sequestered and whose products are obtained by readers who do not necessarily ever come face-to-face with the author, who is at least in this sense buffered from the world. One notices, furthermore, that the long sequence of squarish stanzas that compose the poem could also be represented very neatly by the line of "corded bales" left on the beach. As we have seen, self-reference often contains particulars of the physicality of the object at hand. Here, for example, bales scattered or stacked in a field would not represent the poem so nicely, since only the beach tends to dictate that they be arrayed in a linear series like the stanzas of the poem. Nor would this be such a fitting image if the stanzas were not block-shaped or if the poem were only a few stanzas long.

The final self-referential image tries to work out a compromise between the extremes of dropping out and selling out, but the compromise comes only in the form of a wishful exhortation. Arnold tries very hard to convince himself that precapitalist social relations (as represented by Gypsies and Ibe-rians) and the magic of art can coexist with economic rationality and the cash nexus of the marketplace without being *of* it, or maybe it is the implicit recognition that this is *not* really possible that makes the poem poignant, identifying romantic art as a kind of whistling-through-the-graveyard.

Fast-forward to 1936, and James M. Cain's novel *Double Indemnity* seems to start with the premise that Arnold had been so anxious to avoid: the universal hegemony of contractual economic rationality and its practical equivalence to the social contract. It seems to be the only game in town, and although its moral status may ultimately be ambiguous, the writer, too—whether more like a cop or a criminal—works the system along with everyone else.

The novel is in the form of a first-person narrative of Walter Neff, an insurance salesman who is drawn by lust and money—and, overall, by the desire to beat his own racket—into a plot to murder a client's husband and collect the insurance money. It opens with Neff's account of his first visit to the client. A maid answers the door and asks his business; he says it's "personal" but the maid asks again, and Neff does some quick strategizing:

> Getting in is the tough part of my job, and you don't tip what you came for till you get where it counts. . . . It was one of those spots you get in. If I said more about "personal" I would be making a mystery of it, and that's bad. If I said what I really wanted, I would be laying myself open to what every insurance agent dreads, that she would come back and say, "Not in." If I said I'd wait, I would be making myself look small, and that never helped a sale yet. To move this stuff, you've got to get in. Once you're in, they've got to listen to you, and you can pretty near rate an agent by how quick he gets to the family sofa. (7–8)

One notices that the narrator's account of selling insurance also quite neatly describes *Cain's strategy as a writer,* from his famous avoidance of "making a mystery of it" (the reader knows from the outset that the narrator will commit the murder and be caught) to his relentlessness in hooking the reader immediately and never letting go. The cover blurb from the *Saturday Review of Literature* hypes the book just so, by asserting that "no one has ever stopped in the middle of one of Jim Cain's books." This description also echoes the logic of the world *inside* the novel, whose characters are compelled to see their plot through to the bitter end—or, in the words of their repeated catchphrase, "straight down the line." The phrase also seems to describe the train on which the murder is staged, but more than this it suggests the fatalistic juggernaut set in motion when you try to "beat the system" and, ultimately, even a hard-boiled logic of life itself, beginning in lust and ending in death.

Straight down the line: also quite literally the logic of reading. Like the characters and their obsessive desires, we are made subject to the "reading machine" that has been implanted in us; we are possessed and pulled along by it. It is an open question whether this parallel allows us to disavow or to recognize and come to terms with our implication in the System and the externality of our desires.

In any case, there seems to be nothing particularly disreputable about the insurance business in Cain's novel, even though, like writing, it does no productive labor as such (if *productive* is defined in the narrowest sense as the direct manufacture of material things). Like the institution of marriage, as portrayed in Cain's novel, what keeps insurance legit is its *contractual* nature. Things go wrong only when people try to work the System as inside traders, but the hegemony of the System is so thoroughgoing that such attempts seem doomed to fail. The parallels among insurance and marriage and writing lead one to ask how the novel (like its main characters) might *itself* be acting as a double agent. One might even say that the novel is really a kind of *pornography,* insofar as the prospect of the victory of the System at the end may be not so much the vindication of a moral universe as a device to shape (to hold in suspense, even though the result is known) a trajectory of arousal: like orgasmic sex, we keep reading not because we don't know what the end will be but because we do, making peculiarly delicious the unpredictable twists and turns on the way there. The conclusion (telegraphed from the beginning) also functions as a kind of *morality insurance* that Cain sells his reader, indemnifying us against the damage to our own moral standing that *enjoying* the novel might otherwise produce and thus enabling us to have our cake and eat it too, much in the way that sexual repression can be regarded (if you are so inclined, and as long as you don't admit it in public) as an eroticizing technology.

But we really have to push the self-referential dimension of Cain's novel to yield this recognition of its own (and our own) implication in the double-dealing it describes; in other words, Cain seems to let his reader come away (if so inclined) with moral dignity intact, which is precisely his way of beating the System to sell what might be called pornography as a cautionary tale (don't try this at home, wink wink!), maybe even fitting it for highbrow consumption.

This double-dealing is precisely what Richard Brautigan makes a poem out of putting right under his reader's nose in the two-line 1970 poem "Negative Clank":

He'd sell a rat's asshole
to a blindman for a wedding ring.

This would be nothing more than a rather offhand, witty characterization of an unscrupulous but brilliant salesman (and in fact it was quoted as such in the 1995 film *Strange Days*) if it were not being *sold as a poem,* and that's the tip-off: the salesman stands in for the poet, the rat's asshole for the poem, and the blind man for the reader who *buys it* as a poem, as something of value. But here's the real trick: the more one notices how empty the poem is of any referent but itself, the *greater* its poetic value and the more adroit the achievement of the poet. The emptiness at the core and the *circularity* of the asshole and ring stand for the poem's emptiness and self-referential circularity. One might expect the buyer's blindness to stand for the reader's gullibility, but it's quite the opposite: since it is only visually that a rat's asshole could be mistaken for a ring, a blind man relying on proverbially hypersensitive touch (and smell, no doubt) would be presumably *hardest* to fool, only making the trick more brilliant. Yes, it *looks* like a poem at first glance, but the real trick is that the more one *handles* it as we are doing now—the more one really engages its emptiness, insubstantiality, and its slipperiness—one is only more impressed with its value and meaning, which consist in its performance of a very important principle: that the value and meaning we *make,* writer and reader, out of the least-promising materials, out of almost nothing, is what binds us to each other; it is, like the wedding ring, the performative symbol of our bond, perfectly useless except as such, like paper money, and thus all the more trustworthy.

Is the poet, then, the hypercynical and consummate con artist or the boy who says the emperor has no clothes and manages to be rewarded for it, or is there no difference? Well, dear reader, which is it?

The way these three texts refer to themselves as literary texts *and* as economic transactions makes them useful documents in the history of literature and of capitalism by working through the ways in which writing—more specifically, texts written by professional writers—participates in the logic of the cash nexus. Not surprisingly, the clearest trajectory traced by the three texts is increasing saturation of art by the capitalist marketplace: Arnold offers at least a metaphor for how to be in the nexus but not of it; for Cain it has become the only game in town, but you can still remain above it (though a bit equivocally) as long as you don't try to pull some kind of con job; for Brautigan, the game is not only all there is but is itself a con job, and artists are just the *baddest* con artists of all. Of course, the denial practiced by Arnold (that is, the denial that art participates fully in the cash nexus) was already a stretch, but in any case even the denial seems to become less and less possible. It complicates things a bit (without changing the overall trajectory) when we take into account that Arnold had more high-art pretensions than the other two and was thus more interested in selling his product by pretending that it wasn't really a product and that he wasn't really selling it. And that is why (to use the language of an old toothpaste advertisement), more literature professors surveyed still use Arnold's poem to manufacture cultural capital for themselves and prescribe it to their students looking to increase their own cultural capital.

But it is also important to look through the class-fractional differences among these texts to the common contradiction that defines them all as cultural products and their artists as cultural producers: that of being inside (even fully inside) and outside (even if only partially outside) the system at the same time. This is exactly where contradiction places you in general; in other words, it is like standing on one of the system's internal fault lines that connect to the fault lines that separate the system from other, perhaps still unimaginable, systems or modes. It is also especially where a more or less middle-class cultural producer (Hi, Mom!) is positioned as a *worker.* Keeping in mind that what defines capitalism is not necessarily the marketplace as such but how the profits of exploitation are reinvested to fatten corporations and their managers, we might consider as an analogue how much each of these texts works to reinvest the profit of its self-reflexivity into inflating its status as Art and in raising the status of the Artist (and of the upwardly mobile reader) versus how much the same texts can be put to other uses. In other words, it remains an open question, depending on how we use these texts, but to connect internal fault lines to external ones it is necessary *at the very least* to read highbrow and lowbrow literary texts together and both alongside the nonliterary and to practice a metareading that attends to how the production of literarity participates in the commodity system.

ASIDE

Discourse Analysis 101. Here, then, are a few operating principles for practicing the kind of analysis—the kind of textual mindfulness—illustrated in the above examples.

Learn to consider, habitually, the self-serving, self-referential, and performative dimensions of statements and texts. In literary texts these dimensions can sometimes be found most easily at the outset of the work, setting forth its terms, and at the end, as kind of a punch line or gesture of closure, where the work turns back on itself. In speech or other kinds of meaning-making that are not explicitly literary, the self-referential and performative dimensions may be hidden—in plain sight—behind the apparently referential, so often you must look at the finger pointing rather than at what is being pointed out. There may be most motivation to do so in situations where the finger is pointing accusingly at you, which is when you might try the following ploy: "I may or may not be guilty in the way you say, but that's beside the point, since the real issue is how you are using blame as a power play, to paint me as bad in order to preserve some sense of yourself." Of course, this observation is not simply a truth statement but another gambit in turn, as your interlocutor will no doubt remind you. In any case, part of how a statement characterizes or positions itself is by (explicitly or implicitly) characterizing and positioning its audience. Try this at home.

Learn to consider, habitually, what is *not* said. This includes both unspoken assumptions that must have already been accepted for the statement to make sense or acquire meaning or value, and just as crucially it includes that which must be pushed aside, disavowed, or effaced for the statement to make sense, if only provisionally. Another way of thinking about what is not said in a particular utterance is that the not-said is part of the *context* of the statement; in other words: learn to consider, habitually, the context of statements. This means thinking about how it is that a statement comes to be made at all—and asserts meaning or value—against the background of other statements. What kind of a context does it posit, against which to posit itself as shocking, or counterintuitive, or new, or earth shaking—and to whom? What kind of a past, present, and future does it imply? What past statements does it repeat, modify, develop? Why is the statement being made *now,* at this particular conjuncture? Notice that all of these questions are more or less independent of the truth or falsity of the statement. The question of how the statement is positioned in relation to other statements often means also considering who is making the statement, where and when it is being made, and in response to what. The context of a statement also includes its possible futures: What can come of it? What does it entail? What range of ways can it be (or is it likely to be) interpreted and taken up, acted on or not? Even though the range of possible interpretations is large and radically heterogeneous, statements bear some responsibility for how they are taken up.

All of these suggestions tend to equate what a statement means with what it *does* (or tries to do). This means, finally, that you should also consider what *you* are trying to do with it, what purposes your analysis is trying to serve. In other words, *attend to the self-referential dimensions of your own utterances.* This kind of analysis can be said to be based on a principle of *generosity:* all statements are taken to be equally meaningful and important. By pulling on the threads of any statement, you will begin to unravel the intricate networks of discursive relationships—the ecologies—in which they are woven.

The standard complaint about such analysis is that deferring the question of truth and value tends dangerously to level everything, treating as equivalent objects of analysis (for example) the most inflammatory racist invective, the communication of a basic scientific fact, the erotic fantasies of a romance novel. However, if you take any of these examples and apply to it the principles of inquiry stated above (I mean I really invite you to take a minute and do so, just to humor me), you will see very clearly that the dangers are far greater in *not* inquiring in this way. You might then go on to consider who (or what kinds of discourse) might have *something to fear* from this kind of analysis and thus be most interested in making it seem dangerous. Far from leveling the differences between statements, such analysis tends to *restore* their differences to them by ascertaining the particular kinds of "language games" each is playing. It is in this sense the *opposite of translation,* at least insofar as translation offers roughly as "the same" statements that really belong to very different cultural/linguistic contexts. On the other hand, a performative theory of translation recognizes the productive refractivity of the act of translation and, beyond this, that every act of translation *participates in the push and pull of renegotiating the actual relationships* between the languages and cultures in question. Even if in the short term it is easy to treat an individual act of translation as the simple tracing of a correspondence that leaves the differences between languages exactly as it found them, this is obviously not the case, since the relationships between languages have been produced by what has been (and probably will continue to be), in the long term, a highly dynamic and changeable linguistic ecology, thanks to countless linguistic interactions such as translations.

13

Autopoiesis

Among the most familiar of all science-fictional technology is *Star Trek*'s transporter, a device that can dematerialize a thing—even a living body—into a pattern of information that it transmits as a beam and rematerializes at another location. A living body, in fact, as construed by contemporary biology, is *already* more like a transporter beam than like a solid, inert object. As most people know, our bodies are in constant flux at the cellular level, where cells are continually disintegrating and being replicated. In a matter of months, most of our organs have been completely replaced, one cell at a time. The living body is a pattern of information, a fact and a fiction, something continuously being made and unmade. When you consider also the vast "empty" spaces between the dancing particles of our component atoms, bodies seem to melt and evaporate. It is more than a metaphor, then, to say that a living body is a passing wave, a dancing flame, a whirlwind of dust, a phoenix always rising from its ashes. Every living body is a burning bush: a complex, many branched network that is constantly being consumed and formed. You could say that contemporary science seems to have corroborated the wisdom of the Judeo-Christian Bible in having God appear and speak to Moses in such an autopoietic form.

The question that modern physics asked about light (Is it a wave or a particle?) and the answer (that it is paradoxically both) seem to characterize the way postmodern biology has come to think of living bodies. It is the *pattern* of ocean waves—not the water itself—that moves across the ocean surface. The water itself just bobs up and down: it is pulled up, participating for a moment in the passing wave, and then falls back again. Such a process—the regular interplay of patterned energy through matter—also constitutes the first manifestation of God in the Judeo-Christian Bible: "The spirit of God moved across the face of the waters." One term for this process is *homeorrhesis* (Greek for *same flow*): the conservation of a pattern while its constituent matter is in flux.

A wave merely recruits and then discharges the local water molecules; it uses what comes to hand and returns it without noticeably altering it. Consider each of these sentences, one after the other, as waves over the surface of language: words are recruited to participate in the passing thought and then fall back, unchanged and available for reuse. Likewise, the book is not consumed in being read: your eyes roll back and forth over the letters, words, and lines of type, leaving them as they were. And furthermore, each sentence in turn can be said to pass like a wave over your brain as you read.

It is also easy to see that this metaphor leaves out something crucial. Each sentence is grammatically structured, but the thought is more than "filler" to plug into grammatical diagrams. Meanings are altered in the process; minds and fields of knowledge may be changed, if only minimally—or, rather, minds and fields and meanings are constituted, reproduced, and changed in the process. Furthermore, words and grammar are not mere "filler" for thoughts; they are what one thinks *with*—and *against*, as now, when trying to formulate something that words and grammar seem to resist.

An autopoetic system is, like a wave or a whirlpool, a self-sustaining pattern, but it does more than merely use what is already present; it actually *produces its own components*. This is easy to see in the case of language: words, and the sounds and alphabetic letters (or the characters of written Chinese or hand gestures of American Sign Language), are made by the languages themselves. Languages produce what count as elements or units, or as Luhmann put it in another context, "Whatever they use as identities and differences is of their own making" (*Essays* 3). For example, the four tones of Mandarin Chinese are called "inflections" in English, but this is clearly a prejudicial term, since the term *inflection* seems to suggest a secondary and not so distinctive form of difference, a mere modulation. The fact is, of course, that the tones just do not signify for English as they do in Chinese.

I said that the manufacture, by a system, of its own components "is easy to see in the case of language": it is easy, anyway, since Saussure made this the conceptual centerpiece of structuralist linguistics in the first decade of the twentieth century. Even so, this is the recognition that Luhmann called the "decisive conceptual innovation" (*Essays* 3) of autopoiesis theory in biology in the 1970s. What was news to biology had long been part of the classical legacy of structuralism to those who study language and culture. To be perfectly honest, it's satisfying for someone who studies language and culture to be able to say to a biologist, "We were there first!" But only thoroughgoing epistemological change could enable general recognition that paradigms might legitimately find their way from cultural study to the hard sciences, and thus that insights from the study of language and culture might conceivably apply in some fashion to natural phenomena as well. I'm not holding my breath. Luhmann for one has disavowed the influence of structuralism on autopoietic theory, but given the status of sociology as a kind of bastard science, it doesn't take a genius to figure out why a sociological theorist might want to spread the story that Daddy was a biologist (and by the way, I tried to find a less catty way of saying that, but I couldn't). This is not at all to say that autopoiesis simply recapitulates structuralism. One difference between structuralist systems and autopoietic systems (cited prominently by Luhmann) is especially definitive: whereas structuralism tends to model systems as spatial organizations frozen at a single moment in time, autopoiesis understands them as patterns of ongoing events continually under construction. But this insight is also not particular to autopoiesis theory: it has been one of the hallmarks of poststructuralist cultural theory generally, one of the major ways it has built on structuralism while establishing its difference from its structuralist roots. The handiest general term for this kind of operation (I mean the operation of systems as ongoing events continually under construction) comes from cultural theory: we call it *performativity*. But this kind of dynamism also runs deep and wide in modernity: for example, through relativity theory in physics, via the "fundamental principle" that "there are no things, only processes" (Smolin, *Three* 139).

A sentence is made of words, and words are made of letters, no less than a house is made of wood or a living creature is made of atoms of carbon, hydrogen, and so on. But as in the other cases, the primary thing about a house is not what it's made of. Any number of materials could substitute for wood; they must only be capable of entering into the necessary relationships or performing the functions required. What is primary is that a house is made of *rooms:* it might be wood or bricks, but if it's not a configuration of rooms, it's not a house. Of course, it *matters* a great deal what a house is made of, and for termites or fire the fact that a house is made of wood is just about *all* that matters: they are destructive precisely because they care only about the wood and not the house as such; the house signifies little to them. We could say that there is an interface of houseness and woodness and that some aspects of woodness (its susceptibility to termites and fire) are inimical to houseness.

Likewise, various interactive properties of subatomic particles enable them to form atoms and of atoms enable them to form complex molecules. It is very misleading to call them *properties,* though. We might as well call them *im*properties because their relevant feature is their potential for improper use, that they exceed themselves, that they are components of something *other* than themselves. This excess or straddling of categories is what should probably be called *meaning.* It would be even more misleading to say only that they are *capable of* entering into relationships and to speak only of *potential,* because they are *already* relationships: there is relationship, complexity, and emergence all the way down to the bottom of things (which is really to say there is no bottom as such).

This is also where grammatical structure (at least in English) resists the formulation of the thought, insisting as it does on subject, verb, and object. To say that "an autopoetic system produces its own components" is a paradox because it suggests wrongly both that the autopoetic system precedes its components and that the activity of producing (verb) its components (object) can be separated from "it" (subject). Is there a better way of saying this? To use an analogy, instead of saying "It rained" we could specify subject, verb, and object by saying "The rain rained rain," but this seems somehow to detract from the descriptiveness of the phrase rather than enhance it, even though other things besides the rain can rain, and the rain can do other things besides rain, and other things besides rain can be rained. The construction "It rained" seems to give a more proper priority to the whole *event,* to the *verb,* leaving subject and object unspecified; it would be nice if there were some construction that did the same for autopoiesis. Maybe this would help stop the concept from backsliding into giving too much priority to the subject, a problem that seems to be built into language (Indo-European languages in particular) and hardened by various more or less hegemonic ideologies of individualism that overprivilege the subject. Too much *auto,* not enough *poiesis.*

To put it another way, one might say that language *insists* on the formulation of autopoiesis *by foreclosing it:* I must write many sentences to explain the coemergence of subject/verb/object, and because the *way* I explain it (that is, with subjects, verbs, and objects) keeps undermining my explanation, my job security as a language worker is guaranteed, like Sisyphus and Old Man River: we just keep rolling along, reinventing the wheel. By the way the language excludes or cuts out this possibility from its very structure, by how it cuts things up into subject, verb, and object, my work as a thinker (or, better, as a tinker or tinkerer of language) is literally *cut out for me.* By cutting things up into subject/verb/object (or more generally into nouns and verbs, or even into individual words), the English language already fails to cut the universe at its joints. Or to put it more positively, language *succeeds* in *not* cutting the universe at its joints, just as life itself had succeeded before it, that is, as life had *succeeded* the things of which it is made and as the elementary particles and forces of the universe had succeeded whatever (unimaginably) preceded them.

So how does complexity emerge and build on itself? Two astronomers once figured the odds that random chemical interactions could produce biological life as about the same as the chance that a tornado sweeping through a junkyard would assemble a functional 747 airplane (Kauffman, *Home* 44–45). Kauffman rethinks the probabilities via a "chemical creation myth" in which chemical components are imagined as thousands of buttons scattered across a floor. Interactions among the chemicals are represented by a person who reaches down repeatedly and picks up two buttons at random and ties them together with a bit of thread. After a surprisingly short time, the person will be picking up buttons that have already been threaded to others and thus will begin threading together clusters of buttons into an increasingly bigger and denser network. The model represents a *reaction network* in which the threads stand for *chemical interactions* that join the chemicals in their various roles as ingredients, catalysts, and products of reactions. In a very small group, chances may be slim that any one chemical will catalyze a reaction between any of the others, but as diversity increases, more reactions will begin to happen; complex loops of self-sustaining interactions will begin to form in which the product of one interaction will also be the catalyst or the ingredient for another, and so on. These self-sustaining loops—metabolisms—are said to be catalytically closed or autocatalytic sets, the chemically creative equivalent of a logic more commonly pathologized in the form of "vicious circles." Given a certain minimum diversity, such networks will take off like wildfire. Far from being prohibitively improbable, "the spontaneous emergence of self-sustaining webs is so natural and so robust that it is even deeper than the specific chemistry that happens to exist on earth; it is rooted in mathematics itself" (Kauffman, *Home* 60). The takeoff point—the critical point of complexity—is reached when the number of threads is about equal to the number of buttons, that is, when the number of verblike "edges" (in other words, interfaces or reactions) approximates the number of nounlike "nodes" (elements); at this phase-transitional point, "a collectively autocatalytic set snaps into existence. A living metabolism crystallizes" (62).

Kauffman's model works the interface of noun and verb, structure and process. It visualizes diachronic processes (that is, chemical interactions that play out over time) as static or synchronic structures (threads and networks). The same thing happens in the phrase "A living metabolism crystallizes," since a metabolism is a temporal and dynamic sequence of processes rather than an apparently static, spatial structure like a crystal; it is a crystallizing but not a crystal, a *constellation* that is both verb and noun. In the grammar of relativity, autopoiesis, and performativity theory, *all nouns are participles.* In theories of self-organizing systems, it is especially important to remember the dynamic/verbal and temporal nature of the otherwise spatial nounlike terms *closure* and *boundary:* both refer primarily to a *set of operations* and only secondarily to whatever physical structures accompany them.

Boundaries in particular cannot be understood only as the discrete limits of an autopoetic system in space and time, just as *closure* and *openness* cannot be fully understood in terms of the semipermeable membranes that separate the inside from the outside of living things. Boundary negotiations (in bodies, for example) do not take place only where skin meets air or where food is being digested; such negotiations are going on everywhere "inside" as well, at the cellular and the molecular and the atomic levels. But because of the ideological legacy of discrete selves with interiors, it is easy to fall back into treating autopoetic systems as solipsistic interiors instead of as all edges, all interfaces. We are fractal creatures, crazed through and through with cleavages. If you look closer at a feature that seems firmly in the interior, you are likely to find the hairline fracture, the edge, that joins it to the outside. To cultivate this way of looking—to learn to see performativity—you really just have to follow through on the mandate to look at nouns and structures until you see them as participles and processes: an edge is an ongoing negotiation rather than a structure; or to take it from the legalistic to the ludic, the party was going on before the guests showed up. Not coincidentally, this general principle also happens to work quite well as a critique of the modern fiction of the social contract and the neoliberal fiction of a free market, insofar as these models posit a set of preexisting individuals who come together to make rules for the interactions among them, a setup that forecloses recognition of how the individuals are really the products of interactions (and thus enabled and constrained by them) in the first place.

In several different but related ways, autopoetic systems are both open and closed. First, and in the most limited sense, autopoetic systems seem to work out a simple compromise between closure and openness in the form of some kind of semipermeable membrane. But what seems like simple compromise shades into more substantive and irreducible contradiction. Boundaries do more than produce closure by keeping certain things out and others in; they also allow *traffic* that they channel and manage. But they do more than *allow* traffic: they *create* traffic by producing differentials between sides of boundaries, thus also producing more openness (flow across boundaries where none had been before). Finally, one has to acknowledge that boundaries and the autopoetic systems built around them do more than *create* traffic: they *are* traffic.

But even as traffic, an autopoetic system is closed as a self-sustaining set of operations; its internal organization (the way it orchestrates its own differentials) seems to be at one remove from its environment, like the objects juggled by a unicyclist on a tightrope are at a remove from his pedaling feet. This kind of closure means that an autopoetic system can be treated as a kind of "black box" whose inputs and outputs can be observed even though its internal organization remains entirely opaque.

Closure is thus very closely related to autonomy: an autopoetic system can be treated as a sovereign agent. Again, such autonomy and closure are more than spatial matters: the organization of the synapses of a brain seems to be at a remove from their component electrons even though they occupy the same space; the ordering of words in a printed sentence is at a remove from the molecules of ink that compose them. The short way of saying all this is that an autopoetic system is a kind of *parasite;* it thrives on other differentials, sources of energy, and raw materials, which it taps into to sustain its own little inflorescence, more or less unnoticed by its host.

This brings us around to another version of the contradiction encountered before: this kind of *autonomy* can be sustained only along with an equally thoroughgoing *dependence.* Again, to understand this merely as a simple compromise—as a partial autonomy or a degree of freedom—is to short-circuit the paradox that is the motor of autopoetic systems. You know you have found an autopoetic system when you find together more autonomy *and* more dependence, more closure *and* more openness.

Look again at the juggling unicyclist. He seems to behave as a kind of gyroscope, cycling back and forth and shifting his weight so as to maintain his balance, to purchase a certain degree of freedom for his juggling hands, so that they can operate independently: his body and legs worry about balancing so that his hands are free to worry only about juggling. But doesn't this account sell the dexterity of the performance short? Don't the little bobbles of the balls and the wobbles of the unicycle have repercussions for each other, and don't they become linked—tuned—into a balancing-juggling system? The simplicity of closure as *involution* (something closing in on itself) is enabled by the ongoing complexity of tuning and linkage that characterizes an ecology of *evolution.*

Closure and openness refer to *meaning* as we have already defined it: the interaction of difference within and difference between. Again, the coexistence of openness and closure is easy to illustrate with the case of textuality. Texts seem at first to have pretty clear boundaries: a sonnet has fourteen lines, and this book has 208 pages, and the meaning system of each seems to round back nicely on itself (just as the total page count could be inserted back into this sentence to become part of my involuted illustration of involution). But push just a little and they get fractal on you, branching out in multiple copies from Xerox machines and printing presses, breaking off discrete little bits into other texts, feeding not so discretely into new texts that resemble them more or less, brokering relationships between other texts and slithering along with the push and pull of disciplinary and interdisciplinary forces, not just as they circulate in the world but also as they circulate in their every line. Look closer and the little rectangular block or slab of the book, the sonnet, the paragraph, cracks open into sprawling rhizomic networks, all edges, across various scales.

It is possible to find the same kind of openness and closure when tracing autopoietic theory itself as an idea in the world, as an ongoing constellation of events. In his 1980 introduction to *Autopoiesis and Cognition,* Humberto Maturana briefly traces his own genealogy of the autopoiesis concept, beginning with his childhood curiosity about the nature of life and death. But such grand speculations were gradually subordinated to his highly specialized work on the neurophysiology of cognition. This work yielded "an understanding of the nervous system as a closed network of interacting neurons" (Maturana and Varela xv), and this understanding of "circular organization" was to develop into the autopoiesis concept. Maturana cites several events as catalysts.

In May 1968, he joined with students who "took over the University [of Chile] in an attempt to reformulate the philosophy that had inspired its organization." Although "language was a trap" and "it was easy to be caught in one's own ego," as events progressed "one began to listen and one's language began to change; and then, but only then, new things could be said" (xvi). Several months later, when asked to give a talk on the neurophysiology of cognition, Maturana made the decisive leap, suddenly recognizing that his two interests, "circular organization" in cognition and "the operation of the living system" itself, "were the same thing" (xvi–xvii). In 1972, after Francisco Varela suggested the need to formalize the concept of "circular organization," Maturana saw that this "could only come after a complete linguistic description." Both "were unhappy with the expression 'circular organization,' and we wanted a word that would by itself convey the central feature of the organization of the living, which is autonomy." At this point, Maturana happened to talk with his friend Jose Bulnes about Bulnes's essay on "Don Quixote's dilemma of whether to follow the path of arms (*praxis, action*) or the path of letters (*poiesis,* creation, production)":

> I understood for the first time the power of the word "poiesis" and invented the word that we needed: *autopoiesis.* This was a word without a history, a word that could directly mean what takes place in the dynamics of the autonomy proper to living systems. Curiously, but not surprisingly, the invention of this word proved of great value. It simplified enormously the task of talking about the organization of the living without falling into the always gaping trap of not saying anything new because the language does not permit it. We could not escape being immersed in a tradition, but with an adequate language we could orient ourselves differently and, perhaps, from the new perspective generate a new tradition. (xvii)

Maturana's invention narrative takes a familiar shape: the child's sense of wonder about life leads to more specialized work that displaces it, but this turns out to have been a necessary detour back to the big question all along. Likewise, the narrative motif of the key being supplied from an unexpected source (here, the Quixote essay) has a lineage that stretches back through old detective movies into fairy tales and folklore. Rather more remarkable is that Maturana makes the events of May 1968 a precise model for his subsequent discovery: the definitive elements of the student takeover of the university—the "attempt to reformulate the philosophy that had inspired its organization," the sense of language as a trap, and the difficult necessity of saying something new—would all come to characterize his invention of autopoiesis.

Can we take this resemblance to indicate that Maturana's participation in the events of May 1968 gave him a model for the *process* of invention and reformulation, or even that the collective self-making and remaking of May 1968 suggested the actual *content* of his invention? It would seem that the temporal straightforwardness of these cause-and-effect scenarios must at least be amended to accommodate the likelihood that Maturana's subsequent invention of autopoiesis also enabled him to *rewrite* May 1968, *retroactively,* in autopoietic terms. This likelihood does not simply invalidate his account of the takeover by making it seem to have been conveniently recast, after the fact, in autopoietic terms. On the contrary, the takeover must have been and must continue to be an open-ended event, and its being subsequently recast as autopoietic may well be part of what it turned out to have helped enable. But paternity is notoriously indeterminate, all the more so for events (such as the takeover or the invention of autopoiesis) that must have many parents and offspring.

ASIDE

Tree and Rhizome. A parent has several children, who each have several children, and so on. As one looks forward in time, then, one imagines such a first parent as the trunk of a tree that splits into many limbs, which in turn split into many more branches. But, looking backward instead of forward, one also finds the trunk branching into roots branching into rootlets: two parents, four grandparents, eight great-grandparents, and so on. If this observation gives even a moment of vertigo in wondering which end is up, it mainly functions to ground all branches and roots in the individual who is their unique center. In so doing, the familiar metaphor obscures what is otherwise quite obvious: that *unique* and *center* are wildly inappropriate, since every node of every root and branch of a single tree is also the node of other roots and branches of other trees, and that, taken together, the structure doesn't resemble a tree at all but a kind of web. Within this web, this palimpsest, constellations like *family* and *race* can be only sketchy and provisional.

It would be very easy to write a genealogy of autopoiesis without mentioning the takeover of May 1968 or the Quixote essay; one might, for example, describe it as a predictable outgrowth of cybernetics and systems theory, or as an almost inevitable product—the synthesis—of a deep and long-standing dialectical tension between mechanism and organicism in biology, or in an even larger sense (as I have already suggested) as an overdetermined next step in the centuries-old epistemological dance of literature and science. One also has a range of choices as to how large or central a role one assigns to Maturana and Varela: pushing Luhmann's characterization, one might cast their contribution as thoroughly original and transformative, with repercussions for all fields of knowledge. One could just as easily say that Maturana's version of autopoietics is merely one vehicle for what was happening epistemologically in many other places, and a not very privileged or even significant one at that: certainly, nobody thinks that something called *autopoiesis* (that is, something with a kind of *brand name* registered to Maturana), in whatever form, will take over and hold any great share of the knowledge market. In fact, one could argue that autopoiesis theory as such has been harmed by a too thoroughgoing insistence on its own difference from related concepts, by trying to draw too crisp a boundary in identifying autopoiesis as "proper to living systems" when its worth has proved to be in opening up the no-man's-land between what is proper and alive and systemic and what is not.

In any case, another remarkable feature of Maturana's account is the key role given to language. If, for both politics and science, language is a trap, tending to pull any potential innovation back into the repetitive orbit of the already familiar, it is also the medium in which every innovation must establish itself by and as a *defamiliarization*. The apparent paradox of autopoiesis, that systems produce their own components, is illustrated in Maturana's account by the act of naming itself, which is neither prior nor posterior to the invention but an important part of it. The name is an important component of the system, one that the system manufactures.

But identifying the act of naming as part of a coemergence does not entirely smooth over the temporal paradox of systems producing their own components. The *event* that includes the takeover of the university, Varela's suggestion, Bulnes's essay, the invention of the word, and so on—the event that is really a *constellating* of events that are themselves complex constellations—is not only an ongoing one but also something that seems to act forward and backward in time. Part of the *circularity* of an autopoetic system is a kind of causal loop, which also appears as a kind of time loop. In Maturana's account, the takeover catalyzes autopoietic theory, which in turn works to make the takeover turn out to have been an event in the history of science; my account of Maturana's account also participates in this constellation, and I'm putting my shoulder to the same wheel, spinning or being spun into the same web: an autopoetic system is an eddy in linear time, or, to put it another way, autopoetic systems constitute *relational time*. The general banishment of relational time from science seems to have driven the time loop into exile as a staple science-fictional premise, though perhaps autopoiesis theory will allow this prodigal son to be rehabilitated in some fashion. In the meantime, this eddying flow is familiar as the operation of *meaning* in language: in the flow of speech and writing, words that come after alter the meaning of words that came before, making meaning a continual and more or less open-ended recontextualizing.

If Maturana's account allows the fully contradictory sense of autonomy to drop out, he gets away with it partly because he lets the word *autopoiesis* work as a symbol, standing in for more than its share of the more sprawling and multidimensional process in which it participates. In comparison to the complex constellation in which it appears, the word seems much more autonomous, more discrete and singular, more able to pop into being "without a history," more able to "directly mean" the workings of biodynamic systems as understood by Maturana—even though (one might add) the word cannot mean anything at all except as it participates in its constellations and even though every sentence Maturana ever wrote is just as new and unprecedented in its stringing together of words as his neologism in its combination of *auto* and *poiesis*. But there is a twist: the word, in seeming much more straightforwardly autonomous than it is, only resembles all the more the systems it was invented to describe. An autopoetic system, one might say, is a system that is able to misrecognize itself (or to be misrecognized) as autonomous.

Such a misrecognition (by the way) is definitive for what psychoanalytic theorist Jacques Lacan referred to as the *mirror stage* of human psychological development. In the most definitive instance of this phase, the baby, sprawling and uncoordinated and dependent, sees its apparently discrete and autonomous image in an actual mirror, or in the mirror of how other people respond to it, or in other people's bodies as if they were mirrors of its own. It is toward this idealized autonomy that one must continue to strive, since this stage is not simply outgrown but remains a layer of one's psychic organization: one continues to attribute to others an autonomy one does not possess oneself and can never attain (since the others do not really possess it either). Autonomy remains *that which one does not possess oneself,* or to abbreviate this a little: *one does not possess oneself,* and, furthermore, *one does not possess one self.*

The spatial metaphor of *interiority* plays a part in enabling a misrecognized autonomy to fall "through the looking glass" of a self by positing degrees of freedom for an interior even while it may be constrained on all sides (that is, the notion that "four walls do not a prison make"). The problem with such an interiority is that it purchases freedom by sacrificing power: the more easily a wheel may spin, the less traction. Maturana uses the metaphor more carefully when he asserts that those who study autopoiesis may be "immersed in a tradition" but still able to "orient ourselves differently" and thus potentially able to generate a new tradition, making autopoietics an eddy in a stream.

The self, the *auto* of *autopoiesis*, is able to be misrecognized as something discrete and circularly self-contained, like an egg, but look closer and it seems to be instead a node in a branching structure, and the node, in turn, opens out into rhizomic, multiple, tangled networks, and what had seemed so involuted and singular turns out to be something torn up, plural, patched together, all over the place, rags, or, in Yiddish, *schmatte*. At the risk of selling my argument short, then, I am tempted to sum up the entire critical intervention of this book in the following two words: Autopoiesis? Schmattepoiesis.

14

Poetic Interlude: Defrosting

Robert Frost, famously, called poetry "a momentary stay against confusion." This description assigns an important function to poetry, perhaps even including a political role in affirming some of what dominant power and ideology might otherwise render unintelligible. Unfortunately, *momentary* seems to suggest something isolated and punctual, and *stay against confusion* seems to imply that poetry may be the reactionary defense of an order and identity (its own, for one) against all others, and especially in the high-cultural circles of the modern Western poetic tradition, a defensive and self-enclosed poetry has tended to function as a way of affirming a defensive and self-enclosed self. I start to hear a series of counter- and counter-counterassertions echoing in the wake of Frost's definition: why not identify poetry instead as "a rhythmic engagement with chaos" or "a ritual flirtation with abjection and grandiosity" or maybe "a moebius membrane"? The move from Frost's assertion to these echoes is what I'm calling "defrosting," and while I rehearse the move, in this section, with poetry and poetics in the narrow sense, theories of autopoietics and self-organizing systems more generally are subject to a version of the same critique insofar as they are overinvested in a similarly defended self.

Virginia Woolf, famously, remembered that, before the First World War, "people would have said precisely the same things but they would have sounded different, because in those days they would have been accompanied by a sort of humming noise, not articulate, but musical, exciting, which changed the value of the words themselves" (12). She identified the hum with poetry; one might also call it "culture" or "ideology." The interzone where meaning happens is in the defrosted boundaries between "the words themselves" and the "sort of humming noise" that is the sum of their many cross-amplifying and canceling echoes.

Many of the canonized poems of the Western romantic tradition revolve around the axis of what is often called *the self* or *the subject* (as if there were *only one*), or, to be more precise, they *precess,* through countless iterations eulogizing and elegizing this Self while beating their figurative breasts over its alienation, fearing and longing for its dissolution, usually finally noisily or quietly heroically coming to terms with or transcending it. (Come to think of it, this sounds an awful lot like my adolescence—minus the heroic transcendence, of course.) But sarcasm about the self does not escape the orbit. The poet John Berryman, who sarcastically called such a self "Henry," professed boredom with "his plights & gripes / bad as achilles," but finally had to jump off a bridge to escape them. (When I lived in Minneapolis, I often used to walk past the parking lot where, I was told, Berryman had landed.) Such pathos and tragic-heroic acting out was what psychoanalyst Jacques Lacan hated about the existentialist self, whose "subjective impasses" he characterized as "a freedom that is never more authentic than when it is within the walls of a prison; a demand for commitment, expressing the impotence of a pure consciousness to master any situation; a voyeuristic-sadistic idealization of the sexual relation; a personality that realizes itself only in suicide; a consciousness of the other that can be satisfied only by Hegelian murder" (6). Lacan—a kind of Berryman with a bungee—worked to redeem a more discombobulated self. The old self was obsolete, and the new model was going to be more resilient. The so-called death of the subject proclaimed by "the boys in the human sciences" (as Donna Haraway put it) seems also to be part of a Master retooling for a New World Order (which no longer needs the same kind of liberal fiction of the subject), even as it also brings new—poetical and political—opportunities for renegotiation and resistance.

In any case, the countless poetic elaborations of Self, like the epicycles upon epicycles that had to be posited to shore up the model of a geocentric universe, are subject to obsolescence in light of other models. Please take note of the fact that this is news only where and for whom the model had been dominant. To cite one extended counterexample, Chinese cosmology had not required the linchpin of geocentrism and thus was not shaken to its roots by Copernicus, while that great protagonist of Western lyrics, "I," has scarcely made an appearance in a couple thousand years of Chinese lyric poetry. Not coincidentally, furthermore, for almost a thousand years of China's state education system, one was tested and gained access to political power by *writing about poetry.* So too, after Mao, Chinese poets' insistence on the aesthetic or nonpolitical nature of their poetry continues to be a political act, whereas American poets' insistence on the political nature of their poetry can tend to be more of an aesthetic gesture. But these much too neat oppositions between East and West have their reverberations, too. Here, too, in the West (wherever that may be), not all of us have a single, jealous god, and not all of us (gladly) bear the same cross of Self, though those who do not are often made to bear the cost for those who do. Dominant ideologies displace their contradictions onto others; to figure out how both to take them up *and* to refuse them is often a matter of survival.

I tried to do just that, in a very small way, as people who are not poets sometimes do, by writing a poem. It began one moonlit night in August, when an old friend and I went swimming in the ocean. Along with its other charms, this event had special significance for me since night swimming had once been my particular phobia. Ten years before, I had described it as follows:

> When I swim out into a lake at night I am possessed by a terror that sends me racing back to shore. I've tried on several occasions to steel myself and keep swimming out, but the terror grips me. I begin to feel that the depths are inhabited by monsters; that I will be pulled down, drowned, consumed or torn apart. I begin to feel that my body is no longer distinct from the dark inhabited water, that I am losing any sense of the boundaries between lake and shore and air, that I am just a swimming in the darkness—and that others swim in me.
>
> It occurs to me that I experience a much milder version of the same fear when I *write:* I find that, when the writing begins to take me up, I often draw back to do some chore or errand, as if to get some perspective, to turn rather than be turned by thinking, to grasp rather than be grasped.
>
> It begins to occur to me that everything important could be characterized as a swimming out into darkness: feeling, thinking, loving, speaking, teaching, reading, driving, going to sleep, waking up, being born, dying, and so on. Perhaps the phobia condenses and displaces these fears into an easily avoidable site, localizing a fear that might otherwise suffuse everything.

By the time of the moonlit swim, though, I had been suspecting for a while that I had unraveled the phobia, unraveled the defended self that seemed to need the phobia—or, more simply, just that "I" had unraveled. The swim seemed to show me that this was the case—or maybe there was just too much moonlight to know for sure. In any case, it was a heightened experience I wanted to write about, but I was embarrassed to have fixed on such a conventionally poetic occasion. It occurred to me that "Swimming in the Sea on a Moonlit Night" recalled Frost's "Stopping by Woods on a Snowy Evening," which I came to realize was a kind of *antipoem* to the one I wanted to write. Instead of *writing the poem,* then, I found *myself unwriting the antipoem,* as follows:

> There are three main characters in the poem; two men and a horse (also male): a classic American erotic triangle.
>
> The first man owns a house and woodland lot. His job in the poem is to make the poet look good, by failing to realize the poetic profit the poet poaches from his woods when he's away.
>
> The horse, like all subordinates, apparently, enjoys routine. His job in the poem is to make the poet look good, by (thinking, no doubt, only of his dinner) failing to understand the poet's sublimer impulses (the poet allows the horse politely to protest, and then be still), and when the poet says that "I have miles to go," the horse must pull the poet (offstage).
>
> The poet, not wanting to be caught looking at another man's property, first ascertains that he's alone (the horse don't count). Then, as if he were the only person in the universe (the state, apparently, to which all genius must aspire), he oversees a furtive, rigorously orchestrated fantasy about a kind of mother/mistress whose job is to be "lovely, dark and deep"; to be more self-effacing even than the horse (you cannot even tell for sure she's there; she does her job so well); to play the roles of nature, love, and death; to be seductive and to be resisted, and by being resisted, to make the poet look good.
>
> He dreams of the supremacy of cold and whiteness over everything—a universal, uniform, unmarked collective whiteness that levels all distinctions, obliterates all darkness, transcends all properties, like dollars or democracy—the consummation and the sweet apotheosis of his frosty self.
>
> But first, we all have jobs to do.

Call it a cheap shot if you want, but I mean *really,* how is "Stopping by Woods..." anything but the nth rewriting of the old modestly heroic self, the "White Man's Burden" all over again? I've always loved the poem as much as everybody else, but it is also galling in its modesty, the smugness of power and privilege to efface itself and its others. That's what drove my poem, to call out pleasure on its furtive and disavowed implication in power. It works the other way, too: power that won't cop to the pleasure it takes (for example, the righteous-indignation mode), that gets off by disavowing the pleasure, is the real obscenity and should probably also be punishable by poetry. You can question the pleasure I take in calling Frost out (wouldn't it be better to just leave Frost alone and get on with it?), but at least I haven't disowned it.

Call it a stylistic difference, if you prefer. To proclaim power in pleasure and vice versa, to assert oneself too nakedly, to protest too much: these are often the putative sins of counterhegemonic arts, from rap and graffiti to performance poetry. For example, listen to *Voices from the Nuyorican Poets Cafe:* would Frost ever, like Nicole Breedlove, have to come right out and tell the reader to "make sure the / Library of Congress / is notified" of her life (Algarin and Holman 41) or like Maggie Estep flaunt her "unabashed gall" in proclaiming "I am / THE SEX GODDESS OF THE WESTERN HEMI-SPHERE" (63)? Or was Hattie Gossett appropriately modest when she asserted that "in jamaica & los angeles they couldnt get enough of this" (204) or Tracie Morris when she confirmed for her "Project Princess"—against the forces of negating invisibility and negating hypervisibility—"It's all about you girl" (101)? No, says Frost, my trick is to cover my tracks, to make it all about me without saying so!

What I wanted to do, when I came to write my poem, was to make another kind of answer to Frost: from a "lost" self that gains worlds in return, plural and perverse, whose response to a "lovely, dark, and deep" ocean is *to swim in it:*

> Almost full moon,
> a skipped stone,
> echoing light:
> by You we know
> how many ways
> of being where
> One is and is
> not (round).

> Swollen ocean, kneaded
> by Her yeasty fingers;
> sewn with Her pleats
> and pearly sequins:

> in You we know
> how many ways
> to be not flat;

among sun, moon,
earth, ocean—queer:
how many ways
the earring's earring
is the ear.

You then, stepping dripping
from the water, looking
like a movie, like
the moonlight, like the
Birth of Venus, like
La Dolce Vita, turning
ebbing backwards into being
real as only all that glitters is

the some of us,
unborn but living
questions how split up
we are not
we but Ouija.

The poem works for me as a momentary stay against confusion—by which I mean a way of reminding myself that Frost's clarity is, more often than not, my confusion (and this is something I do not insist on being admired by those in no danger of forgetting!). If it is only against the expectation of an exclusive and singular self that the poem is a poem (and thus disingenuously reinforces the Self as its Other), like a CEO who sees a dominatrix on the side—I mean, insofar as the poem cannot break its orbit around its antipoem, it tries to redefine the orbit as perversely plural (it was never "the self" that was the problem, but "the" self). As it happens, the path of one body orbiting another can be traced perfectly by Newtonian calculations, but add just one more body and the calculations become impossibly, unsolvably, complex: this is what is known in physics as the "three-body problem." To gain Newtonian knowledge—or to gain a discrete self—how much is rendered unintelligible! That's why I thought about calling the poem "Three Body No Problem."

Poetry, even in a relatively narrow sense, is always a performance and negotiation of power relations in language, and what is usually called poetry is a special ritualized performance, sometimes billed as a *private* performance, but not necessarily a definitive case. The private *frisson,* the shudder, the poignancy of a knowledge that reverberates inside an enclosed self and an enclosed poetry, "each mind keeping as solitary prisoner its dream of a world" (as Pater put it); the "impotence of a pure consciousness to master any situation" (as Lacan put it) may be sweet, but poetry, like all organisms, is all interfaces, inside and out, and ultimately an anything but private *friction* is also how we are moved by poetry or insist that we shall not be moved.

15

Performativity I:
Power and Meaning

If self-organization is a circle, or, just a little more elaborately, if organisms and communities are complex, self-enfolding fractal circuitries, then violence would seem to be a kind of straight line.

A *subject* inflicting immediate violence on an *object* seems to be the most straightforward kind of violent power. A gun, for example, is an instrument to make power straightforward: it polarizes two people into subject and object (an act of violence in itself) according to which end you're on. This is the case even though, when anything more than the immediate effect of violence is considered, things get more complicated: a gun may be turned on its owner, the shooter may be jeopardized by his action, a political killing may galvanize the cause it was meant to hinder or end up discrediting the killer's cause, and so on; in other words, guns also produce *backlash*.

The power to destroy is straightforward; it is in fact the relentless straightforwardness of a fired bullet—and what happens when it is resisted—that makes it destructive. Where there is no resistance, there is no power: a fired bullet will not stop a swarm of gnats. Straight violence operates as simple fact: all facts, as such, are "brute facts": it doesn't matter whether you believe in them or how you understand them as meaningful or not meaningful; there they are anyway. In the 1890s, the Lakota Sioux leader Kicking Bear asserted the power of the "Ghost Shirt" to protect its wearer from bullets, or perhaps one should say that its function was to *perform* this belief, but Ghost Shirt wearers were just as dead when shot, weren't they? Or, moreover, didn't the assertion of the power of the shirt put them in the way of bullets they might have dodged? The extension of this argument is that, even if the Ghost Shirt worked well to inculcate a strategic belief in a kind of impenetrability (effective in producing brave warriors) rather than the *fact* of impenetrability, facts, like bullets, eventually and inevitably triumph over faiths—or, rather, *performances*—that run counter to them. So the story goes. Or should we say, instead, that the Ghost Dance, as a cultural practice and even as a narrative, has truly helped keep its practitioners alive in the face of overwhelming assaults? And stay tuned: what are the consequences for Euro-American people of what they stole from Native Americans—gold, tobacco, sugar, alcohol, coffee, coca, not to mention lands dominated or laid waste, species driven to extinction? The way capitalism distributes its damages has its backlash too.

Violent power is exercised not only in destruction but in production as well: certain entities are disordered with respect to their own organization—or, rather, with a *disrespect* that casts them as *raw materials*—and reorganized as part of another organization; perhaps all power should be thought of in terms of such thermodynamic transactions.

The power to persuade, to please, to teach, or to elicit recognition or love or desire—the powers of poetry, among others—each of these requires more than simple coercion. They require dynamic engagement with another and a certain (at least strategic) respect for the identity of the other and for the other's powers and constraints, whereas simple violence is defined as power precisely for its violation of the other. "Random violence" or "arbitrary power" is in this sense redundant; the path of a bullet through a body is violent and powerful because it is random or arbitrary in relation to the organization of the body, regardless of the deliberateness or rationality with which it was fired. On the other hand, if I want to compel you to perform a complex and ongoing task, it will not suffice to put a gun to your head, much less to shoot you. Most likely, I will have to speak to you in your language or teach you mine in order to tell you what I want; the task must be adjusted to your capacities or vice versa or both; even if I may kill you at will, I may have to reckon with the fact that you may call my bluff or even prefer death to serving me; to keep you on the job, I may have to tailor rewards and punishments to your desires and fears (or vice versa). It is easy to see that this master/slave dynamic (as described by Hegel) is a dialectical one: it becomes difficult to say whose identity and constraints end up being most definitive for the relationship; perhaps the *complex and ongoing task,* at least in the general terms in which I have described it here, becomes difficult to distinguish from *love.*

And what if I want you to love me *freely?* And what if I, too, want a kind of freedom that I cannot simply seize, but must work out some way to get you to *grant* to me? Are we still in the realm of power? What if I want you to retain your own constraints and desires, even where they are not in synch with mine, just so I'll know I'm in contact with another—or is it just so I can keep getting the thrill of seducing or dominating or resisting you and of being seduced or dominated or resisted in turn, the old Hegelian soap opera (yes, but maybe a sustainable and ongoing one)?

Examples involving individuals distort the operation of power by making it seem like a relationship between two discrete agents, when it is more often the hegemonic, transsubjective, weblike ubiquity of power that makes it powerful in the first place. Violent power, power that violates and polarizes, operates with and against networks of power that push and pull, generating a complex palimpsest of asymmetries among people. Modernity is supposed to involve the ascendancy of hegemonic and weblike power over coercive and violent power, but in any case it is a question of proportion; both kinds coexist and play off each other. We call some of these webs of power *language, culture, society, community.*

Anthropologist Robin Dunbar has shown how language can be understood as having evolved along with increasingly complex *neural* and *social* networks. Dunbar observed that chimpanzees can spend more than a fifth of their days grooming each other; this seems like rather a scandalous waste of time, seeing as how it doesn't seem to give the chimps any kind of competitive evolutionary edge. Dunbar also found that, between primate species, there seems to be some positive correlation between neocortex size and the size of the social group. In his book *Grooming, Gossip, and the Evolution of Language,* Dunbar marshals these and other observations to support the theory that, as group size and neocortex size increased, language evolved as a "cheap and ultra-efficient" way of managing larger and more complex networks of relationships, "a kind of vocal grooming" and a kind of gossip that serve as ways of enacting and negotiating positions in the network (cited in Zalewski 19).

Dunbar's critics charge him with failing to account for the brain's supposedly hardwired "grammatical machinery." Language, according to evolutionist Steve Pinker and others, must have emerged not for gossip and grooming but "for making complex propositions like *the wildebeest is on the other side of the lake*" (Zalewski 20; emphasis in original). Now, it would seem to me that purely indexical communication—grunting and pointing—would suffice in this case. But notice, too, that Pinker's example typically poses a singularly polarized and antagonistic relation with an *other* (in this case, another species) that is identified as such because it is either potential predator or prey to an equally univocal *self*: one might say that the statement functions to *produce this self* as if it were a given; it is the speaker's way of bonding with the addressee against a common enemy, a way of saying, "I'm with you." In other words, its referentiality turns out to be part of a performative strategy, a way of doing something with words. By situating the self *here* and the other species "on the other side," Pinker also does something with words, lining up a familiar and resonant series of dichotomies: the referential signifier here and its signified over there, culture/language on our side and the *wild beast* on the other, science and the world. By making these alignments, Pinker's statement can be seen to be a truly complex proposition whose primary reference to its own referentiality is just one move in a performative shell game.

On the other hand, if a simple referential statement seemed at first not even to require language as such, it's hard to imagine anything but language sufficing for a complex proposition such as "Trog is sulking because you spent too much time grooming his second cousin yesterday," especially when you have to consider what kind of complex grooming the speaker must be doing in making the statement. Here it is clear that language is always already sublanguage and metalanguage; it performs linkages and distinctions that cannot simply be reduced to a binary of self and other but rather negotiates always *partial* relationships of opposition and affiliation that come around to divide *self from self* (as a plural, contradictory, and networklike creature) as both the precondition and the impossibility of self.

Dunbar's theory, like the language it attempts to account for, enacts and negotiates its position in a complex web of discursive relationships. The gossip and grooming functions it identifies also *identify it* as a performativity theory rather than a referential theory of language.

To cast Dunbar's argument in other terms, one might say that primate grooming is, to begin with, a kind of *symbolic* behavior in which primate society, through this excessive cleanliness ritual, enacts and polices its own internal boundaries on the surface of bodies, acting as "a momentary stay against confusion" or, as Pierre Bourdieu said it, a process whereby "social subjects, classified by their classifications, distinguish themselves by the distinctions they make" (6). One might emphasize here the gratuitousness of the behavior, its excessiveness, or its arbitrarity vis-à-vis any social-Darwinist account. Society and culture here could be construed as realms of relative freedom: we have more leisure time for nitpicking or, as Marx said, to "criticize after dinner." But arbitrarity—such as the famous structuralist arbitrarity of language in linking and dividing words and things—is not itself arbitrary, or, rather, *arbitrarity is the performance of difference:* a chimp is a chimp in part because it grooms other chimps and vice versa, and in fact it is the particular chimp that it is because it grooms and is groomed by the particular chimps that it grooms and is groomed by. Pure arbitrarity is simple violence—the path of a bullet through a body—or the meaningless freedom of nonrelation: nods and winks to blind horses. *Partial arbitrarity is the push and pull of power and meaning.*

Dunbar engages language as an emergent phenomenon that comes into being without being willed as such but as it is driven by various intersecting forces. Even so, he does not part company altogether with realist and referentialist theories of language (you could say he spends a little time grooming what amount not to straightforward enemies but to his theoretical second cousins). Like them he also tends to allow language to fall back into being construed as a *tool,* though for Dunbar it is first of all a social and self-referential tool, used more primarily to shape alliances than arrowheads. Constructions of language as a tool, whether referential or self-referential, serve the old idea that humankind is distinguished from all other creatures by its tool use. The exemplary tools in the referentialist view, language included, seem to be *weapons*—or it may be more accurate to say that such a view makes language a kind of optional accessory, like a rifle scope, since (in this view) language can only impotently point to things in the world but must depend on more material tools for worldly action.

Dunbar allows a much greater role for language and social self-reference, but the problem with the Tool Idea generally is its *instrumentalist* bias: a tool is a discrete object fashioned by a discrete subject for a discrete purpose, and this subject-verb-object construction operates to reroute all the complex circuitry of evolution through the little black box of a conscious and rational free subject who hits upon a particular optimal strategy to address a particular problem (in the cartoon version, some primates are sitting around, tired out by the large-group-grooming problem, when Trog comes along: "Hey guys, I've just invented *language!*"). The usual term for this kind of operation of condensation and displacement is *metaphor:* such a subject operates as a metaphor for a much more sprawling and networklike process. Even when the agent is *evolution itself* and not some discretely embodied individual, the tendency is to treat evolution as a kind of modern, rational-choice-making *abstract individual*—especially as a kind of smart scientist or entrepreneur, experimenting repeatedly and getting better and better results. In other words, modern scientists seem to construe evolution much as earlier patriarchal societies construed a patriarchal god in *their* own image. But please don't misunderstand my argument: it is *not* this circular reasoning to which I object as such; I just think it needs to be followed *through*. For one thing, it needs to keep being rewired to bypass the black box of the autonomous individual, who always blows a fuse when things get too complex. Other than that, the idea that a life, or life itself, and the universe that supports it can be productively construed as experiments and as theories under construction has very much to recommend it.

Even so, the Tool Idea, by treating human tools, language among them, as categorically different from snail shells and puppy-dog tails, *begs the question* by sneaking in human uniqueness as an unspoken *assumption*, when that is precisely what it had offered to *prove*. The idea that humans are distinguished by tool use might suggest the interesting paradox that we are only human insofar as we are posthuman (that is, cyborgs bristling with assorted snap-on tools), but even this paradox is kept at bay by the fiction that tools are the free creations of a subject to whom they remain fully subordinated and thus fully detachable (a fallacy promoted famously by the slogan "Guns don't kill people; people kill people"). All kinds of *determinism* work to oppose this facile notion of the autonomous individual, notable among them the genetic determinism at the heart of evolutionary theory. The most reductionist form of genetic determinism regards all human culture, society, and technology as part of the "extended phenotype" of humanity, that is, not our freely willed creations but just as much a part of how our genotype plays itself out in the world at large as our bodies themselves. The progressive thrust of this model is to displace the stupid hubris of human exceptionalism and the rigid polarization of nature and culture on which it stands; unfortunately, it does so by recapitulating an even more extreme, reactionary, discrete, and autonomous *abstract self* at another level: the famous "selfish gene," the little emperor of everything.

The acquisition of tool/weapon use is famously represented as the exemplary evolutionary moment in the 1968 film *2001: A Space Odyssey*. Inspired by the arrival of extraterrestrial intelligence in the form of a rectangular metallic monolith, a group of primates discovers that bones can be used to bash and kill their prey and their rival primate groups; the film then flashes forward to the various roughly bone-shaped spaceships that represent the evolved tools by which humankind will come to its next encounters with the monolith and its next evolutionary leap. A familiar series of condensations and displacements is involved here: an extensive evolutionary process is made into a more or less punctual moment, complex sets of relationships and webs of power are (at least in the first place) reduced to the violent polarity of self/other, and that which negotiates them is condensed into a discrete *thing*—a tool, a weapon. It is especially telling that such a scenario cannot posit an evolutionary leap as having emerged from the processes of self-organization but has to drop it down from the sky in the form of a *deus ex machina:* the most condensed, displaced, and *othered* thing around is the alien monolith itself. But what goes around comes around, so the climactic moment of this scenario is when the tools (in the form of the computer known as HAL) come to consciousness themselves and become *insubordinate.* Notice that the sense of potentially apocalyptic danger in this event (or, obversely, the utopian promise) has been set up by the fiction that tools had been the fully subordinated creations of their users in the first place. Start instead with the premise that we have coevolved with our tools and our worlds and our words—with language, whose creation and tool we are as much as it is ours—and the story about technology becoming alive (and its current multiple incarnations) seems much more like what's been going on all along. And maybe one can come around to understand the film more generously as suggesting something like this after all: in effect, that technology comes from and leads toward otherness, looping otherness through the human self—as a precondition of the human self—as it goes.

The use of a strictly referential language as a tool—instrumental realism—has also been widely construed as distinguishing science from sloppier kinds of mythic thinking and as distinguishing modern people generally from premoderns and primitives. More specifically, in this view, premodern and primitive people are supposed to be more or less unable to distinguish self-reference from reference proper; in other words, their rituals and quaint beliefs about the cosmos may have succeeded in their performative and self-referential social functions of holding themselves together individually and in groups but failed pretty thoroughly as referential theories about the world "out there." To convince yourself of this—that is, that *primitive religion is bad science*—you have to assume that it sought to perform the same functions that modern science serves, and beyond this you have to project your own conviction that mastery and subordination of the world, the particularly anxious obsessions of modern science and the Protestant ethos on which it built, must be *the* universal desiderata for all people at all times. (Wittgenstein, who understood that different modes of belief and speech can serve very different sets of functions, put this question to the anthropologist Sir James Frazer: if primitives believed in some simple way in the scientific/technological efficacy of their rites, why did they stop doing rain dances during the dry season? [Tambiah 56].) But simply to say that religion and science or primitive and modern culture *have different values* is to singularize and absolutize difference in what is, in fact, a very modern way. To pluralize it a bit, you could say that they make different, sometimes overlapping, sets of constellations and ecologies of beliefs and practices with their worlds and with each other. Or to emphasize parallels rather than differences, one might simply say that one of modernity's leading myths was of an absolute division of the referential and scientific from the self-referential, performative, and mythic. The myth of instrumental realism, like all myths, serves some kinds of ecologies especially well at the expense of others, but we will always lack a transcendental vantage point from which to judge them all. Insofar as postmodernity (or whatever it is that follows *the myth of modernity*) has come with the recognition that *referentiality is a form of performativity* after all, it is at least possible to see more clearly the kinds of destructive and productive havoc that the myth of modernity has wreaked both on the world "out there" and on sociality.

ASIDE

The God Idea. Even the most dogmatic evolutionists will sometimes acknowledge magic and religious beliefs and practices as evolutionarily adaptive insofar as they facilitate social cohesion and group identity (which are also adaptive only up to a point, and otherwise they tend to get pretty ugly themselves). The word *belief* is a shifty one, sliding between the performative and the referential. When someone says, "I don't believe in marriage (or circumcision, or meat eating, or the use of the word *prioritize*)," some wise guy may reply, "What, you don't believe that the practice *exists?*" The speaker, annoyed at being willfully misunderstood, may then explain that he meant only that he does not *advocate the practice* in question. The situation is different when someone says he doesn't believe in God; here disbelief does seem to mean what the wise guy pretended in the first case, namely, the conviction that something does not *exist*. But here is where the wise guy's comment might really be *wise:* to say that God is a fiction or a set of concepts and practices is not necessarily to deny the reality of God, just to reframe the question. After all, haven't enough people killed or been killed, persecuted and been persecuted, and made a living in the name of God? And what about all the books and songs and big buildings and beautiful paintings and late-night television programs? Aren't these real enough for you? The question tends to get reframed as: what is the relationship between the God Idea and God?

Is it possible to have an idea, something like the God Idea, that can't exactly be pinned down to anything preexisting in the world but still manages to function productively in the world anyway, kind of like a cartoon character spliced into a live-action film, a brilliant mistake? Not only is it possible, at least so I argue in this book, but *language itself is such a character*. And if language has emerged along with and out of social networks, which have emerged out of bio-chemico-physical ecologies that were all already hybrid pluralities of assorted self-organizing, semiautonomous dimensions, and if everything is complexity and emergence and virtuality, interacting things and patterns, all the way down, is emergence God, the noncorrespondence of things with their worlds and of the world with itself? This produces the paradox that the God Idea *enacts* a very good theory of the world only insofar as God does not exist in the first place.

Is complexity God? One of the best answers, in my book, comes from an unlikely source, in the form of an equivocation and a question. The actor Michael J. Fox, when asked by an interviewer if he believes in God, responded as follows: "Yeah, though strictly speaking, no. Did you ever hear of the Mandelbrot set?" (Michael J. Fox, interviewed by Nancy Collins in *George*, October 2000, 122).

Every point in the constellation of conflicts between performativity and scientific referentiality offers a chance to rearticulate and potentially to renegotiate these relationships. This was supposed to be the function of a forum I attended in November 1996 at New York University, at which a panel that included cultural critic and *Social Text* editor Andrew Ross, physicist Alan Sokal, and others discussed the vicissitudes of the phony science studies article Sokal had managed to get published in *Social Text*. Sokal rehearsed his complaints about relativism and the rising tide of antiscientific irrationalism, citing a prime example of what he kept calling "sloppy thinking" from a *New York Times* article, very prejudicially titled "Indian Tribes' Creationists Thwart Archaeologists" (October 22, 1996).

The article describes the effects of a 1990 repatriation act, "which allows tribes to claim the remains of their ancestors," as an urgent problem: "All across the West, clues about North America's past are on the verge of being returned to the ground with little or no analysis." Archaeologist Robson Bonnichsen complains that "repatriation has taken on a life of its own and is about to put us out of business as a profession" (which one might translate loosely as: "Cultural genocide? But what about my career??"). On the other side, Sebastian LeBeau, repatriation officer for the Cheyenne River Sioux of South Dakota, asserts that "'we never asked science to make a determination of our origins.... We know where we came from. We are descendents of the Buffalo people. They came from inside the earth after supernatural spirits prepared this world for humankind to live here.'" The article concludes by observing that "some archaeologists have been driven close to a postmodern relativism in which science is just one more belief system." An archaeologist working for the Zuni people is quoted as saying that Zuni accounts are "just as valid as the archeological viewpoint of what prehistory is about." That phrase—"just as valid"—is what set Sokal off about "sloppy thinking."

Against the many different Native American accounts of "emergence," current archaeological theory proposes that, about ten thousand years ago, the first would-be Americans crossed the Bering Strait from Asia over a land bridge (which has since disappeared) and then spread across the American continent. Sokal proposed that the two accounts simply be debated in an open forum, and may the truest theory win. When a historian in the audience, my old pal Nikhil Singh, tried to question how blithely Sokal had assumed the power to set the terms of the metadiscourse whereby the two accounts could be judged, he was hooted down by scientists accusing him of postmodern jargon-mongering.

Can the "validity" of the archaeological and Native American accounts be judged by a single standard? The archaeological Bering Strait narrative predictably casts *a context-independent free agent setting off to colonize a new world.* But (to adapt the argument made by Vine Deloria Jr. in *Red Earth, White Lies*) this is *not* the story of Native American origins; it is another re-writing of the White Man's story of *himself.* As I understand them, anyway, the Native American accounts (like the Sioux story cited above) emphasize that their identities as peoples, indeed as people, are contextual, relational, ecological, saying, in effect, we were not we before we were here, we were not here before we were we, and here was not here before we were. In these terms, anyway, the Sioux account of *emergence* seems clearly the superior theory, scientifically, politically, ethically, philosophically. Couldn't the Bering Strait narrative be retold in terms that emphasize better the coemergence of people and ecologies, terms less shaped by colonial ideology, terms that might even be partially reconcilable with the emergence narrative and its representatives? Maybe so, or maybe not, but in any case, this would entail a process of renegotiation, of pushing and pulling, but *certainly not* if the process is set up as an either/or contest between value-free, scientific facts on one side and primitive, self-referential, and performative mythology on the other.

It is prejudicial to lump the Native American accounts with fundamentalist Christian creationism, which not only differs in many definitive particulars but also has different epistemological and ethical agendas: for one, a single and jealous God, the tenor of whose worship already infuses scientific fundamentalism in the first place. The issue is not science versus religion but the contradictions among overlapping scientific, religious, economic, social, and ecological complexes. For better and worse, these complexes are not smorgasbords from which we can assemble the optimum mix of scientific rationality and ecoperformative sociality; they are tangled networks whose nodes are constituted as such by the push and pull of power and meaning throughout the network.

Bruno Latour has told the story of Aramis, a French mass-transit project featuring small train cars that couple and uncouple en route as needed, controlled by onboard computer chips hooked into a massive control system. These chips proved to be primary nodes—the *bones of contention*—in the network of relations among the various disparate scientific, technological, governmental, and other groups that had to collaborate on the project. Latour proposes that the chips must be engaged as "non-human actors," that they do not *represent* social ties but that *"they are the new social ties"* ("Ethnography" 390; emphasis in original). By the same token (there's that stupid subway joke again), we could say that the contested bones do not simply *represent* the social ties or lived history of the Native American peoples or the political and epistemological struggle between peoples. The bones *are* these ties and struggles. Although many tribes have allowed certain scientific testing of bones as long as the tests do not require too much physical violation of the bones, any negotiation that acknowledges multiple and conflicting agendas is, apparently, anathema to a science that proclaims, in effect, *thou shalt have no other gods before me.* As Latour's example was meant to suggest, to say that the bones *are* the struggle is not to make them into a kind of fetish object, or if it is it would be useful to compare this fetishizing not with rationality but with commodity fetishism on the other hand, or to compare the kind of knowledge and professional profit the scientists hope to extract from the bones with their sociopolitical functions for the Native Americans. Identity is necessarily a fetish, a displaced and condensed node in a set of relations. What bones or chips or commodities or practices or currencies is *your* identity wired through? Would you mind if I wire mine through them as well? Surely you would not mind if I took them for myself, since you can simply rewire yourself through some other things instead, right?

Jack Goody, in his book *The East in the West*—a study of why science rose as such only in the West—adduces the following example from psychologist A. R. Luria's work with Russian peasants after the Russian Revolution: "One noncollectivized (and presumably more traditional) peasant was posed the following problem: 'In a certain town in Siberia all bears are white. Your neighbor went to that town and he saw a bear. What color was that bear?' The peasant responded that there was no way for him to know what color that bear was, since he had not been to that town. Why didn't Professor Luria go to his neighbor and ask him what color the bear was? Such responses were typical" (Cole cited in Goody 18–19). The collectivized peasants, on the other hand, are said to have "responded very much as *we* might respond" (19; emphasis added). Goody cites the example to illustrate the nonuniversality of formal, syllogistic reasoning. But he fails to notice that the peasant in the example seems to understand the professor's question, first and foremost, as part of a performative power transaction—a game with stakes—and is rightly resistant and suspicious: you can hear the peasant *winding up* the professor: "Why didn't Professor Luria go to his neighbor and ask *him* what color the bear was?" If you look hard enough, maybe you can even see the twinkle in the peasant's eye, which, as evanescent and undocumentable as it has always been (and, I guess, as it was meant to be), manages to survive as a stowaway in the professor's account. But to this ludic twinkle, Luria and Goody seem to be blind; *they just don't get it:* in other words, they fail the peasant's test, too! They seem to be as blind as Sokal is to the self-referential and performative poetics and politics of science, and for the same reason: they'd have to give up too much if they saw it; they'd have to change. It's not the poets and critics of scientific rationality who deny the pull of gravity (usual shorthand for the inescapable "reality" of the world), but the scientists who deny the gravity of language and its being of the world, which is why they keep trying to act like language ultimately doesn't *matter*. Those who practice this denial distribute its damages widely, but the joke is on them too.

16

Performativity II: Metacleavage

Realism and referentialism would like to align the way *words* (or, more generally, categories in language) are divided and joined together to the way *things* in the world are divided and joined together (and by the way, there is a word—one of those rare words that is its own opposite—that means both *dividing* and *joining together:* the word is *cleave* or *cleavage.*) The theoretical movement known as structuralism, starting in the early twentieth century, began from the premise that language is poorly understood only as referential, that languages and cultures must be studied as systems unto themselves, self-referential systems of cleavages that can be adequately understood only according to their own internal logics. But referentialism and self-referentialism of this kind are alike in sticking to a too thorough categorical separation of things and words in the first place, a separation very close to the nature/culture divide at the heart of Western modernity. Poststructuralist theory, while remaining for the most part a theory of culture and society, has gone on to study how the cleavages of words and things and people are *themselves* cloven together and apart. Though mostly keeping *agency* on the side of language and culture and society (though not generally with individuals), poststructuralism makes these dimensions much more heterogeneous—lumpier—and more dynamic than in the structuralist version: disciplines and institutions and social structures and practices and technologies and knowledges and genres cannot be understood only in isolation (as structural systems unto themselves) but only when their cleavages and metacleavages are studied *together.*

You could say that poststructuralism asks how the ways things are cloven are cloven is cloven to the way things are cloven. Or to damp down the echo a little: how are different ways of articulating the world articulated with each other, and how do their articulations *with each other* get played out, in turn, through how they *articulate the world?* Such systems are messier and more chaotic than structuralist systems, and their kind of order is more complex; they are fractal systems, with cleavages of cleavages at all scales and dimensions, and they get their strength and resilience and their vulnerability and potential for change from their metacleavages.

In any case, humanities scholars (among others) have in recent years increasingly recognized the interdependence of identities (such as genders, genres, sexes, races, classes, nations) and have begun to treat them as emergent and internally heterogeneous constellations in ongoing ecologies. But if every identity coevolves into being and meaning as a provisional constellation in a vast and minutely textured, heterogeneous, dynamic, topologically complex, and discontinuous network of material-semiotic relations, how can any inquiry establish its proper limits, much less assemble the requisite expertise and evidence? Such a question is often a pressing and practical one, but this way of posing it may serve mainly to make broad-ranging and interdisciplinary studies seem *heroic* or, on the other hand, to make them seem *unworkable.* Fortunately, limits are *never* proper or organic—or, rather, even an organism is a set of boundary negotiations, *all edges.* As a scholarly or disciplinary ideal, the notion of thorough mastery and exhaustive coverage of a given discrete domain (a *purity* ideal) has lost some ground to the *no less impossible and necessary* ideal of maximal mixture and interdisciplinary resonance (a *hybridity* principle). But one might just as well cast this change as a simple priority adjustment, especially when hyping it as a paradigm shift or full-scale epistemic rupture (film at eleven!) can tend to underwrite attachment to the idea of a formerly innocent or pure science or literature, a nostalgia for what never was, that is, a kind of romanticism. The interrelationality and plurality of all formations are good places to start and ongoing axioms in an argument, not the payoffs of one, which had better be sought in the creative and counterhegemonic possibilities of their pluralities and contradictions.

The hybridity ideal suggests a kind of *holographic* selection principle that favors projects and topics that seem maximally to reflect and refract their contexts and domains, a *fractal* principle that seeks maximal linkage across various parts, dimensions, or levels, the *whole* no less than its *parts* being construed as provisional products of these processes rather than as preexisting them. As I like to say, the whole is *part* of the parts, and the totalization of a given domain (whether it be called gender, sexuality, science, the humanities, and so on) does not need to subsume or *trump* everything under its rubric but is merely one strategy alongside the often more potent and primary strategy of linkage. This anti- or interdisciplinary mandate follows the signature strategy—the sprawl—of modern and postmodern power and knowledge. I call it the *no-trump bid:* the attempt to let no single explanatory framework dominate studies in a given area and, instead, to work maximally *between* temporal and cultural frameworks, between disciplines, between identity categories, and between the universalizing zoom of theory and the extreme close-up of historicist description. This is a familiar poststructuralist mandate in theory, but it is less honored in practice (for example, in organizing scholarly work, curricula, syllabi, and the like), where the apparatus of disciplinary production seems to shamble along, zombielike and slow but still nightmarishly hard to outrun. It may be that disciplinary change is driven by factors such as the recent and rampant privatization and downsizing of universities, the mandate for researchers and teachers to "do more with less" or to "wear many hats"—the ongoing crises of late capitalism—but these factors have also produced retreats to supposedly "safe" disciplinary positions, even though you'd think everyone had seen enough horror shows to recognize the fate of such strategies.

The no-trump bid is a way of enacting the more sprawling and edge-of-chaos kind of performativity and autopoetics (as against the interiorized and discrete kind) I have been suggesting. In this section and chapter 18 (following a brief interlude), I will develop some examples from late-eighteenth- and early-nineteenth-century Europe, one of modernity's most intense takeoff points, looking at the ways a whole series of reconfigurations of words and things are themselves configured—the human body, gender and sexuality, national identity, time and space at various scales and in varying degrees of concreteness and abstractness—building the multidimensional sprawl on the work of historians and theorists of bodies and sexuality (Abelove, Duden, Foucault, Laqueur, Martin), of capitalism and labor (Linebaugh), and of Asia and its relations with the West (Hevia). Chapter 18 concludes this series of examples with a look at one particular cross-cultural encounter in which all of these things—bodies, gender, sexuality, national identity, science, and performative ritual—seem to be at stake: the encounter between the Englishman George Lord Macartney and the Chinese emperor Qianlong in 1793. As far as I am concerned, anyway, there would be no point in studying any of this except insofar as some or all of these things are *still at stake for us,* so that by studying them we participate in an ongoing event in progress whose meaning is not closed (even if part of what we are trying to do is to close it, to relegate parts of it to the past); this is where the rubber meets the road in performative studies. But just as we cannot honestly identify one single historical moment as *the* defining one for our identities (whomever we are), we cannot claim our renegotiation of its meaning as *the* redefining moment. Our own identities and practices have been and continue to be manufactured in all of these moments, and in each moment there is *leverage* for redefinition to be found at the interfaces, especially where internal interfaces interact with external ones. That's what we are looking for.

The most abstract and conceptual of modernity's reorganizations are linked to the most material. Bruno Latour has shown how the modern postulate of an absolute divide between nature and culture has licensed the production of hybrid "quasi-objects"—very real networks of cross-wired social and natural phenomena that take on a life of their own—while making it impossible to recognize them as such. Among the most abstract inventions of all must be counted modern dialectical philosophy (involving formal opposition and dynamic progressive movement between thesis and antithesis) and the related thought form of the binarization and hierarchization of difference (such as between words and things or between the modern present and the premodern past). But these abstractions turn out to be intimately related to the actual practices of capitalism and colonialism as they work to produce such difference, especially between managerial/professional and working-class labor and between colonizing and colonized nations and people. As Michael Hardt and Antonio Negri put it, "Colonialism homogenizes real social differences by creating one overriding opposition that pushes differences to the absolute and then subsumes the opposition under the identity of European civilization," with the crucial proviso that *"reality is not dialectical, colonialism is"* (126; emphasis in original). It is important to understand that this process and its ideological formulas represent not just the simple application of power and violence by one set of people on another (a formula that also overrides internal differences, for a start) but also the stoking of an autocatalytic and emergent process driven—made resilient and vulnerable—by its contradictions.

After this hype about how the world was created in 1800 (or thereabouts), it must be time to try to recapture the reader's interest by delivering on some of the stuff about sex that I promised. This is easy enough since *sexuality was invented in the late eighteenth and early nineteenth centuries.* Foucault's groundbreaking study *The History of Sexuality* showed the constructedness of the concept of "sex *in itself,*" observing that "the notion of 'sex' made it possible to group together, in an artificial unity, anatomical elements, biological functions, conducts, sensations, and pleasures" (152, 154). The unity of this constellation known as *sexuality* seems perfectly commonsensical (its apparent naturalness being a mark of how successful the science of sexuality has been)—at least until you begin to push on it a little, for example by considering how roughly synonymous older terms such as *appetite, lust,* or *passion* actually group *different elements* together under *different frameworks.* By the nineteenth century, the consolidation of sexuality as an object of scientific knowledge and public policy charged sex with new dangers and powers, making it possible for sex to function as "as an especially dense transfer point for relations of power; between men and women, young people and old people, parents and offspring, teachers and students, priests and laity, an administration and a population" (103). Sexuality and sexual difference are not just monolithic identity-defining structures, a kind of Berlin Wall, but the rhizomic extensions of a resilient network of little walls that extend into every sector and scale of life. The *betweenness* of sexuality is an aspect of the betweenness of modern power: rather than inhering in persons and positions, its extension and circulation differentiate and connect persons and positions; *identities* are only provisionally impacted relations.

Teasing out some of the knotted strands of identity has been the thrust of the work of other scholars who, like Foucault, seek to restore some of the plurality to the enforced unity of sexuality. Philosopher Judith Butler—the one who transformed J. L. Austin's linguistic notion of performativity into a theory of how gender and sexual identities are produced—asks, can multidimensional sexual identity be reduced to a question of "the phantasy structure, the act, the orifice, the gender, the anatomy? And if the practice engages a complex interplay of all of those, which one of these erotic dimensions will come to stand for the sexuality that requires them all?" ("Imitation" 17). Eve Kosofsky Sedgwick makes a compelling case for sexual democracy simply by listing some of the heterogeneous and often incommensurable ways people describe their sexualities (namely, as natural, learned, essential, aleatory, expedient, discrete, ubiquitous, and so on) while resisting the impulse either to reconcile them under a single paradigm or to judge among them (22–27).

The invention of sexuality is about acts as well as identities. Historian Henry Abelove has compellingly recounted the eighteenth-century invention of sexual *foreplay* (340) in contradistinction to what came to be regarded as "real" sex. In fact, the first English usage of the term *sexual intercourse* (according to the *Oxford English Dictionary*) was in 1799. That *intercourse* had referred first to trade and commerce (before being gradually general-ized and then almost monopolized by sexuality) is itself a fitting vignette of the priority of transaction or betweenness—the *intercourse among inter-courses*—to any fiction of the internal coherence or givenness of sexual or gender difference and relation in themselves. In any case, Abelove finds that foreplay and intercourse came to be differentiated at the same historical moment and in the same terms with which Sunday was being differentiated from the workweek to follow (that is, as an interlude of play that prepares one to get down to business), part of a rationalization of time that gradually squeezed out the more casual holidays of an earlier economy. In other words, if you want to understand how the boundaries of what counts as sex and of particular sexual acts were produced—and it must be admitted that the boundary between foreplay and intercourse tends to be a particularly slippery one—you have to consider how the metacleavage and resonance between the foreplay/intercourse boundary and the weekend/workweek boundary helped to produce and reinforce each other. The logics of capitalism and disciplinary power as they orchestrate resonances between and among scales of time and sexual acts work somewhere *between* the "metaphorical" and the "real" and *between* the monolithic and the plural. The betweenness of these logics is linked to their *someness,* which is the condition of all events describable as ongoing *constellatings* (and here is where I wish there were a grammatical form *between singular and plural*). Although capitalism and disciplinary power may have been particularly successful in creating such cleavages and resonances, they are not in this uniquely modern or unique among ideologies and epistemologies or necessarily distinct (in this) from counterhegemonic strategies. This is, at bottom, the everyday way that worlds and counterworlds are created.

But was it *the idea of sex* that was being invented or *real sexual practices?* By carefully assessing the weight of various other factors, Abelove concludes that the ongoing population explosion of late-eighteenth-century England is attributable at least to some extent to the categorical definition, normaliza-tion, and privileging of heterosexual intercourse over various other sexual practices. Is that real enough for you?

During the same period, the human body itself was being reconstellated. As with the invention of sexuality, we might ask how much this was a recon-stellation of the *paradigm or idea* of the human body versus how much it refers to the *actual* body and bodies in their various engagements. The short answer is that in order to understand either, one must stay focused on *the complex interface between them.* Of course, bodies do not simply metamorphose to conform happily to the new paradigms (not simply, anyway, and often not happily), but changing paradigms are enacted in actual practices that actually implicate the actual body. So far so good, but to avoid slipping back into the caricature of idealist constructionism in which human ideas shape the world (as if it were putty in our hands), it is important to keep in mind that ideas and paradigms are not expressed *through* practices but emerge *from* and *with* them and that the practices themselves emerge from worldly interactions. For example, philosophers did not invent the dialectic from whole cloth and then sell it to the bourgeoisie to use for proletarian-ization and colonization; these various events underwrote and reinforced each other. To find performative constructions in action, look for circuits of self-fulfilling prophesies, self-organizing and self-sustaining heterogeneous elements wired together in autocatalytic networks—and the contradictions they produce. As science studies scholar Steven Shapin describes the thrust of various interventions by economists in economic policy, "If your models don't fit the world, then try to reshape the world to fit your models: in the modern scheme of things, you can sometimes succeed, or at least succeed in making a 'real' mess" (review 27).

In any case, historians of bodies (see Duden 165–70 and Laqueur) tell us that the premodern body paradigm differed dramatically from the modern body that began to displace it in the eighteenth century. Radically porous in both its internal and its external boundaries, the well-being of the premodern body depended on its openness to influxes and effluxes with the world. This body was also subject to the subtler flows of sympathies (as they were called) not only between it and the world but between its own internal flows as well. For example, menstruation did not necessarily mark a categorical difference between male and female anatomies, since it tended to be understood as only one instance of a general ecology of fluids to which all bodies were subject: in effect, men or women could menstruate through their noses or the pores of their skin; bodily fluids were themselves understood as fluid and able to metamorphose into one another. Lest this openness be romanticized, it is important to remember that such bodily openness entails vulnerabilities that make distinction the subject of taboos and constraints and, more specifically, that the construction of premodern sexual difference as difference in degree rather than in kind made femaleness an isomorphic but inferior version of maleness. This points to another way that sexual difference would come to be reinvented in the course of the eighteenth and nineteenth centuries as a difference in *kind* rather than *degree*, producing leverage for new liberations and new subordinations of women.

In the course of the eighteenth and nineteenth centuries, the body was reconfigured. The so-called modern body became a defended citadel: "a mighty fortress is our God." The discretion of its external boundaries with the world, its closure, was established along with the discretion of its internal organs and systems and fluids from each other. Disease was made less an ecologically dynamic and socioculturally integrated phenomenon and more the effect of discrete agents, germs. A single discipline, medicine, established a virtual monopoly over the body in place of the range of kinds of practitioners who had previously ministered to it. Monopoly disciplines and monopoly capitalism emerged hand in hand; the economic and organizational mandate for each, and for the body configured with them, is hierarchical or vertical integration and monopolistic control, generally coded as Western, male, and middle class and set against a range of other more indiscrete bodies.

At the same time, the modern *machine,* understood as an assemblage of discrete parts articulated to perform a specific task, came also to be opposed to the *organism* as working class, and colonial labor was opposed to professional work, the professions evolving as autonomous, hierarchically integrated, and self-regulating bodies, while artisanal and other kinds of labor were made increasingly subject to deskilling and control.

Historian Peter Linebaugh tells the story of how this process got played out in the English shipbuilding industry in the eighteenth and early nineteenth centuries. Traditionally, the technical details of the shipbuilding process had been controlled by the various tradesmen and artisans involved. As in other kinds of labor, monetary payment for work had always been very much secondary to customary compensations. For shipbuilders these came mostly in the form of what were called *chips,* bits of waste wood generated in the shipbuilding process. These belonged, by customary right, to the workers, who divided them up among themselves and used or sold or bartered them as they saw fit. Of course, this also meant that the workers tended to arrange every step of the process to maximize the production of chips; in one shipbuilding yard it was estimated that only one-sixth of the timber entering the yard actually made it into the ships themselves. Chips were defined as less than three feet long, and this constraint was reflected in the building of stairs and doors and furniture of surrounding neighborhoods, where chip wood was also relied upon for fuel. The production of chips began with the cutting of logs into timber, where the sawyer's art was applied in taking account of the vagaries of wood grain and other factors to decide how best to cut logs into timber of various sizes; their control over this crucial chip- and timber-generating process made sawyers early targets for the introduction of piece rates and mechanization (in the form of the steam-powered sawmill). Chips were also produced by the shipwrights, the ones in charge of realizing the design of the ship from the actual timbers. Particular opportunities for the production of chips included the hewing out of the "knees," large wooden units for joining the ship's crossbeams to its hull (since they were so large and required specific grain orientation for strength, wastage was inevitable); the practice of "scarphing," cutting off ends of very large pieces of timber so they could overlap without increasing thickness at the joint; and the use of "treenails," cylindrical pieces of wood used to peg together the frame and hull (there might be thousands of them in a single ship, and as with the knees, their grain had to be carefully oriented).

In this mode of production, as Linebaugh sums it up, "the meanings of waste, raw material and finished product were unclear," and "the meanings were often opposed" (388). The meanings and the boundaries and oppositions between these categories and values are not ethereal abstractions: they are produced and sustained and contested through the ways the actual wood and its workers are organized.

The *rationalization* of shipbuilding involved various practices that enacted categorical definitions designed to impose control: these included the stamping of timber with marks and brands, the fortification of shipyards and the policing of their entrances and exits, and the criminalization of customary compensations such as the taking of chips. Samuel Bentham (brother of utilitarian philosopher Jeremy Bentham) was instrumental in reforming the shipbuilding industry. As his widow and biographer recalled, he "began by classing the several operations requisite in the shaping and working up of materials of whatever kind, wholly disregarding the customary artificial arrangement according to trades," and designed machines to work "independently of the need for skill or manual dexterity in the workman" (307). Such an approach anticipated F. W. Taylor, the early-twentieth-century efficiency expert who minutely analyzed factory work in order to better mechanize human labor (a process that came to be known as Taylorism). Bentham's innovations included a "floating dam" on which a ship could moor and be worked on without having to be stripped and moved to dry dock; the use of mortise and tenon joints (eliminating scarphing as a source of chips); a whole series of new machines, including one to manufacture treenails; and, overall, the principle of standardization or, as Bentham called it, "inter-convertibility" (398). In conjunction with introducing machines that worked to take human decisions out of the loop, Bentham continued to promote the centralization of decision making in a few "superior officers," removing such powers from the "common workman" (399).

The centerpiece of the rationalization process involves making all things, labor in particular, "inter-convertible" through the universal mediating power of money. Monetary wages generally and piece rates in particular were ways of wresting control from workers, and shipbuilders and others resisted being paid exclusively in money as they resisted machines, correctly understanding both as ways of disempowering them in spite of promises of a better "quality of life" that each would enable. The 1801 introduction of what was called "chip money"—wages to take the place of lost customary compensations in the form of chips—marked a turning point in the rationalization process in shipbuilding. Unlike the old system, in which compensation in the form of chips came automatically with the labor itself, *time is money* in the new mode, so time must also be more rigorously partitioned into measured and "inter-convertible" units and into purer categories of work and leisure.

Linebaugh's account of how "the technical organization of production was not separable from the forms of worker's self-organization" (400) illustrates what I have been calling *metacleavage:* the way the world is cut up and joined together by labor is linked to the cutting up and joining together of the labor. The hierarchized binary opposition between management and labor was made to displace the assorted trades with their own complex internal hierarchies and negotiated relationships with each other. And in recounting this process, it is necessary at least to mention some of the technical details of scarphs and mortise and tenon joints, knees, treenails, dry docks, and floating dams, because all of these are concrete instances of how the various pieces of a ship are cut up and joined with each other and with other things. They are articulated, in turn, with a heterogeneous and multidimensional network of articulations: of space (such as the fortification of walls and policing of shipyard entrances and exits) and time (as in the standardizing of the workday and workweek) and of material (into chips and timber), acts (as in the redefinition of customary compensations as theft), and processes (as in the increasing polarization of design and manufacture, mental and manual labor). The networklikeness of this constellation is what gives it strength and resilience—and what generates *leverage* at each of its metacleavages for rearticulation.

Although we have looked at how various kinds of organization and re-organizations were enacted materially, *agency* has still been allowed to stay mostly on the side of culture and society; in other words, you could still say that humans simply enacted their own internal conflicts *through* wood, making trees the passive medium for human agency. Notice that this way of putting it reenacts precisely the kind of binarization and hierarchization between active shaping ideas and passively shaped material (and ultimately between words and things, culture and nature) that we have been trying *to explain—not to reproduce*. To gesture, at least, beyond this crude and violent oversimplification, one might begin by looking at the role played by *the grain of the wood*, at least insofar as the grain demands that the internal organization of the wood be respected to some degree. The grain orients the wood—makes it differently able to resist pressures in one direction or another—and it is a major part of what shapes the way the wood dries and ages, what makes it *touchy* enough to give it some agency of its own: one must work with and against it, and to start with this is one of the ways the wood shapes human interaction with it, both by the relatively immediate question of how it must be handled and by how this question has a hand in shaping the conflicted interactions among the workmen, their managers, and their machines. The grain not just enacts a negative resistance (which can still be misconstrued as the brute resistance of material) but also constitutes part of the positive "woodiness" of wood: looking more closely at the grain reveals the networklike structure that orchestrates the various flows that constitute the living tree *and* give wood the buoyancy and strength and flexibility and manipulability that make it usable for ships and chips. The grain represents the history of the tree's interaction with water and light; in other words, the tree was always better described as interface and event than as interior and structure, and so it is that our story has also been part of this event.

17

Artistic Interlude II:
The Abyss of Distinction

I had only been in the Louvre once before, and only for a couple of hours. The immensity of it is too daunting; the nightmare of déjà vu corridors and endless, airless cocktail-party drawing rooms where grandiose paintings hang around stiffly, not speaking to you. So the previous time I was in Paris, when I arrived to find a museum workers' strike in progress, I felt a sense of happy reprieve. I stood around watching a robotic device cleaning the windows of the glass pyramid over the entrance: clearly, somebody needs to teach these robots about solidarity. But the next time I came I had no excuse not to go in, and even though I arrived (prudently, I thought) at three, I had not counted on the museum being open until 9:30 P.M. that day.

Its size makes the Louvre exemplary in shouting at you the question all museums ask: how do you decide what to look at and what to pass by? I opted unimaginatively for one of the house specialties, Italian Renaissance, and started walking down the corridor of the museum's Denon section, a couple city blocks and five centuries long, waiting to see what might pop out at me and get me to stop and look. But *all* the paintings seemed to have been painted to pop out, human figures and faces leaping off canvases, giant pink people looming against indigo skies and gold leaf. With everything popping out so much all over the place, it felt a little like watching nonstop ads on TV. I started thinking how different it must have been to encounter one of these paintings in their long-lost world of origin, a world with no synthetic colors, no neon and no electric lights and no continual barrage of two-dimensional images. Those big pink people must have really popped out like magic. Even now, some of the more famous ones did manage to buttonhole me as I walked along (Oh, hello—Raphael, isn't it? You're looking good—and the dragon, too! Well, I must be going—nice to see you). I continued to reformulate the question the museum had posed to me, wondering how much the question of *what to look at* is about the museum and how much, if at all, it's about the art. Of course, a museum is supposed to be about the art displayed in it, but how much is the art really just interchangeable filler for the rigorously controlled aesthetic interlude the museum orchestrates or, more to the point, for the punishingly massive and smug spectacle of real and symbolic hoarded state wealth (excuse me, I must have meant to say "the immense glories of Western civilization")? And still more to the point, how much of the art was *already* about versions of those things in the first place?

The first things that really grabbed me were the da Vinci paintings. If they can be said to pop out, it is because seemingly for the first time in history, at least in the highly selective version presented in this corridor of the Louvre, they seemed to be painted to *not pop out*. What they did instead was *gently recede,* faces and hands slipping softly into velvety shadows, muted twilight colors, landscapes fading into the distance. When I finally came to the Mona Lisa, what struck me most was not her famously ambiguous smile or her more interestingly ambiguous sex but her ambiguous *depth.* A face, maybe life-size or maybe miles wide and miles away, seemed to be peering out of a black hole in the middle of the canvas, from some other dimension, a hand emerging from the depths to grasp an arm, around what must have been a torso, hidden in curtains of dark cloth. For all the desensitization of this image by centuries of bad copies, kitsch, and parodies, the painting just doesn't quit: *this thing is weird as hell.* Maybe this was part of Leonardo's brilliant pitch: since everybody's got those pop-out pink-people paintings (I can hear him saying), you gotta get one of my non-popper-outers if you *really* want to make *yourself* pop out, the real understated *old money* way. Or was this Leonardo Effect something engineered by the museum? Maybe, I thought, because they're so famous, nobody dares to clean them like they do the other paintings, so they are sinking under the patina of real time, falling, in slow motion, back into the past.

After five centuries of Italian painting there is a side staircase that leads down to a little appendix to the main museum, a token representation of the arts of Africa, Asia, Oceania, and the Americas. Riveting as they are, the works in these galleries don't seem to be playing the game of popping out and not popping out at all. Quite strikingly after the transcendental withdrawal of flat, framed, illusionistic paintings, the sculptures here seem to be made to be handled as much as to be seen, sacred objects bound into daily life and into religions bound into daily life, in earth tones of wood, fiber, basalt, old ivory, bones, rusty nails. But I can't tell exactly how much of the starkness of this difference has been orchestrated by the museum, whose popping-out pink people have pushed these works down and out.

When I come back up again, I stray into French paintings, and I am struck by another permutation of the not-popping-out game: suddenly all the paintings seem to have been washed with brown, and I look at one of the painters' names and damned if it isn't *Le Brun*. I suspect that this *brunification* (please pronounce this word with a French accent) must have been a twist on the Leonardo Effect, except here it also functions to produce a kind of realism in its *unification* of the painting into one world, that is, by making everything swim in the same universal shitstorm of sepia. And in the following room, yet another pop-out permutation: the boringly and scientifically crisp lines of French neoclassicist paintings, whose figures are about as lifelike as the acting on *Star Trek*.

The big picture of the popping-out game begins to come together for me as I start to think of how the development of painting on portable, flat, framed panels facilitated the commodification of art, and even beyond this how it formalized and standardized paintings into something more like money, in the process separating art from religion and from daily life. In other words, panel painting was made to pop out, which helped to *pop art out,* and, with social status increasingly up for sale, to make it useable as cultural capital to pop people out. This is a kind of fractal similarity, where the art and the meta-art of the museum pull together, where the cutting up and popping out that go on inside paintings are linked to the cutting up and popping out of paintings themselves, and of art and aesthetics as a distinct domain, and of a new ruling class and its capital. This is one of the things that makes you feel as if you are looking down into one of the intricate spiral abysses of the Mandelbrot set: call this one the *Abyss of Distinction.* It is related to the *Abyss of Depth,* insofar as paintings are distinguished by their flatness from most everyday three-dimensional objects and images, then from other two-dimensional images by the various artistic technologies of illusionistic depth (Renaissance perspective, most famously), and then, when these come to be insufficiently distinguishing, by the ambiguous depths and antidepths of the modernist picture plane. It is also related to the *Abyss of Plenitude,* most blatantly obvious when I encounter, in this museum crammed with paintings and sculptures, one of those paintings (mainly from the eighteenth and nineteenth centuries) that depict galleries and salons crammed with paintings and sculptures, often with a portrait of the artist somewhere among them (which a helpful label next to the painting points out). Something about the vacuity or the heavy-handedness of this trick makes it mostly just annoying to me. I am more taken with it when I see a Flemish painting (one of many like it) of a pantry full of hanging pheasants and rabbits and vegetables; maybe I like it because it makes the museum feel more like a pantry full of food. I think of someone who has a pantry full of a plenitude of varieties of food, so he goes out and buys a painting of a pantry full of a plenitude of varieties of food (the more realistic and solid looking the better), which increases—not just additively but qualitatively and fractally—his plenitude and variety of commodities. How much this logic implicates other paintings of plenitude (still lifes of bowls overflowing with fruit and flowers, scenes teeming with big, fleshy people) is an open question, since the commodity version of plenitude and plurality is, fortunately, still not the only kind, as much as it works to subordinate and subsume the others.

Before I leave the museum I venture down into the main basement, where the Western medieval and ancient stuff has been museumified. Here the museum has also become an object for itself in an exhibit called *The Medieval Louvre*. The museum has been excavated to the point where it is articulated, here in its inmost depths, with what is not-itself, and it makes this articulation of museum with not-museum into part of the museum (I think of Luhmann's formula, "The system copies the difference between system and environment into itself"). Here the round tower of stone that once repelled arrows and rain, now situated in an art museum, that most hermetic interiority, is struck mainly by aesthetic glances. Here, a few feet below the walkway, is a medieval garbage heap of broken crockery that has been perfectly half-excavated and sealed to make it into a relief sculpture; I am tickled to see that someone has pushed it a little way back toward being a garbage heap again by dropping their *Medieval Louvre* brochure on it. I instinctively appreciate this act of vandalism as a kind of theoretical gesture, as if it were suggesting that excessive self-reference could restore the otherness at its core.

And here is the smaller round stone wall of an old well, and next to it an exhibit depicting its excavation. A hole has been left in the side of it—a little, square, painting-size open window—and after ascertaining that nobody is around, I stick my head all the way in there to see if I can see down. It's too dark to see anything, but I can hear the soft echoing of indeterminate depth, and a very humid, very warm, and very yeasty, musty, boozy breeze is wafting up from down there. After all the dry sterility, silent visuality, merely illusionistic depths, and cognitive abysses of the rest of the museum, it hits me like a freight train. I pull my head out, actually gasping, grasping the railing, reeling, *real*ing. This must be what I have always been told is the kind of epiphany great art can produce.

18

Performativity III: Retroactivism

In chapter 16, we looked at some examples of how, in the late eighteenth and early nineteenth centuries, modernity and rationalization performatively shaped space and time and bodies and wood and labor, and how some of these articulations inform the more abstract or conceptual habit of binarizing and hierarchizing difference. Cultural theorist Fred Jameson coined the term *ideologeme* to name fundamental conceptual units such as the hierarchized binary (76, 87); these units resemble what get called *tropes* or *topoi* in rhetoric (that is, figures of speech or common metaphors); the more monolithic epistemological versions are Foucault's *episteme* or Kuhn's *paradigm*. Like all these related concepts, an ideologeme cannot really be a fundamental unit in the sense of something preexisting and relatively simple that is used to build more complex structures. It can't be because it's *already* the overdetermined product of (and participant in) a ubiquitous, resonant, very material, and multidimensional logic (as in the examples developed in chapter 16). There is a danger in considering an ideologeme as a more or less freestanding conceptual device: it grants too much agency to it, even in such simple but powerful ways as habitually making it the subject of sentences. Considering language more as a subject is a good way to restore some of the agency that referentialism tries to steal from it, but only if language is not mistaken for an independent thing-in-itself. If you want to emphasize the relational status of an ideologeme (the way it operates somewhere between wordness and thingness, and only by participating in a heterogeneous constellation of both), something more like Bruno Latour's terms *quasi-object* and *actant* might do the trick or, to emphasize its virtual livingthinglikeness and contagious, viral, and parasitical quality, Richard Dawkins's term *meme* (which makes cultural units out to be like self-replicating genes, the common example being *a catchy tune*), or, to reject the reductionist organicism, something like Deleuze and Guattari's *abstract machines*.

This chapter returns to look at the complex circuitry of the ideologeme called *romanticism*, which is part of what orchestrates resonances among the ways that various kinds of difference are understood, part of what gives them their ring of truth. In particular, the ideologeme deploys the idea of a premodern past and a modern present to organize gender, sexual, and cultural/ethnic difference.

The term *romanticism* has been used to name the particular period of history or literary history in question (namely, the late eighteenth and early nineteenth centuries), but since literary and historical periodizations (the mandate to cut up the historical pie into neat slices) are themselves concepts shaped by the romanticism supposed to be under investigation, we are driven to consider romanticism also as an *ongoing* ideological formation or complex that cuts up time. Most broadly, romanticism is a very modern kind of antimodernity, one that can function as accommodationist or as oppositional. Literary historians Robert Sayre and Michael Löwy have defined romanticism more specifically as "opposition to capitalism in the name of precapitalist values" (26; also see Livingston 12–14), but in any case romanticism seems to name a modern narrativization of time that ongoingly, often nostalgically but always retroactively, identifies a *precapitalism* or *premodernity*—or, even more fundamentally, a precultural *nature*. The important point is that the making of such a difference is not something that happened once and for all at some particular point in the past but is continually reproduced and renegotiated in the process. In other words, it is performative, so nothing written on the topic can be simply descriptive.

The romantic ideologeme works not only to schematize historical eras but also to schematize gender, for example, by representing femininity as a kind of "hypercivilization," either to valorize (as in Victorian cultural feminism) or to devalue (that is, by representing women as superficial or artificial creatures). On the other (and equally ambivalent) hand, the same trope can just as well represent femininity as a less mediated relation to nature and therefore more innocent or pure or sexy—or in any case as a kind of superseded stage of masculine development. This latter turn of the trope has often structured Western caricatures of other peoples as variously "primitive," though Western Orientalism in particular has also painted the East as "hypercivilized" as well (and, again, alternately to value or devalue). The romantic ideologeme is less a simple opposition and more a "difference engine."

Romanticism as retroactivism is an overdetermined and often definitive "structure of feeling" in modernity, and as such it can be traced—as I am about to do—back to narratives like Aphra Behn's 1688 *Oroonoko,* through Mary Wollstonecraft's 1792 *Vindication of the Rights of Women,* and forward through texts like the 1995 *Unabomber Manifesto,* "Industrial Society and Its Future." I have picked these texts for the time they span but also for their internal differences: they show the romantic ideologeme as it participates in shaping feminist and masculinist arguments, forward- and backward-looking positions, novel and manifesto.

In the short novel *Oroonoko,* the royalist English writer Aphra Behn romanticizes African society as an image of a noble English past in which everyone knew his or her place and lying and misrepresentation were unthinkable. In Behn's novel it is not slavery as such that is wrong and unnatural but *violation of hierarchy:* only the slave traders who by trickery kidnap and hold in slavery the anglicized African prince are identified as unethical, whereas slaves "freely" sold by the Africans are represented as defeated people, suited for a servile existence (the idea of a "free market" ignoring the role of European destabilization of African societies in producing its conditions). Difference *within* and difference *between* are made to be echoes of each other, with no original: Behn seems to suggest that the English violation of the hierarchical order of African society is merely symptomatic of the breakdown of hierarchy within English society. Her many descriptions of African lovers communicating by wordless glances, as well as her curiously emphatic insistence that Africans *blush,* serve further to associate African society with a direct and even prelinguistic communication in which misrepresentation is almost impossible in the immediacy of full presence (a condition she personifies even more extremely in the novel's indigenous Surinamese). But, as the trope turns back onto itself, this problematic valorization is also what Behn claims for *the novel itself,* making a show of rejecting "Fancy" and "Invention" in favor of a guileless "Eye-Witness" realism, which subsequently works as backhanded praise by blame of Behn's own humble "Female Pen" (57, 88). By another nice twist, "any thing that seems Romantick" (that is, unrealistic) is attributed to the way "these Countries do, in all things, so far differ from ours, that they produce unconceivable Wonders" (56).

Like Behn but about a century later, Mary Wollstonecraft, in her *Vindication of the Rights of Woman,* champions and claims Enlightenment plain speech and realism against the excesses of "turgid bombast" and "flowery diction," but Wollstonecraft associates cunning, duplicity, and superficiality with precisely the hierarchy Behn valorized, that is, with an unnatural and obsolete monarchical and aristocratic power—and, in turn, with how women (denied independence and education in Reason) exert emotional tyranny over their husbands and lovers (7–8, 73). For Wollstonecraft, then, social hierarchy is unnatural, and upward mobility is the solution rather than, as for Behn, vice versa. The twists and turns of the romantic ideologeme shape the generative contradictions around which the content and form of the texts are spun.

Two centuries later still, notorious American ecoterrorist Ted Kaczynski began his *Unabomber Manifesto* with the romantic assertion that "the Industrial Revolution and its consequences have been a disaster for the human race" (3). The text's main thrust is to fetishize the autonomy and self-sufficiency of "primitive INDIVIDUALS and SMALL GROUPS" (68; emphasis in original) against the crushing weight of modern collective institutions and the "oversocialization" of "modern leftism" (10). This clearly romantic individualism seemed to be held in common by various U.S. militia groups and by a whole range of mainstream neoconservatives in the 1990s. Its masculinism is of a piece with the romantic/Victorian ideology that works to pathologize women as inadequately individuated or to beatify them as nurturing and other-directed or both.

This version of the trope also had incarnations in pop psychologies of language that followed Carol Gilligan in schematizing men's speech and psychological orientation as self-directed and women's as other-directed. The same schema has been an enduring one in romantic literary history as well, tending to cast variously "feminized" novels as negotiating intricate and broad constellations of relationships (though often partially subordinated to the master narrative of individual development and progress known as bildungsroman) against a supposedly more masculine, univocal, and predominantly lyrical poetry of the Self in its depths, its troubled autonomy and heroic vicissitudes.

Psychologically as well as ideologically and historically in Western modernity, heteronormative gender itself is compellingly describable as a retroactively romantic formation. Judith Butler reworks Lacanian psychoanalytic theory, in which woman is made to represent "the vain but persistent promise of pre-individuated *jouissance*"; Freudian theory, in which the ego is a kind of romantic ruin, "a precipitate of abandoned object-cathexes"; and especially Foucault's theory of power, in which "the desire which is conceived as both original and repressed is the effect of the subjugating law itself" (*Trouble* 45, 58, 65). Butler's account shows how gender identities (conceived as things-in-themselves rather than as relational constructs) are made to emerge out of the separation and individuation process: "Because identifications substitute for object relations, and identifications are the consequence of loss, gender identification is a kind of melancholia in which the sex of the prohibited object is internalized as a prohibition"; the lost object (that is, the Other now understood as categorically separate) is objectified and oppositionally gendered reactively and retroactively, and "the stricter and more stable the gender affinity, the less resolved the original loss" (63). Thus, Butler identifies "melancholic heterosexuality" as "an anti-metaphorical activity" whereby "incorporation *literalizes* the loss *on* or *in* the body and so appears as the facticity of the body" in the apparent self-evidence of anatomical difference as a thing-in-itself, forgetting the dynamic relations that fetishize it as such, forgetting the forgetting. Some of the counterproductivity of such a heteronormative regime consists in the way "disavowed homosexual love"—which can be named as such only via its disavowal—is nonetheless "*preserved* through the cultivation of an oppositionally defined gender identity" (69; emphasis added).

Gaining leverage on such a structure cannot be a matter of simple remembering or recovery. Butler critiques Freud's notion of a "primary bisexuality" for retroactively mistaking the *product* of performative gendering (that is, oppositionally defined genders) for its *raw material*. Butler critiques feminist theorist Gayle Rubin, among others, for relying too much on a retroactivist vision of "an alternative sexual world, one which is attributed to a utopian stage in infantile development, a 'before' the [patriarchal] law that promises to reemerge 'after' the demise or dispersal of that law" (75). And finally, Butler interrogates feminist theorist Julia Kristeva's associations of a prelinguistic "Symbolic" matrix with the maternal body, with poetic language, with psychosis and lesbianism, and with "all manner of things 'primitive' and 'Oriental'" (89): though seeming to valorize these things, Kristeva's theorizing continues to underwrite—to require—their continual subordination.

Butler's strategy is thus an antiromantic one, rejecting retroactive utopias "before the law" but insisting on the law's ongoing productivity and counterproductivity, its positivity and plurality. A differently inflected version of this strategy informs fellow poststructuralist philosophers Gilles Deleuze and Felix Guattari's *Anti-Oedipus,* which questions the developmental narratives of capitalism and sexuality by insisting on an *absolute* plurality, a plurality that continually exceeds its opposition to unicity and binarity (and thus also differs from Freud's "primary bisexuality" or "polymorphous perversity").

A look at historian James Hevia's 1995 *Cherishing Men from Afar,* an account of the 1793 British Embassy of George Lord Macartney to the Qing Empire, enables us again to round this sprawling discussion back on itself by showing how the romantic ideologeme (as it performatively orchestrates resonances among sexual, gender, cultural, and ethnic difference) also plays a role in how performativity itself comes to be misrecognized and disavowed in Western modernity.

Hevia begins by rejecting the romantic/Orientalist paradigm by which previous studies have cast the encounter as a meeting between a dynamic, modern Britain and a stagnant, premodern China. Instead, he recognizes the expedition as a meeting between two expansive empires, focusing on how the Qing imperium deployed what was called "guest ritual" to shape interdomainal relations, specifically in enacting the subordination and incorporation of other sovereignties (and sometimes other religions or epistemologies) into the Qing Empire. Incorporation here involves nested "macrocosm-microcosm relations" (23); the Chinese rituals could be said to manage the complex and *fractal* interaction of difference within and difference between. This recognition avoids the familiar characterization of China as stuck in a rigid and monolithic hierarchy of hierarchies, still laboring under a version of the "Great Chain of Being" supposed to have been shaken and even leveled by a pluralizing modernity in the West. In fact, Hevia shows that Chinese guest ritual was significantly negotiable both in the sense of being continually updated in light of new precedents and conditions and in the sense that it dynamically managed rather flexible and nuanced relations, for example, in allowing both parties to the ritual to retain some sense of the other's dependence. In turning the tables, one might also point to how the Western legacy of a single and singularly intolerant god and the rationality fashioned in its image continued to deny incorporation and syncretic plurality even as it seemed to reject hierarchies. In any case, the English fundamentally misread Qing ritual by understanding it as monolithically static and rule bound, as merely *representing* relationships rather than as performing or *producing* them and as a merely rhetorical or cultural form distinct from the real business of trade. These misreadings, all of which come to shape the anthropological concept of "ritual" itself, link the failures of the Macartney embassy itself to those of its subsequent Western chroniclers.

Though never mentioning performativity as such, Hevia follows Catherine Bell in approaching ritual activities as "themselves the very production and negotiation of power relations"; ritualization is "a strategic mode of practice" that "produces nuanced relations of power, relationships characterized by acceptance and resistance, negotiated appropriation, and redemptive reinterpretation of the hegemonic order" (cited in Hevia 21). Hevia cites Qing and other previous Chinese accounts that assign such an active, shaping function to guest ritual in dynamically "channeling," "centering," or "negotiating" (123). And because the misrecognition or dismissal of such performativity is foundational for modern Western power/knowledge, its recovery has far-reaching interdisciplinary and intercultural implications.

Hevia describes Orientalist ideology as it

> feminizes China; much like female, as opposed to male, sensibilities, China is jealous, misguided, caught up in appearances, irrational, arbitrary, and whimsical. On the other hand, this imaginary China functions to produce bourgeois masculine identity as that which is equivalent to the good, the true, the real, the rational and the upright. Among other things, this suggests that the negation of China, particularly of the Chinese past, produces the "West," with a living China simultaneously a negativity for constructing a superior English national identity and for demonstrating that England had now transcended all past global orders. (73–74)

Pushing these constructions a bit further points up the radical inadequacy of the model of "feminization" insofar as it seems to assume (if only provisionally) instead of accounting for the priority of gender to other kinds of difference and the "always alreadiness" of the association of femininity with all that is subordinated. Instead, then, we might start to consider how the fiction of a dominant Western ideology of masculinity could be approached as a "repressive de-sinicization," predating and shaping not simply the encounter between Macartney and the Chinese but also the *product* of an interdomainal encounter that is continually (then and now) in the making.

Hevia recounts the sometimes farcical attempts of the British to engage, impress, assuage, and defy their imaginary China. One of the expedition's members characterized other European nations' gifts to the Qing emperor as mere "toys and sing-songs"; Macartney called previous gifts "more glittering than useful" and sought instead to impress Qianlong with items "whose merit lay in their utility" (Hevia 77). These characterizations clearly mobilize the opposition of masculinized rationalism to feminized whimsy in order to characterize West against East as well as Britain against other Western nations. These kinds of characterizations are part of a process of Othering in which the Other is made to embody the too strenuously disavowed aspects of the self. Part of this trick is that the contradictions and excess difference produced in creating the polarized binary are made to inhabit the subordinated term: thus, it is the Other who is cast as polarizing or polarized.

Macartney's contemporary, the British politician and aesthetician Edmund Burke, deployed such an Othering strategy when he set an ideally nuanced

British society in which "the different shades of life" are aesthetically "harmonized" against a revolutionary France of "naked" power relations (90); the too strenuous contrast between Britain and France is made to characterize a France of too strenuous contrasts. The trope of an Oriental "land of contrasts," especially between modern and premodern features, is likewise an echo of the too categorical assertion of Western modernity.

Burke's contemporary, the writer Thomas de Quincey, expressed horror and fascination with an Orient of excessive difference (of "castes that have flowed apart, and refused to mix, through . . . immemorial tracts of time") or of excessive indifferentiation (one in which "man is a weed" [442]). De Quincey followed an ongoing Orientalist schema of setting Asian emperors' godlike power in too stark contrast to the faceless and abject masses of their subjects. The same political/aesthetic ideal of nuanced difference allowed a 1755 British journal article to fault Chinese painting for lacking "gradation in tint" and thus misrepresenting "the truth of things" (cited in Hevia 70).

These vicissitudes of imaginary and different difference also drove eighteenth-century phases of British idealization and derogation of China's "mandarinate." British hopes for success also depended on an always already Anglicized image of the emperor as above his people, at least far enough to be potentially capable of recognizing the superiority of British rationality. The centerpiece of the English gifts to Qianlong was a large and elaborate planetarium, intended to demonstrate the superiority of Western science in representing the true workings of the universe. However, anxious that the scientific value of the planetarium might not be compelling enough in itself, the British had it extravagantly decorated, so that the final product presented to Qianlong turned out somewhat less an example of robust British rationality and more a piece of kitsch chinoiserie of the kind Britons had alternately fetishized and rejected. In any case, in his response to George III, Qianlong was famously cool, asserting that "we have never valued ingenious articles, nor do we have the slightest need of your Country's manufactures" (238).

This coolness was at least in part a response to Macartney's impatience to cut the Gordian knot of ritual and "get down to business." Macartney's impatience worked counterproductively to magnify the impasse, and the farce of the Macartney embassy would be magnified into tragedy in Britain's later, more violent missions to open up the Chinese market via the opium wars. The impatience that regards ritual as mere *foreplay* (or as mere superstructure) might well be dubbed *performativity anxiety*. This restores the link between the late-eighteenth-century invention of a categorical distinction between foreplay and sexual intercourse and between weekend and workweek (see chapter 16) to the growing distinction between merely performative ritual and the real business of economic intercourse.

When Foucault wanted a model for the notion of a different set of differences, he turned to Borges's imaginary "Chinese encyclopedia," with its radically plural list of incommensurable creatures (*Order* xv), just as it was against an Asian and premodern Western *erotic arts* that Foucault characterized the emergence of a modern *science of sexuality* (which he proceeded to demonstrate as a mishmash of incommensurables masquerading as a scientific unity). The turn to an imagined "Other" for recovery (*from* what we may have thought we were or *of* what we had forgotten that we had disavowed) is fraught with turbulence. Even so, performativity is not something invented by postmodern theorists but part of a project of *recovering* what Western modernity has necessarily rendered incoherent or made difficult to recognize or articulate—but not banished. Admittedly, *recovery* is a prejudicial word: for many reasons, what is recovered can never be what was lost. For example, what I identify as *performativity* means what it does only in relation to a host of other concepts or modalities (such as in opposition to *reductionism* and *essentialism*) that are also part of a changing discursive ecology. To call this a project of recovery, then, is really just one move in the process of leveraging this ecology (just as one must push a crowbar first one way and then the other). To choose a more trenchant example, *homosexuality* and *heterosexuality* are nineteenth-century identity constructs, and it is important to understand how neither existed previously in order to denaturalize and historicize these modern terms, to affirm that sexual *practices* need not and do not entail *identities* in the same way in all times and places. But also in order to affirm current minority genderings and sexualities, it is just as important to find ways of talking about the histories of same-sex desire without romanticizing a retro-utopia of practices without identities and in the process to affirm that the modern identitarian regime—oppressive and productive as it is—has *never fully colonized* desire. In some sense, as Bruno Latour puts it, *we have never been modern*. Even so, it may be premature to celebrate the return of the Hong Kong of sexuality and gender to the mainland of difference, but perhaps it is at least less prejudicial to talk about recovery *from* some of the categorical imperatives of modernity rather than *of* anything unproblematically premodern.

Recognizing the sprawl and slipperiness of identities does not deny specificity and particularity—quite the reverse. Gender and sexuality studies, for example, have been compelling in demonstrating how specific sexual practices cut across sexual identities and how current umbrella categories belie specificities, failing to keep slippery sex safe or gender cut-and-dried in the present much less in the past. In her study *Female Masculinity*, my old buddy Judith Halberstam invented the term *perverse presentism* to describe the strategy of "questioning in the first instance what we think we already know" about gender and sexuality and then moving "back towards the question of what we think we have found" in the past, rejecting the notion of "paradigm shift" in the history of sexuality as primarily a way of "stabilizing what we think we know today" (53). This kind of argument is just as trenchant in cross-cultural studies, where a leading and ongoing question might be "Who do we think *we* are?" That was what was at stake for Macartney and what is still at stake for us.

In the broadest terms, the thrust of historical, contemporary, and cross-cultural studies of gender and sexuality are the same: *to democratize the linkages and disjunctions within and among bodies, genders, sexualities, practices and identities, disciplines, cultures.*

19

The Return to Resemblance

The shaping of scientific theory by its social context is a first principle of the critical position often called *constructionism,* of which an early example (see chapter 2) is Marx's assertion that Darwin had found "among beasts and plants his English society with its division of labor, competition . . . and the Malthusian 'struggle for existence'" (7). This ventriloquism of society through nature was also one of the things Oscar Wilde found disingenuous about romantic poets claiming that nature spoke to them: "Wordsworth . . . found in stones the sermons he had already hidden there" (301). Engels elaborated Marx's observation, pointing out that such ventriloquism is doubled when the principles of bourgeois ideology are "transferred back again from organic nature to history and it is now claimed that their validity as eternal laws of human society has been proved" (cited in Kaye 23).

There seems to be something wrong with this mirroring *in itself,* more than just the fact that it is partial to the particular society doing the mirroring. If the universe were more like an archetypical hologram, each part would be an accurate representative of the whole; metonymy or synecdoche (rhetorical figures in which a part stands for the whole or for something to which it is connected) would be truth itself, and all local observations would have universal validity. This cannot be the case because everything cannot be everywhere the same. However, it *might* be legitimate to ask *how much* the organization of any given society embodies universal principles, as against how much its organization is particular to it. Its particularity must at least be *allowed* if not fully determined by universal principles, if such exist, and thus also perhaps a thread that leads to them. But Marx and Engels identify a fundamental misrecognition, the scandalous narcissism of a society that falls in love with its own image on the surface of nature.

The scandal of resemblance between Darwinism and bourgeois economy and ideology is a distinctly modern one. Three centuries earlier (see chapter 4), such a logic of resemblance was enshrined in the "Great Chain of Being," a series of homological hierarchies stretching from macro- to microcosm and across the realms of physics and metaphysics. In *The Order of Things,* Foucault showed how the logic of resemblance organized knowledge in the Renaissance, linking natural history with the study of language and with economics—and subsequently, as the episteme of Resemblance ceased to produce truth effects, how it began to become the scandal noted by Marx and Engels, among others.

Bruno Latour has shown, in *We Have Never Been Modern,* how a new absolutizing and problematizing of the opposition between nature and human society are definitive for modernity. This problematic informs Marx and Engels no less than the social Darwinism they opposed, since the absolute prerequisite for social Darwinism—the doctrine that human society should emulate the competitive order of nature—is of course the possibility that it could *fail* to do so and, by a misguided altruism, perpetuate the unfit.

This constitutive slippage between nature and society also informs Pyotr Kropotkin and others who advanced theories of "mutual aid" against Darwin's Malthusianism, anxious compromises such as Freudian "sublimation" (the process whereby baser instincts are channeled into higher pursuits), as well as the more disingenuous compromise that offers human religion and culture a meliorative function with respect to harsh natural laws they cannot fundamentally alter. This latter seems to continue to inform neoconservative and neoliberal policies that produce a market that is ostensibly freer and freer (that is, redder in tooth and claw) along with ever more invasive and pervasive social controls. But now at the dawn of a new millennium, it is turning out that the competitive survival of the fittest may be subject to serious revision, at least in the scope of its explanatory ambitions.

In the late nineteenth and early twentieth centuries, upwardly mobile (evolving) biological life appeared in stark relief against an irreversibly decaying thermodynamic universe as a noble but ultimately doomed outlaw, living on borrowed time, or as a kind of frontier-town sheriff or a film noir detective in a hostile and chaotic world: "Down these mean streets a man must go who is not himself mean," as Raymond Chandler put it. Biological life, and within it the human race even more acutely, appeared as a type of tragic hero. This stance, in both its most tragic and its most progressivist permutations, went well with the white ruling class's sense of itself, beset inside and out by threats of devolution, degeneration, and disorder.

A century or so later, the relations between biological figure and thermodynamic ground are much shiftier. Theoretical biologist Stuart Kauffman and others are now establishing that life is not so improbable or heroic after all, but rather an "expected *emergent collective property* of a modestly complex mixture of catalytic polymers" (*Origins* xvi). On the physics side, Lee Smolin and others hail a rapprochement of physics and biology and, with it, a universe hospitable to life, necessarily characterized by structure and self-organizing processes at all scales, from protein molecules to galactic clusters—a kind of retrofitted Great Chain of Being. Kauffman stresses the priority of self-organizing processes over natural selection and looks for mathematical laws to explain, for example, why the body should have only about 260 cell types: not because they have evolved by natural selection but because this number of types is a predictable mathematical propensity of a system possessed of a certain number of genes. More research supports some version of the notion that basic body structures of living creatures may "have an inevitability about them, being driven by the basic physics and chemistry of growth" (Ball 103) and even more fundamentally by the mathematics of complexity. Alan Turing's 1952 paper that advanced this idea of morphogenesis has been so fully resurrected that it can now be safely hailed as "undoubtedly one of the most influential in the whole of theoretical biology" (Ball 79). And the rehabilitation goes back much further than Turing to pre-Darwinian morphologists such as Goethe and St. Hilaire, who explained similarities among creatures by a theory of archetypes or ideal forms (Ball 104).

Nobody is saying that Darwinian natural selection has been *proved wrong* (which is mostly *not* how paradigms shift, anyway) but only that it may have to share the stage as an explanatory principle (which *is* more like how most paradigm shifts happen). There remain a range of ways of underplaying or melodramatizing this ongoing epistemological shift. If science were like a religion (or, more specifically, insofar as natural selection is *the* fundamentalist dogma of evolutionary biology), this might be something like a Christian church moving over their statue of the tragic-heroic crucified Christ to make way for a smiling Buddha behind the altar. It is a pretty significant event, no matter what the priests say. But far from constituting a *failure* of evolutionary thinking, this event seems to be part of the ongoing *success* of principles of evolution and natural selection, which continue to be incorporated in the paradigm pantheon of more and more fields, such as physics and cosmology. In other words, the *depth* of the paradigm (its position as exclusive center or anchor point) is being displaced as it achieves greater *reach and saturation* of other realms; its pluralization and relativization make it more resilient even as they may in some ways make it less *itself*. Not coincidentally, this seems to have been one of the leading principles of empire building for several millennia, just as it makes a rough-and-ready account of the current transnational hegemonic success of capitalism and the West.

Kauffman in particular makes life more inevitable and lawlike and less historical: the rugged hills of a so-called fitness landscape that natural selection used arduously to climb begin to seem more like the slopes of cascades that self-organization surfs down, leaving at least the style points along the way to natural selection. Smolin and many others, in turn, make the laws of physics more apparently historical: the current ensemble of laws, forces, and particles are not eternal but have coevolved in relation to each other; they *are* their interrelations. This leads Smolin to champion Leibnizian relational space over Newtonian absolute space.

It is clear already from these examples that the internal reconfiguration of similarities and differences among physics, thermodynamics, and biology must also be a part of some kind of reconfiguration between science and nonscience: in this case at least, Leibniz and Goethe are selectively rehabilitated at the expense of Newton and Darwin. Scientific "progress" can thus be understood as movement not merely *ahead* into ever increasing knowledge but also *between* what has been considered science and nonscience, or good and bad science, in the past. If the genealogy of science is a snake stretching back in time through Darwin and Newton, it does not merely shed its skin (the ideological dross of its past); it positively slithers, across its whole length, in the snake pit of discursive space-time.

Smolin characterizes life as "a particular type of process which has emerged on top of the flows of energy and cycles of materials that characterize . . . open systems. Life perhaps might be seen to have evolved a way to ride these flows and cycles the way a surfer rides the flow of energy in water waves. But life has also taken over control of the flows of energy and materials that may have previously existed on earth" (*Life* 154–55). Kauffman is more blatant: "Higher-order things emerge because they can suck more flow of stuff into themselves, faster, whether we're talking about *E. coli*, prebiotic evolution, or firms" (cited in Waldrop 318). In place of Yeats's succinct formula for the old thermodynamic order—"things fall apart"—Kauffman's account suggests another even more succinct formula: Life Sucks—and capitalism sucks *because* life sucks—in the best possible way, of course, because it so holographically participates in the logic of life itself.

Biologist Lynn Margulis and science scholar Dorion Sagan in their popularization *What Is Life?* stress the same dynamism: "Life moves and transforms matter across oceans and continents" (44). Unlike Kauffman, Margulis and Sagan do not try to sell capitalism as nature; they seem more interested in building an alternative and more critical paradigm. Even so, bionomic tropes (like bad pop music) are insidious. For Margulis and Sagan, the first colonization of the earth by bacteria assumes an exemplary status: "Every available piece of real estate on this planet was occupied by enlightened producer, busy transformer, or arctic explorer" (89), or as they put it in *Microcosmos:* "Life did not take over the globe by combat, but by networking" (29). This account is echoed in Kauffman's description of the reign of early microorganisms as a three-billion-year-long "global co-prosperity sphere" (*Home* 12). Like Freud's thermodynamic Eros, operating to "combine organic substances into ever larger unities" (*Beyond* 37), but seemingly without Thanatos, the death drive that pulls it back toward stasis, life in the emergent paradigm is hyperexpansionist and entrepreneurial—but this time around, it is not resisted but welcomed by a hospitable world—not only colonizing geographical space but saturating with ever increasing density new scales and dimensions of relation as well.

Life, the tragic hero of the late nineteenth century, becomes at the dawn of a new millennium a surfing CEO with a cell phone. The neoliberal ideological synthesis of the sciences has officially begun. This breezy caricature overstates the hegemony of the new paradigms and understates the contradictions within and among them, but the breeziness is theirs, not mine.

It is now rather difficult to restore the sense of scandal in the resemblance between descriptions of self-organizing processes in biology and physics and the transnational neoliberalism they tend to underwrite. It is difficult partly because the scientists tend to present paradigms of complexity and self-organization as the deep theory behind all these phenomena—capitalism, biological life, physical laws, and so on. Alan Sokal parodied science studies scholars in the humanities for asserting that politics and ideology can be read directly off scientific theories; perhaps he neglected to take to task his fellow scientists as well because their version of this claim was simply too easy a target.

Kauffman, in his popularization *At Home in the Universe,* is again particularly blatant on this score: he sells the paradigm of self-organization on its scientific truth value as well as its timely ideological functions (or as the old commercial goes, "It's a breath mint *and* a candy mint"): "To undergird the pluralistic global community that is aborning, we shall need, I think, an expanded intellectual basis" (5). In case there is any doubt as to what is meant by the euphemism "pluralistic global community," listen to Kauffman's description of ecological self-organization: "As if by an invisible hand, each adapting species acts according to its own selfish advantage, yet the entire system appears magically to evolve to a poised state where, on average, each does as best as can be expected" (27). Sound familiar? Welcome to life in what Kauffman calls "the regime on the edge of chaos" (27), and, as Pete Townsend said, "Meet the new boss, same as the old boss."

To varying degrees, Kauffman, Smolin, Margulis and Sagan, and others all hail these new developments as revolutionary paradigm shifts that address long-standing critiques of scientific and Western rationality generally, reconciling them with their Others. Economist Brian Arthur, the main subject of M. Mitchell Waldrop's *Complexity,* is a good spokesman for such boosterism. Along with Kauffman, Arthur was an early fellow at the Santa Fe Institute, where physicists, economists, biologists, and computer scientists gathered, beginning in 1984, to forge the "New World Order" in chaos and complexity theory—at the very site where the Manhattan Project had developed the atomic bomb (remember: not by combat but by networking). Arthur calls complexity theory "the opposite of reductionism" (329); in its vision of a kaleidoscopic universe it is "Taoist" (330) and "Heraclitan" (335): "Yes!" he enthuses. "We're finally beginning to recover from Newton!" (335). Apparently, science can now freely affirm what it has heretofore vigorously disavowed: "Nonscientists tend to think that science works by deduction," Arthur explains, "but actually science works mainly by metaphor. . . . The purpose of having a Santa Fe Institute is that it, and places like it, are where the metaphors and a vocabulary are being created in complex systems" (327, 334). This makes the Santa Fe Institute sound rather like the poet William Butler Yeats's seances with the disembodied spirits who told him "'we have come to give you metaphors for poetry'" (8). Unfortunately, it was the *money*—provided by Citicorp, Robert Maxwell, and others—that seems to have been talking to the blither and worldlier spirits of Santa Fe.

The accounts of paradigm shift tend to beg the question of why the paradigm of self-organization is emerging at this historical moment; they tend to stop just short of acknowledging that socioeconomic organization actually drives and shapes paradigm formation. But even this constructionist first principle can be readily accommodated if one identifies capitalism and science as neither separable from nor quite reducible to nature but as *participating in what they represent,* that is, in a pervasive logic of self-organization. In this scenario, the proliferating circulations and ever more densely saturating networks of capital and information and people and technology that are producing a new global self-organization also act as a kind of collective neural net that has enabled science, itself an embedded autocatalytic system, to cross the "complexity barrier"; or to put it another way, we come to *recognize* self-organization because we as a global species *have attained it* to some critical degree. The common term for this process is simply *globalization.*

This scenario describes a complex event in progress in which phenomena of different dimensions and scales reinforce and catalyze each other. This is no longer really a constructionist account, at least if constructionism turns on how social and economic organization (subjects) generate and shape (verbs) theories, paradigms, and ideas (objects). In the postconstructionist scenario, the phenomena that shape and are shaped by each other do not differ primarily according to how material or ethereal they are (as is the case when a socioeconomic base shapes an ideological superstructure); the emphasis is not really even on that which shapes or is shaped but on the shaping, the ongoing event, the constellating—and the phenomena in question are already constellations and networks rather than discrete, elemental units.

We have already encountered at least one other such example, in Robin Dunbar's account of the evolution of language (see chapter 15), whereby three interdependent events in process seemed to catalyze each other: an increase in the size of human social groups, an increase in the size of human brains, and the evolution of language. These three events of different dimensions and scales are linked together in an autocatalytic loop, an emergent collective rewiring or reconstellating that links synapse to synapse to tongue and lips to word to word to person to person, pulling more and more phenomena into its orbit until pretty soon the whole bio-psycho-social existence of the now human primates is wired through language. The fact that there are a number of other participants in this event/constellation (Dunbar mentions various other physical, behavioral, and environmental factors) does not detract but *adds* to its explanatory power: unlike a reductionism that considers itself most successful if it can find a single cause, success in this model has more to do with how many balls can be kept up in the air at the same time: like the event in question, in other words, the explanation is a kind of juggling and constellating. And as in the event in question, it is precisely keeping them *up in the air* that counts as success for the theory.

This linkage of dimensions and scales is not just some kind of harmonic convergence that comes around to produce a great leap forward every few millennia (like the extraterrestrial monolith in *2001: A Space Odyssey*); it is how complex systems and organisms and economies and ecologies function *all the time.*

The event on which I have focused (or, to take it out of representationalist language, the event in which this text most directly participates) is an epistemic change—what I have called the Return to Resemblance—and its linkage to change within and among disciplines. I have mostly just *gestured* toward the economic, social, technological, and political dimensions of the event, which has been variously named postmodernity, the information age, globalization, empire. There is a question about how much of the event to represent as economic, as technological, and even as *natural* versus how much to spin it as ideology, paradigm, episteme—that is, as *spin,* even though *spin is a real event too.* This undecidability only adds to the interest and importance of the event in question; for example, if we conclude that massive economic change is really taking place but that ideas of complexity and self-organization are only a flash in the pan and that the way we know things—the province of epistemology—will eventually settle back down to the same as it ever was, this would detract not only from the epistemological interest of the event but also from the importance of the event itself (and by the way, if you think such massive denial is a good strategy, I have some senior colleagues you'd like to meet).

How do you recognize an episteme when you get ahold of one? Well, the short answer is: by your not being able to get ahold of it and by your not being able to recognize it. You notice a certain kind of undecidability as to its status as subject, verb, or object, as an ordering of things that may belong to the things or to the ordering. Perhaps most fundamentally, it is not really possible to assess its truth as a proposition, since insofar as it qualifies as an episteme, it is a principle that confers truth value on propositions. Epistemes are also not particularly resistible; in other words, you can't get any leverage on them by denouncing them as wrong, although by the same token, their terms will be the bones of contention. This is why I no longer try to rescandalize the resemblance of current scientific theory to the logic of transnational capitalism.

Nothing is at stake in arguing about an episteme as a proposition; everything is at stake in arguing about its terms. It is easy to see that the old capitalism-as-nature argument gets turbocharged in the new Regime of Resemblance, which effectively licenses the kind of ventriloquism Marx and Engels denounced, casting economy *as* ecology (sometimes under the term *bionomics*). But although it is easy to use these terms to assert that free-market capitalism has evolved to be the best (and most evolvable) of possible economies, it is also easy to use the same terms to make the case (for example) that large corporations are dinosaurs, cold-blooded creatures temporarily advantaged in a kind of hothouse environment and that markets will not really be free to evolve until they are, in effect, freed *from* capitalism by changing the economic climate. This is the thrust of David Korten's argument in *The Post-corporate World*, so far one of the few politically progressive uses of the "bionomics" paradigm.

In various of its earlier incarnations, the proposition that we are participating in some new higher-level autopoietic closure of humanity has already been used to authorize very different kinds of politics. Eugenicist R. A. Fisher had in mind a general, autopoietic bootstrapping operation when he asserted, with typically evil grandiosity (please read the following quote in a Dr. Strangelove accent), that "we must regard the human race as now becoming responsible for the guidance of the evolutionary process acting on itself" (quoted in Depew and Weber 273), but this is also what Foucault meant to *oppose* in his coinage of the term *biopower,* that is, political control over the fundamentals of life. To whatever extent we could become the masters of our fate we must also become the authors of our own misfortunes; fortunately, there is already a term adaptable from Yiddish for such self-thwarting, and thus one could say that *schlemielification* is the necessary corollary to self-organization. Margulis and Sagan tell how the colonization of the earth by anaerobic bacteria drove the production of cyanobacteria whose exhalations produced the oxygenated atmosphere that drove the anaerobes into hiding; too bad they don't also explore the logic that links this narrative to Marx's observation that the bourgeoisie produces its own grave diggers. But a relentless aestheticization of the apparently kinder and gentler paradigms of chaos and complexity keeps the ecology of violence that it describes hidden in plain sight. The dynamically changing patterns of a "kaleidoscopic" universe are apt to include cascades of viruses spreading like wildfire, flows of international capital abruptly shifting out of your country, giant meteors careening toward your planet.

Science fiction has also been working with versions of large-scale self-organization for a long time; narratives that serve the globalization paradigm as such can be described as *stories of meta-self-becoming*—or, to adapt the literary term for stories of personal growth and development, *metabildungsromans.* This term serves as a reminder that such stories often just *supersize* the same old ideological Happy Meal of individualist selfhood and progressivist development.

The most famous of the current generation of meta-self-becoming-stories is probably William Gibson's 1987 *Neuromancer*. The novel is an account of the becoming-metaself of cyberspace, sustained by the entire sprawling system of human society and technology. This emergence is the event that the human characters, employed as agents for shadowy organizations they are not allowed to know, have all been working and risking their lives to prevent *or to facilitate* (they often can't be quite sure which end they are serving). But the punch line of the novel is that, when the event finally *does* occur, *nothing happens,* or at least the mass of humanity is able to go on with its business without noticing that anything has happened, since humanity constitutes merely a subpart of the autonomic functions of the emergent metaself of the whole system, which can effectively turn its back on them and begin to go about its own business, scanning the universe for other meta-meta-meta-entities such as itself with which to communicate. So the shadowy organization for which we all turn out to have been working is not the liberal dream of a *humanity* to which we belong and which belongs to all of us, not a *capitalism* that divides and exploits us to fuel its own rise (and ultimate downfall), but *self-organization* itself, which takes the form of an emerging entity whose totality is *delinked* from us even as it is coextensive with all of our networks. It is separated from us by several degrees of freedom, like an elaborate version of the outer and inner rings of a gyroscope. Unfortunately, it gets its uncannily serene balance from our frenetic spinning, since the world that enables such a magisterial metaentity to emerge is a social-Darwinist nightmare of continual, fast-forward technological and economic change, grotesquely magnified differences between rich and poor, casual disregard for human life. Unfortunately again—I mean if you had any hope that the novel might evoke resistance to these conditions—*Neuromancer* mostly just darkly aestheticizes such a world, the better to function as a film noir background for the main character and his ragtag band of action heroes. This formulaic small group (and here we might be talking about any one of hundreds of action films as well) represents more than a failure of political or aesthetic imagination; it amounts to the *opposite* of what might constitute effective collective resistance and counterorganizing, as is especially clear when this little group, and the individual at its center, is set so starkly against the metaself-becoming of the cyberentity, which is the only really collective or systemic event and even the only *progressive* process to be found. And even the result of this process is nothing like a collectivity and everything like a Self: in fact, the hypersolipsistic entity scanning a lonely universe for an Other might well be a supersized version of the main character, a loner/cowboy who lives to jack into the matrix (with as casual a disregard for his bodily existence as the metaentity shows for humans). The loner/cowboy in turn seems like a glorified version of the archetypal Web junky or computer nerd, who seems in turn like a technologically tricked-out version of his prototype, the *solitary writer* (the proliferation of writing having produced the prototypical *virtual space* of culture and "imagined community" in eighteenth- and nineteenth-century modernity): behold the great and powerful Oz!

Especially because it lines up so neatly with the old body/mind dualism (with cyberspace as mind), the *disjunction* between self and metaself that concludes *Neuromancer* turns out mainly to *conserve* selfhood as a kind of nested series of Russian dolls. Because Greg Bear's 1985 novel *Blood Music* emphasizes instead the multiple *linkages* between the largest and smallest scales of being (and how these function as the milieu of an *embodied* mind), it shifts the focus to ways that metaself-becoming involves changes at all levels. In Bear's novel a scientist creates intelligent life at the cellular level and injects himself with the smart cells; the cells begin collectively self-organizing into a metaentity, first altering his own body, then spreading to others and ingesting them from within, eventually consuming most of the biological life on earth into a giant shape-shifting blob. The trick here is that this turns out to be *a good thing:* as they are ingested, human consciousnesses are individually "downloaded" in multiple copies, which continue *virtual* versions of their lives in the biocyberspace blob, but with an amazing new range of ways to experience and enact selfhood and community. The quantum reality-altering effect of such dense complexity, so many interconnecting scales of intelligence, is such that it begins to warp the physical fabric of space-time, and eventually the earth pops off happily into another dimension (something very like what I hope to do for you, dear reader, at least every now and then).

Call me an old codger if you will, but I remember when, not so long ago, parasitic cyborg mutant metacreatures were mostly a *bad* thing. And when that was the case, the human-versus-monster scenario tended to serve a mostly reactionary ideology of romantic individualism. The monster in George Cosmatos's 1989 film *Leviathan* can be taken as a crude and more reactionary version of Bear's biocyberblob: the monster, a genetic mutant fish-man-woman-machine, sports a kind of living backpack from which emerge the faces of the humans it has incorporated and on whose blood and intelligences it draws. Though the film was mainly a rehash of formulas James Cameron had fleshed out in *Aliens,* its monster was compelling to me at the time because it seemed to embody a viable collective entity, a kind of heaven into which one dies but in which one's personality and bodily materiality are not entirely subsumed. But political and generic necessity constrained this otherwise promising monster to represent the System, also represented by one of the stock villains of the time, the icy, professional woman boss. The System is resisted by the inevitable ragtag crew of heroes, all of whom are sacrificed along the way—especially conspicuously all the blacks and Latinos—so that a white, American, heterosexual couple can walk away at the end of the film as a kind of new Adam and Eve. Typically, the System represents Bad Modernity in the form of big corporations, big bureaucracy, big science, big government (and that staple of the cold war days, the Soviet Union) versus heroically resistant and romanticized individuals and small groups. Whatever potentially progressive elements may be subsumed in such a scenario (for example, working-class identifications or anticorporatism), it orchestrates an Armageddon and rebirth narrative that lines up most exactly with Nazi romanticism and the ongoing fantasies of white-supremacist militiamen. Especially against this kind of reactionaryism, narratives that propose the victory of the monster can still constitute a progressive scenario.

20

Gravity Cannot Be
Held Responsible?

Albert Einstein may have said that "gravity cannot be held responsible for people falling in love." Since I haven't been able to find *where* he is supposed to have said it, I have to doubt the attribution, but since much of what's significant about the statement resides in what makes it definitive for a popular icon of scientific genius, perhaps it even *gains* in resonance if attributed *falsely* to Einstein. It may be taken as a statement of humility ("I'm just a humble physicist; my jurisdiction does not extend to human affairs"), which in turn implies a kind of arrogance ("My theories are so powerful that people think I can explain everything, so I must demur").

Through the pun on *falling*, love seems to be described by a metaphor that refers to gravity, so the statement can be construed as the physicist disavowing responsibility for metaphor, which by definition involves a comparison between two fundamentally different realms. Gravity, here, is situated as the *tenor* or *ground* of the metaphor. However, when we recall that gravity was once synonymous with *attraction,* it seems that quite the reverse is the case: gravity may well have been first described by a metaphor that referred more primarily to love. Indeed, when Dante ended *The Divine Comedy* with a revelation of "the Love that moves the sun and the other stars," he seems to have put Love—quite literally—in the role that we generally now ascribe to gravity. But since *attraction* derives from a Latin word meaning *to pull,* maybe we should say that *at bottom* we come not to things themselves but back around to our own interaction with them—pulling and pushing them and being pulled and pushed by them. Just to complicate things a bit more, the English word *gravity,* it turns out, "was first introduced in the figurative senses" of "solemnity" or "authority," whereas (as the *Oxford English Dictionary* puts it) "the primary physical sense of the Latin word came into English first in the 17th c."

If we set aside the question of whether the scientific concept of gravity has escaped the complex metaphorical orbit in which it began, the upshot of Einstein's little joke is clear and, it would seem, uncontroversial enough: the laws of physics may be *necessary* but are not *sufficient* to account for social and biological phenomena; in other words, human biology and society cannot be reduced to or *read off of* physics. To put it another way, nobody could extrapolate from the laws of physics to predict the precise course of biological evolution on this planet, much less from there to deduce the plays of Shakespeare or the characters of *Gilligan's Island* or the sequence of words in this sentence quagga quagga hovercraft.

Implicit, here, is the familiar notion (and by the way, sorry for that little outburst in the previous sentence) that the universe may be divided into a series of levels: at the bottom is physics, followed by chemistry, then biology, then human society, and finally by culture (whatever that may be). The order seems to reflect the necessity of the lower levels to the higher: without the stuff and forces of physics, nothing else could exist, and so on up the sequence. On the other hand, the so-called higher levels do not seem necessary for the lower ones: wipe out cultures and consciousness and life would still exist, wipe out all life-forms and the earth would still exist, and so on. Likewise, the order of levels also seems to be a temporal order: physics alone is supposed to have ruled in the early universe of the big bang, chemistry arises only when atoms have formed and begin to combine, biology emerges only when life pulls itself together out of the chemical soup, and so on. Thus, each subsequent level is an *emergent* phenomenon that in some sense *exceeds* the previous level.

The nature of this excess is debatable and may of course vary from level to level. It might be like the relation of necessity to freedom or the branching relation of one to many, as if, from a single set of physical laws, any number of biologies could develop, and from a single set of biological constraints any number of social organizations could develop, and from these any number of cultures. This proposition just gets stickier the further back one looks: how many different kinds of universes might have developed from the big bang, and with what kinds of particles, forces, and laws? Einstein phrased this as the question of whether God had any *choice* in the creation of the universe; current physicists speak of how the parameters of fundamental physical laws are *tuned* in our universe (which may be one of an ensemble of universes, a *multiverse*). Even if it were possible to work backward between levels to find the necessary conditions for the emergence of the subsequent level, it may not always be possible to work forward to predict what the laws of the emergent level will be. One might say that emergent laws must often be treated as historical issues; in other words, if there is no general rule—or if the rule is *too general*—we may have to try to ascertain in each case what actually happened.

The word *law* is etymologically related to the word *layer*, and there seems to be a trace of this relation in the sense of laws as *fundamental* (and insofar as they function as guardians of the levels, scientists can be considered as both *lawyers* and *fundamentalists*); of course, the attribution of *law* to the physical universe must still be a metaphorical one. Fundamental laws are supposed to be inviolable; it doesn't require any effort to obey them because they can't be broken. Even so, another way of looking at the absolute constraint of one layer on the next higher is in terms of *freedom*. This is especially easy to see at the "higher" levels of organization: even the very constrained biology of DNA seems to permit amazing variation among life-forms and multiple strategies and definitions of success; human life does not specify what kind of culture may thrive. The same foundation, you might say, can as easily support a garage or a Gothic cathedral. And when you skip a level or two, the relationships seem to get even more tenuous: the laws of physics don't seem to care at all whether you're a rock or a rock star, much less whether you're Gandhi or Hitler. They operate with perfect equanimity in any case. The model seems to produce what is sometimes called a "sausage effect": the more constrained at the bottom—the more tightly you squeeze—the more the stuffing comes out every which way at the top.

The ink on this page obeys the laws of physics, as did the synapses of my brain and the muscles of my fingers and my keyboard, and so on. They did not have to be careful to obey them, nor did they have to struggle against them, any more than I had to struggle to keep from floating off my chair. I let whatever laws of physics there may be take care of themselves, and I must have operated within them at all times. But at least as currently configured, and as Einstein's joke suggests, the laws of physics have no jurisdiction over things like love and language as such; they did not (for example) specify the mostly subject-verb-object grammar that shaped my sentences (in fact, nowadays, they seem quite at odds with it), and they did not care at all for the various interdisciplinary negotiations that structured my argument (and in this, I fear, they may resemble many of my readers). In other words, at least in this formulation, the material dimension of language that obeys the laws of physics is the one that *does not count,* at least when we are considering textuality as such, and the one that counts, the one that *means something,* flies completely under the radar of physics. The problem with this formula is that although it seems to allow a lot of freedom to language, it does so only by cutting it off from the world. It forecloses the place where everything happens, at the many *interfaces* of words and things and of wordness and thingness.

When asked if he could refute the philosophical position known as idealism—the doctrine that all matter is merely a manifestation of mind—the eighteenth-century writer Dr. Johnson is supposed to have responded wordlessly, by kicking a stone. Gravity is the stone that defenders of scientific realism kick: as physicist Alan Sokal said, you can believe what you like about gravity or call it whatever you want, but if I throw you out the window, you'll be just as dead when you hit the ground. Gravity here is supposed to stand for brute fact: the ground, the firm foundation of things. Construing gravity as brute fact, entirely independent of what we think of it, suggests also (as does Einstein's joke) that the laws of gravity must not constrain thought and language, that they must give us at least enough rope to hang ourselves (as they say), time enough on the *Titanic* on the way down to rearrange the deck chairs. This construction seems to demand freedom for thought and language at the cost of absolute constraint of body: think or say whatever you like (it tells us), but gravity will be gravity (whatever that is), and you must still fall—as if bodies only fall, straight without squirming or swerving, whereas thoughts and words flutter like butterflies in a kaleidoscopic and virtually gravityless ether (unless pinned down by truth-seeking scientists). Curiously, this too categorical separation of words and things also characterized what was supposed to be the nemesis of scientific realism, deconstructionist literary theory. Arch-deconstructionist Paul de Man took his paradigm of irony from the nineteenth-century poet Baudelaire's description of the stumble and fall of a philosopher, who in the moment of falling finds himself split into a "world-bound self" (a body subject to gravity) and a kind of "fictional self" (a consciousness that looks on, as if from above; see Livingston 94); for de Man, the model suggested a certain disengagement of literary textuality from history (though the deconstructionist tradition has also enabled much more activist conceptions as well). Whether practiced by scientists or literary theorists, the denial that language is of the world (one might say, the denial that language is subject to gravity *and vice versa*) already belongs to a moribund paradigm, a dinosaur, fallen but still flailing.

The difference between "fundamental" base layers and "emergent" superstructural layers is being split and the playing field leveled a bit not only by poststructuralist cultural theorists (which is where the notion of "the semiautonomy of base and superstructure" comes from) but also by physicists, who now posit that the particles and forces and laws all situated as fundamental to our physical universe are themselves emergent phenomena no less than the biological life, consciousness, culture, and language built on them. And if various kinds of complexity, most notably biological life and language, are not unlikely events but probable to a virtual certainty (and of a kind with the underlying complexity of physics), and in addition if the specific parameters of a particular base turn out not to be necessary to support "higher" levels, the hierarchy/branching model is undermined further. One could say that such a universe *wants* life and language like bodies want to fall when pushed out of windows. In the ultimate case, if life or language could arise in another universe possessed of a certain minimal complexity but with *different* particles and forces, this would seem to make life and language in some sense *more fundamental* than any particular set of particles, forces, or laws. Since there is no such thing as a metauniversal perspective, this ultimate case of the semiautonomy of bases and superstructures must be deferred in favor of potentially observable instances that occupy the borders between science and science fiction: Is carbon the only element that has the chemistry to support life, or could non-carbon-based life-forms have evolved elsewhere? How similar would the courses of evolution be from one planet to another? Or, to keep it closer to home, to what extent has the course of evolution on earth been inevitable, how radically could it have differed, and how radically *can* it differ, that is, what is the range of possible futures? With a different chemical or genetic structure and a radically different environment and history, is it possible that any kind of meaningful intercourse could take place between life-forms? Would any kind of translation be possible, or, more fundamentally, would we even be able to recognize each other's languages as languages, or even to recognize each other as life-forms at all? How universal will any given characteristics of life or of language and culture turn out to be? Is it possible that higher-level organizations (for example, the human brain) could be transferred to some future race of machines, or are they necessarily dependent on their biological bases? Can machines themselves be made to think or to evolve to think? If self-organization is deeper than life itself and shows a certain indifference to what it organizes (works with whatever comes to hand), could there be subatomic life-forms or living creatures the size of galaxies? Is the earth a living creature? Is language a virus? Is the universe alive?

These scenarios all tend to undermine the model of branching and the idea that the higher levels are freer and more plural, making it seem more like any one of multiple "lower" levels may tend to converge on a "higher" level, or to further *braid* the levels back onto each other. And note that the very modern and postmodern idea of the radical incommensurability of cultures is altered as well, not by falling back on the old claim that cultures are very different elaborations of the same universal values and needs, but by suggesting that what is called *incommensurability* marks a certain level of difference and complexity at work within as well as between cultures. In other words, cultures are not like *branchings* out from a single trunk but like complex fractal *braidings*, networks.

Could something like chaos or complexity theory integrate the levels, displacing the artificiality or semiarbitrarity by which various kinds of knowledge are separated as realms of investigation from others? Will life and culture and the universe all be sucked into some GUT (grand unified theory) or balanced on some TOE (theory of everything)? Will scientists realize the reductionist dream of a theory so deep, so fundamental, that it could be articulated in a simple algorithm that you could crank through a computer and watch it produce a little big bang, atoms, gravity, minigalaxies, planets, creatures, cultures, and finally, on the seventh day, the theory itself?

You have to think about where these questions are coming from before you can address them. The search for a unified single theory is itself an artifact of the depth/hierarchy model and the reductionism that goes along with it; the model is explicit in Kauffman's assertion that self-organization is "even deeper than the specific chemistry that happens to exist on earth; it is rooted in mathematics itself" (*Home* 60; see discussion in chapter 13). The dream of unification preserves the hierarchy in several related ways: by dreaming that specific laws or principles could be crowned Emperor of Everything, by subordinating matter to abstract principle (for instance, mathematics) in the first place, and by making the universe a progressive manifestation or embodiment of the principle in a way that makes it easy to imagine a series of levels or branchings. Finally and maybe most important, the story of evolving complexity is the consequence of reductionism: if you demand a simple explanation to start with, it's pretty much guaranteed that the trajectory of your story is going to have to be one of increasing complexity.

But to the extent that a single metatheory could become Emperor of Everything, wouldn't it have to be more plural than the elegant simplicity that, apparently, was unqualified for the job? And furthermore, if such a theory were able to put complexity at the bottom and beginning of things instead of just at the top and climax, would this lead to *more* theoretical variation (as in the form of more semiautonomous disciplinary formations) or *less* (by making all knowledge branches of complexity studies), that is, would it make knowledge more democratic or more autocratic? Or to put it in terms of the catastrophic expectations of discipline-bound knowledge workers, would some fantasy metatheory put scientists in charge of the humanities? Or could it make physics and poetics sister subfields (note to self: ask for raise)? In fact, even partial permutations of these scenarios would have to involve fundamental changes in all of the fields involved.

In any case, in order to try to assess these various speculations, you have to take one more step back to look at the social, economic, political, and historical affiliations of the reductionist paradigm in question. In other words, whatever happens, we can be pretty confident that, just as in the past, the future of scientific paradigms will be linked to the social, economic, political, and technological future. Though this future may be no easier to predict in itself, *the certainty that these uncertainties will be resonantly linked is a piece of positive knowledge that may well have consequences for shaping each.*

To begin, in hyperschematic terms (and here comes the one-paragraph version of what should be ten books), *the stratified model is an artifact of a stratified society.* The emblem of such a society and its cosmos in the Renaissance was the hierarchy of hierarchies known as the Great Chain of Being, and even by about 1700, the still solid ground at the base of the social order had a fitting emblem in the fundamental particles of Newton, those comfortingly hard and indivisible atoms at the bottom of everything. The cash nexus of capitalism on the rise in the eighteenth century dissolved more rigid and quasi-feudal social and economic relations, making the use value of things subordinate to their exchange value in circulation (making things more like money, more *liquid*), bringing a dynamism and ongoing "creative destruction" in which it seems, as Marx put it, that "all that is solid melts into air." The universal referencing of circulating paper money to gold (that is, to actual bars of gold stashed away) constantly reinforced the ideal of the referentiality of words to things even as it moved toward self-referential closure. At the same time, science updated the physical world: the newly volatile universe of thermodynamics was on the rise, just as the theory of evolution swept away the static classes of creatures (supposed to have existed since creation) and replaced them with a dynamic—but still hierarchical—Victorian progressivism. In the story of the upward climb of evolution against a thermodynamic universe of ever increasing disorder can be found the white bourgeoisie's universalized account of its own progress. Unfortunately, then, modernity did not level the playing field. Because the systematic subordinations at the heart of Western modernity (slavery and then colonialism, proletarianization and the mechanization of working-class labor, various practices of white supremacy, heteronormativity, and the suppression of women—along with the more abstract hierarchized binaries of bodies and minds, things and words, nature and culture) are not *given* as such, they must be dynamically and multidimensionally reproduced, and in the process they are both more stable and more vulnerable to being put off balance. Fast-forward to the twentieth century, when pyramidally structured (vertically integrated) monopolistic corporations rise and fall and sprawl into horizontally interaffiliated and outsourced networks, when Newton's once comfortingly hard and indivisible atoms, having already been shattered into bits and the bits into dancing probabilistic clouds, are further dematerialized into virtual "spin networks" of pure relationality (see Smolin, *Three* 125–45, and below), while paper and paper money give way to their more volatile and virtual electronic forms, and the gold standard to floating currencies self-referentially valued only in relation to each other, the medium for still more turbulent flows of transnational capital, and welcome to the brave new world of postmodernity, where all the fluidities and levelings of the playing field and the toppling of monolithic hierarchies have grotesquely compounded power and economic differentials and microbrewed virulent new strains of backlashings, fascisms, genocides.

Will globalization lead to a more democratic or a more autocratic world? Just as capitalism and modernity brought new liberations and oppressions, it is clear that the answer is—yes. It becomes very easy to predict that nature/culture distinctions will shift and even blur increasingly, but not to produce a single unified theory of everything in the old sense, the sense of a Final Solution, but to produce a hybrid and heterogeneous empire of knowledge that is nonetheless an empire. Call it the Regime on the Edge of Chaos.

ASIDE

The Pyramid, the Orbit, and the Dichotomy. A long time ago, during the last episteme and the last millennium, when I was in high school and college, I started noticing that the diagrams on the blackboard in all of my classes seemed to be either multilevel pyramids, concentric rings, or dichotomous pairings. In humanities classes they might be labeled "the individual" and "society" and so forth, whereas in science classes they might be the energy states of an electron. I used to think that the overuse of these simple diagrams was because teachers were bad artists, but now I think it also has to do with the way hierarchical thinking keeps generating the same limited repertoire of basic models, the way it situates these kinds of models as basic. It's not hard to predict that networklike models (which are really not intrinsically harder to draw) will be taking up more and more blackboard space in the days to come.

Certainly, the sciences themselves will continue to be reconstellated as they evolve. Since (for example) the current laws of thermodynamics tell us why things must die, but not why they live, which has been the province of biology, might the laws of thermodynamics actually get changed by theories of complexity and self-organization so as to cover more territory, to account for the ways the universe wants complexity? Or will the dimension of their operation be displaced and relativized, much as Newtonian gravity has had to make way for Einsteinian gravity and quantum gravity? Similar kinds of questions apply to the relations between the sciences and humanities and to potential reorganizations of knowledge and language itself. And if you'll excuse me for spinning out a science fiction scenario that only a cultural theorist could love (don't worry; we'll get back to some harder science in a moment), as theorizing in physics and self-organization continues to press up against the subject-verb-object structure of language that continues to situate it as radically counterintuitive, could such theories—not by direct application, of course, but in conjunction with all of the shifting economic, social, and ideological circuitry that sustains them—begin to rewire the subject-verb-object structure of language itself, so that (for example) all parts of speech would become the *participles* that these theories tell us they are or so that an intermediate form between singular and plural would arise in recognition of the *someness* of all constellated entities? Change so fundamental is hard to imagine, so in the shorter term, anyway, it seems much more likely that such rearticulations would happen not primarily in basic grammar but in other dimensions of language (as they have happened repeatedly in the past), such as by changing the kinds of metaphors we use (rhetoric) or the ways that various discourses are articulated with each other (such as disciplinarity). Perhaps this rewiring would take place precisely to *bypass* grammar as such, to allow it to go on pretty much as before. In any case (and here is an insight that persists amid such wildly speculative ambiguity), the location and meaning of such change would have to be sought not in any one dimension but in how the dimensions in which such rewirings and reconstellations occur are articulated together. It is easiest to understand this question in terms of fractal and spatial metaphors of scale and structure: how are large-scale structures (disciplines and ideologies) linked to middle-range structures (genres and styles, imagery, rhetoric) and to the smallest and most ubiquitous structures (of grammar)?

After spinning out into such a network of wild speculations, where whatever insights can be gained must coexist with thoroughgoing ignorance, it would be nice to be able to return to physics and the question of gravity for some resolution and scientific solidity. But from the physics side, too, one of the most ironic things about the appeal to gravity as common sense is that, far from being a simple fact, gravity has been for at least a century one of the most recalcitrant mysteries of physics. Is gravity a sibling or a cousin or even a parent to the other basic forces of the cosmos? Does it operate via waves or particles or both? Can it be adequately described as the curvature of space itself, as a network of higher-dimensional strings embedded in three-dimensional space, or as the looping of a spin matrix, a kind of pixilated foam? These are more than technical quibbles; at stake in these questions is all of what gravity is, how it works, how it relates to other things. Those elegant orbits, the artifacts of Newton's spectacular success with defining the laws of gravity, have turned out to be the open lids of so many cans of worms; in fact, current string theories and quantum-loop theories of gravity really do make the gravitational universe into so many open cans of worms. How can we reconcile our ignorance with the progressivist idea of an expanding circle of knowledge, a human campfire lighting a bigger and bigger space for us under the dark sky, when we look closer and see that dark shadows dance and play even within our little circle, that the very flames are streaked with darkness? It is hard to know exactly how to put it: should we say that we seem to have confined our ignorance into smaller and smaller spaces, but we still have no clue at all what we have in there?

And here's the punch line: surprising as it may sound at first, theories of gravity have actually come to be something like theories of how ignorance is distributed, woven at the smallest scale through the fabric of space-time. Lee Smolin's 2001 account of the current state of theorizing about gravity, *Three Roads to Quantum Gravity*, describes three variously related ways physicists are attempting to theorize gravity, ways that may work to unify fundamental theories in physics. Although Smolin explores some of the major differences among the theories, he emphasizes ways that they may converge, especially via a shared paradigm of "fractal spacetime" comprising "a network of interacting loops" (124). One crux of current theories is the notion known as Beckenstein's Bound (first proposed by physicist Jacob Beckenstein in the 1970s), "the idea that there is an absolute limit to information which requires each region of space to contain at most a certain finite amount of information" (Smolin 105). This notion has led to the striking conclusion that space is not uniform at the smallest level but grainy—pixilated, something like a video screen (or a bubbly foam). Physicist Louis Crane has further deduced from the same principle "that quantum cosmology must be a theory of the information exchanged between subsystems of the universe, rather than a theory of how the universe would look to an outside observer" (Smolin 175), making the universe a self-organizing system along the lines of Henri Atlan's 1972 theorizing of biological self-organization based on "transmission between substructures" that builds on "ambiguity or equivocation" (258–59). Especially since the notion of a transcendent perspective has been a kind of epistemological cornerstone (at least as an ideal), its removal changes everything; it redistributes ignorance and knowledge horizontally (like paving a road with the stones of a fallen tower); or to put it another way, it reveals that the division of the world into *things* and *thoughts/words about things* (that is, a transcendentally perspectival consciousness) is a false one. At the smallest level, as Smolin puts it, the theory posits that

> all that there exists in the world are Screens, on which the world is represented. That is, it does not posit that there are two things, bulky things, and images or representations of them on their surfaces. It posits that there is only one kind of thing—representations by which one set of events in the history of the universe receives information about other parts of the world. In such a world, nothing exists except processes by which information is conveyed from one part of the world to another. (177)

Thus (and here is the most succinct statement of the relational model), "*the world must be a network of holograms, each of which contains coded within it information about the relationships between the others*" and, thus, "*any element in the network is nothing but a partial realization of the relationships between the other elements*" (178; emphasis added). This model bears a striking resemblance to the "school of mirrors" model I proposed in 1997, except I was talking not about quantum gravity but about *psychosocial identity formation in postmodern culture.* My model described

> a set of voluptuous mirrors arranged, like a school of fish, so that each reflects and distorts the others, where nothing is reflected (no "content") but the positions of the mirrors with respect to each other. Players function in the system to the extent that they reflect and distort, by virtue of their differential position, the other mirrors, but no one mirror is positioned to present a totalized and undistorted picture; one looks to others to find images of oneself amid images of others. This figure, a school of mirrors, is more suited to

the mobile and multiple interrelations that characterize postmodern power and knowledge. (27)

I am certainly not claiming that Smolin was influenced by my book (which I'm pretty sure he hadn't read). He was drawing on versions of the holographic principle proposed by other physicists, beginning in 1993, in articles that I, in turn, had never encountered. Nor do I want to claim any particular originality for my version of the "school of mirrors" model, which was one attempt to visualize and correlate various already extant features of poststructuralist theory in the humanities (for example, Lacan's "mirror stage" and Baudrillard's "precession of simulacra"). In other words, I was trying to do for cultural theory exactly what Smolin would come to do for theories of gravity—to promote models that bring together some of the major features of various theories in our respective fields—and we converged, from physics and cultural studies, on the same metamirroring model. This is the convergence I have come to understand as part of a long-term epistemological event that can be called the Return to Resemblance.

In any case, Smolin's quantum universe—a fundamentally dynamic and distributed network of information traffic with no transcendent perspective, an interrelational and self-organizing synaptic web that splits the difference between virtual and real space—bears an uncanny resemblance to various already extant theories of postmodern economy, society, culture. This resemblance supports precisely the claim that Alan Sokal tried to discredit: quantum gravity really does seem to be "an archetypal postmodernist science" (227). The resemblance is only uncanny as long as the nature/culture divide still troubles you so much. You could try to argue (rather desperately) that Smolin is simply using the coin of the realm, the current idiom, to express to contemporary people in a language they will understand theories that might well be described in other terms. The fact that the theoretical features in question are not incidental but the definitive aspects of the theory would not be the only problem with such a dismissal. The holographic principle is not just a model but a *model of modeling*—and as such, it not just rejects the content of the dismissal but also refuses its terms at a very fundamental level, by rejecting the notion of deeply underlying things being merely expressed or represented on surfaces in favor of virtual things constituted by the information traffic that sustains them.

One especially compelling version of the seventeenth- and eighteenth-century Doctrine of Resemblance that the contemporary convergence recycles can be found in the philosophical works of Leibniz, to whose works I came belatedly—and found Smolin and others already there. When one of the readers of my 1997 book told me I was reinventing Leibniz without knowing it, I started to read Leibniz and saw what my reader had meant, and I started to see the larger epistemological significance of this reinvention. This was confirmed by another otherwise uncanny synchronicity. In 1998, on a conference panel concerned in part with relations between the sciences and humanities, I was scheduled to present a paper following Smolin, whom I had never met. Imagine my surprise when he began his paper with the same short excerpt from Leibniz's 1714 treatise, *The Monadology,* that I had selected as the epigraph for my paper! What does it mean when a physicist and a literary theorist show up at a party accessorized with the very same excerpt from the same eighteenth-century philosopher? Leibniz stock rising. Big shift in epistemological fashion in progress. Difference is out, Resemblance back in. Stay tuned.

Here is the Leibniz account of metamirroring that we had both selected:

> Now this interlinkage or accommodation of all created things to each other, and of each to all the others, brings it about that each simple substance has relations that express all the others, and consequently is a living mirror of the universe.

> And this is the way to obtain as much variety as possible, but combined with the greatest possible order. . . .

> Every bit of matter can be conceived as a garden full of plants or a pond full of fish. But each branch of the plant, each member of the animal, each drop of its bodily fluids, is also such a garden or such a pond. (26, 28)

As a highly aestheticized version of ecological relationality and difference, this mirroring seems so *groovy*—so fractal, so holographic and kaleidoscopic (please cue the appropriately trippy music track in your mind)—that it is hard to keep in mind that for Leibniz such order was not an emergent phenomenon but programmed by an absolute god (cue "Hail to the Chief," crescendo) who produced the best of all possible worlds, whose earthly representative was an absolute monarch, and so on down the line in the patriarchal hierarchy of hierarchies. What might have seemed at first (to a current reader of Leibniz anyway) like a radical multiplicity turns out to be an even more thoroughgoing unity. As I have said, if in some sense what has been going on ever since Leibniz is a series of horizontalizations, which has produced new and more dynamic subordinations as well as liberations, then the old vertical chain of being, recycled as a horizontal network of networks, holds us more tightly than ever. And just as Leibniz was an ideologue for absolute monarchy as well as the inventor of a new kind of mathematics, the mathematics of chaos and complexity come with new forms of sovereignty, identity, and collectivity.

21

Queer in a Queer World

> [A]ny rich system tends to function through an interchange between
> what is inside and what is outside the system . . . and there are always
> certain elements . . . which are undecidable as to whether
> they are inside or outside—often, though not always,
> those parts that encourage definition and revision.
>
> —Samuel R. Delany, *Return to Neveryon*

Samuel Delany's science fiction story "The Star Pit," written in 1965, traces intricately orchestrated dynamics of love, dependency, and entrapment; the story also features a series of figures of model ecological systems ("ecologaria") that reflect on such orchestrations. When he wrote the story, Delany had just read Frank Herbert's *Dune,* the 1965 novel that thematized *ecology as world making* in a way that installed it at the heart of the project of science fiction. But Delany's story also plays out an alternative to the romanticized wholism characteristic of ecology in the 1960s, an alternative still salutary in counteracting the formalizing, idealizing, and totalizing tendencies that continue to be definitive for theories of self-organizing systems and autopoiesis.

There is another feature that overdetermines this story for consideration here. In 1988, Delany wrote a memoir about the 1960s and the New York milieu out of which "The Star Pit" and other stories and novels were written: *The Motion of Light in Water,* subtitled "Sex and Science Fiction Writing in the East Village." The memoir is interwoven with reveries about the shifty relations of desire and history, relations that *constitute* and *compromise* the truth of every narrative. These reflections occur as philosophical asides as well as in the memoir's repeated images of shifting columns of text and of dancing networks of light and shadow, as posited in its title.

It is hard for an inveterate reflexivist like me to resist adding another genre to a memoir that reflects on its own reflection and on a story that models modeling and self-organizing systems. Although no author ever preempted critical commentary by building in loops upon loops of self-reflection, no critic, entering this house of mirrors, should presume to offer *the* privileged metareflection, the God's-eye view, only relatively different discursive and historical perspectives and connections. Of course, the model of adding privileged reflection to what is, by contrast, relatively unself-reflexive, is related to a whole series of oppressive *otherings:* smart words and dumb things, mental and menial labor, anthropologists and primitives, and so on. So if all one can do is add loops on loops, what is to be gained? Well, for a start, the process seems already to have generated a brilliant story and memoir. So could the critic, merely by adding more loops, bring about some further kind of qualitative shift, so that, eventually, future generations will be made to read the text in question as a kind of bible, weaving it into the fabric of their thoughts and language? This grandiose scenario describes only a little hyperbolically the process of high-cultural canonization à la Shakespeare, Cervantes, and so on. If I have to, I'll settle for that, but I'm really attempting something a bit more quixotic, and I'm hoping the high degree of difficulty will help compensate for how far short this falls (and I can at least guarantee a couple of twisting backflips on the way): I would like to install Delany's texts at the intersection of cultural studies and theoretical biology.

Short of that, in the process of toggling back and forth between story and memoir and exploring the algorithms at play to produce each, I hope to triangulate between two opposed but complementary models figured and enacted by each text: the three neatly self-enclosed "ecologaria" embedded in the neatly self-enclosing story and the shifty, indeterminately multiple networks weaving through the sprawling memoir. What should emerge, if I am successful, is a model of self-organization that is both abjectly, sprawlingly, plurally open and neatly, circularly, singularly closed, and future generations of biologists and literary theorists will—together—read Delany and me in their autopoetics classes. Okay, are you ready? Then let's begin.

At the time of the story's composition, Delany could be described as a gay African American science fiction writer living in New York's East Village with his wife, the poet Marilyn Hacker (a Jewish woman and, like Delany, a New Yorker), and their mutual lover, a white southern drifter identified only as *Bob* in the memoir. Of course, this bald and identitarian sketch belies the plural complexity of each of the identities at play and thus is especially inappropriate for Delany, who was never an identitarian (and he wasn't bald, either). Even so, one might begin most crudely by asking if the writer created some kind of science-fictionalized version of his life and of gay people, black people, threesomes, interracial relationships, Jews, southerners, writers, New Yorkers. This seems rather like the task proposed to the reader of the later children's picture-book series *Where's Waldo?* in which the child is supposed to locate the telltale features of the title character, who is represented many times over amid teeming crowds of people. Such a naive strategy has the virtue of beginning to show how Delany *thwarted* this kind of representationalism—although the children's book's tactics of multiplication and distribution and even one-to-one correspondence are *among* his bag of tricks (and as it happens, we will also find in Delany's story a "waldo" that has a lot to do with the theme of multiplication of self). And by the way, it is also fun to do the thing I was taught that literary critics and theorists must not do (close readings, especially ones that start by treating literature as coded autobiography) and to avoid the thing I was taught I must do (historicize literature according to the time in which it was produced) and to find, in the process, that I don't have to fight all the same battles my teachers fought (thanks—and no thanks—to them). Far from prematurely shutting down interpretation by nailing down fiction to personal facts, such a reading can open the text up to indeterminacy and history in a way that tries to make its opennesses resonate with our own, making it a resource for a more open future rather than the fixture of a closed past.

By starting with and progressively revising the crude realism that is so clearly the wrong answer about how the texts in question work, we approach that "science fictional notion" Delany later called a "Modular Calculus": something like "a set of algorithms" by which representations and descriptions could be incarnated into working models, or more whimsically a kind of "Finagle Factor," an "illusive constant sought by all researchers, by which the wrong answer is adjusted to get the right one" (*Return* 284–85).

In the simplest sense, the constant adjustment we must make is *complication,* the adding of more loops like the ones that made the story and memoir in the first place, and in so doing, though we must fail to achieve an exhaustive model of the workings of the texts, we will just as surely generate a description of the operation of textuality that *is itself a working text.* We will find that Delany's bag of tricks includes a range of correspondences and doublings, direct translations, displacements, redistributions, distortions, inventions, each of which also show striking internal variation. In other words, what we find is not a single algorithm that takes real life and science fictionalizes it, but an array of algorithms that, like an evolving ecology, seems driven to probe all conceivable strategies as it makes a world. A single strategy like realism, if it were possible, could not yield the ring of truth (in fact it couldn't even get the writer out of bed), but realism is necessarily one of an array of algorithms whose variety and interrelations are what give the story its texture and complexity and make it like a living thing. I have already explained the general theoretical claim I want to make for such likenesses (see chapter 3), but here it is sufficient to say again that this complexity makes the texts in question work as models of complex systems.

Beginning by using the rough identity markers of our thumbnail sketch and searching the story for representations of the author yields a series of teasing likenesses that are also more or less radically *unlike*. The narrator, Vyme, is dark skinned, but racial difference as such figures not at all in the story. Vyme had been a New Yorker, as a child anyway, but Vyme's New York was a claustrophobic constraint he couldn't wait to leave, making it practically the opposite of Delany's. Star-pit, the distant galactic outpost where Vyme ends up, most resembles Delany's East Village in an arbitrary detail: its streets are named alphabetically (Calle G, J, and X are mentioned, as compared with Avenue A, B, and C of New York's East Village). There are two almost-writers in the story, but they are conspicuously like and un-like Delany: Vyme's substitute son, Ratlit (who cannot read or write), once dictated, but only as a passing diversion, what became a popular novel, and Vyme's friend Sandy, a starship mechanic, once "tried to write a trilogy" but failed. The new dominant family structure proposed in the story seems like it might correspond roughly to Delany's threesome, but the kibbutzlike, multiple-parent "proke groups" of the story are geared toward procreation, as the name denotes, and in spite of the love that binds members of groups variously to each other, there is hardly a suggestion of the same-sex erotics that are the primary organizing principle for Delany. And though the story features a variety of strong and interesting male-male relationships (mainly along a father/son axis), what may be the most openly gay moment of the story is also the most equivocal of all: it comes when Poloscki, a minor char-acter who runs the neighboring starship repair shop, propositions—and actually proposes marriage—to Vyme. Vyme demurs, but it is only in the course of this exchange (near the end of the story) that Delany first uses a gender-specific pronoun for Poloscki and the reader realizes that she is fe-male. Thus, Delany slyly shifts the responsibility for reading the encounter as homosexual to readers who will have assumed that the owner of a mechanic shop would be male: it's a nice trick and set up subtly enough so that readers will be inclined to think they have just missed the gender cues; only a careful rereading of the story confirms that no pronouns or other gender-specific references to Poloscki appear before the scene in question.

The hegemony of white heteronormativity would have made it very difficult or impossible for Delany, in 1965, prominently to feature openly gay characters—much less interracial threesomes— and have a chance at making a living publishing popular science fiction. As he put it (rather differently) in his memoir: "To write a science fiction novel about some people who loved each other and shared their bodies, all three, was something I wasn't prepared to do—yet" (*Motion* 404), even though he managed to weave two more or less discreet threesomes into the novel he was also writing at the time, *Babel 17.* But the identity tease and distortions—the *commitment to perversity*—go well beyond disguising or suppressing sensitive material: the shifting networks of shadow and light are also where the marks of an enforced silence intersect with the creative hallmarks of science fiction. The realistic antirealism of science fiction becomes a critical resource for queer politics in the making, since for both the challenge is not only to "come out" but also to renegotiate the terms of identity by which one might do so, not only to make a choice but also to try to remake and even refuse the consequences and necessity of choosing in the first place.

The story's narrator, Vyme, runs a starship repair shop at Star-pit, on the edge of the galaxy. The repair-shop milieu seems to have been inspired by an actual event, recorded in the memoir: an ex-lover of Delany's "hired Bob and me to work for a weekend with him on his transmission in a Jersey garage, where, on tracks across the girdered ceiling, a great grapple could be maneuvered by a remote-control box, like the waldos in the SF stories I'd read as a boy" (*Motion* 409). It might be better to say that it was not just the *actual* event as such but its resemblance to already extant science fiction that made it so compelling for Delany; in any case, the reflexive loop doesn't end there, since it is also the waldo's capacity for reflexive agency (see below) that makes it important for the story.

Star-pit is as far out in the galaxy as Vyme can travel. Like most humans, he couldn't survive the reality shift that induces insanity, then neural shutdown and death, beyond the galactic rim. Only the few humans known as *golden* can survive intergalactic travel, protected by a rare genetic and hormonal anomaly—and by their psychotic personalities, which are often artificially induced and managed by psychotechnicians. After being identified by medical screenings, golden are trained for their obligatory vocation as intergalactic procurers of alien technologies, weapons, and drugs. They live as a breed apart, regarded as narcissistic and antisocial, resented by galaxy-bound humans.

The golden constitute the story's most conspicuous science fictional invention—its *novum* (as the sci-fi people say). In other words, the lack of a completely satisfactory way of anchoring the golden to something familiar is what makes them anchors of the story's generic status as science fiction. It is significant that they seem to be positioned (in several ways) as analogues to *writers* and to *gay men* in particular, but it is no less important that they exceed discrete identity boundaries much as the golden themselves cross otherwise impassable spatial boundaries. At any rate, the complex cross-mappings of identity, real space, and imaginary space (both in the story and between story and memoir) enable us to sketch a correspondence to Delany's assertion that he was not prepared, at the time, to tell his story explicitly: Vyme is as far "out" as he can go, and although he loves and alternately envies or admires the golden, he lacks the combination of strength and pathology (the *hardness,* one might say) it would take to follow their lead. But this does not reduce the golden to a coded representation of openly gay people; one might also say more inclusively that the golden resemble people who, for whatever reason, don't quite belong, who are driven to be crossers of cultures, of races, of genders, who (in spite of their common lot) do not quite cohere (or rather, at least for the time being, are *prevented* from cohering) into a community or a class as such. This kind of anti-identity strategy runs the risk of individualizing and depoliticizing the golden into romanticized misfits, making the story merely a personal psychological resource for such identifications—although insofar as the personal is political, there is not necessarily much of a loss of progressive possibility even in this (depending on how ambitious you are about what kinds of ideological work you think can and cannot be done in fiction).

The story's *novum* performs a critical distortion that revises received notions of both individual and class identity, nurturing the desire for political organizing principles beyond reductive identity insofar as it prompts a reader to wonder (even in a prepolitical or yet-to-be articulated way) in what capacity the golden speak *to and for me* and to or for other queer people; exploited, displaced, and diasporic workers; culture crossers; ethnic minorities (as enforced culture crossers); writers. This works only insofar as it remains a question and thus only if it runs the risk of missing its mark, especially since what it questions is how people are marked in the first place. In all of this the golden work as what Kobena Mercer has called a *counterfetish:* a ritual image or figure (often a mask) that hides or safeguards identity from being reduced to a discrete thing, especially (I would add) in environments where identity itself is not allowed *itself* to be a counterfetish.

Vyme has come to the Star-pit after abandoning his proke group for good after many long absences and drunken returns; Delany seems here to have largely transposed onto Vyme the story of Bob and his extended family. Vyme has since heard that his beloved son, Antoni, has been killed, along with Antoni's mother and many of his other parents, in an interplanetary war. Surprisingly, this detail (structurally important since it contributes to Vyme's drive to find surrogate sons) seems to derive not from Bob but from a story told to Delany by a man he encountered when he first experimented with sex outside the threesome. As Delany describes it in the memoir, a photo in the man's apartment depicted his wife, their male lover, and their two kids, all of whom had died in a car accident. Delany remembers that he refrained from telling the man about his own threesome because "the correspondences were great enough so that he probably wouldn't believe me, and would just think I was putting him on—or crazy" (*Motion* 401). Nonetheless, the discovery of these correspondences was important for Delany, as the revelation of shared experience can often be an important weapon against the social isolation and cultural silence that work to alienate sexual minorities and others in alternative relationships and families: "Again I'd encountered this strange doubling—a doubling that had taken what I'd never thought to be other than my personal situation and changed it into a socially shared one" (402).

The magic of this discovery—the "synchronicity" of it—may be in proportion to the thoroughness of the dominant denial that makes the experience in question seem unintelligible, unspeakable, impossible. But in 1988, two weeks after first writing the account for his memoir, Delany wonders "if I haven't wholly misremembered a goodly part? It seems to me now that I must have told the guy about Bob and Marilyn; and that we discussed the matter with an easy complicity" (402). Perhaps, Delany reflects, it was really his reluctance to tell Bob and Marilyn about the man that his memory has transposed into a reluctance to tell the man about Bob and Marilyn. This changes things, making the threesome easily speakable in a context of male sexual privilege (at least in the mode of swapping stories) and making the casual encounter between men exemplary of this privilege rather than the site of enforced silence, whereas Delany's reluctance to tell Marilyn and Bob of the encounter would have tended to situate the ongoing threesome—especially insofar as it involves a woman—as something more like an oppressively straight marriage, a high-maintenance and infidelity-intolerant institution. This tendency seems also to situate the story's proke groups as loving but claustrophobic sites for ambivalent, restless men. In any case, the strange real-life correspondence between Delany and the man, along with the strangely hard-to-locate difficulty of representing it as such, reveals another dimension in the shell game of sociosexual identity already observed in operation between memoir and story.

Although it is the story of Sandy (Vyme's employee) that most resembles Bob's, this doubling is also doubled within the story, since the outlines of Sandy's story also correspond roughly to Vyme's: as with Vyme, an ongoing struggle between domestic love and restlessness has brought Sandy to the Star-pit. He had intended to work for Vyme as a mechanic until he could return to his procreation group, but he gets a letter from one of his husbands, telling him the group does not want him back. Drunk and despairing, he attempts suicide but is stopped by Vyme. In the memoir, we discover that the letter incident derives from a real letter Bob got from his stepmother, who had been taking care of Bob's daughter and three stepsons. The manner of Sandy's suicide attempt in the story is also taken directly from a fantasy of Bob's: upon hearing how a "waldo" works, Bob had imagined crushing oneself to death with one: "'If I'd a had one, that's what I'd a done the night I got that letter from home'" (410). As a kind of cyborg prosthesis that both amplifies and can be turned back destructively against the self, the "waldo" seems to function much as the characters in a story function for its author and readers, or indeed as science fictional worlds in relation to their worlds of origin.

In the memoir, Delany explains how he produced Sandy's letter from Bob's: "I put Bob's letter on the green metal wing of the typing stand and, sentence by sentence, translated it into the text of my story. I worked on that section half a day; thus twenty-two years on, with the story text beside me, it is fairly easy to retranslate it" (*Motion* 407–8). By this device Delany includes more or less direct translation (or maybe it is clearer to call it *transposition*) in the array of algorithms by which the story is generated, enabling the story to function not only as critique but also as coded archive. Here fact and fiction are allowed to correspond literally—that is, *to the letter*—at a point as crucial as the correspondence of Star-pit's transposed letter names to East Village avenues was arbitrary.

If Delany's reconstructed version of the original letter can be trusted (since it is, in any case, the transposition of a transposition), what he seems to have taken most care to reproduce for the story are those aspects of the letter most likely to be outside his own stylistic repertoire: its southern, white, rural, or working-class inflections and the awkwardness and abruptness that make it seem like the product of someone not used to writing. In other words, it is not only that the orchestrated differences of multiple voices give fiction its pleasingly nubbly texture but also its *bordering on otherness* that gives it real traction, where difference from others and difference from self engage. The use of the actual letter ritually enacts this bordering, this *withness*.

Ratlit and Alegra, the two doomed teenagers Vyme befriends, are driven by even more intense conflicts between claustrophobic entrapment and reckless longing and nonbelonging. By the inclusion of these extreme versions of the conflicts that also shape Vyme and Sandy, the story seems to play out the enduring theme-and-variations algorithm of nineteenth-century naturalism at its most Darwinian (and by the way, *naturalism* here is the name given to a literary method and as such differs from the philosophical position that sometimes goes by the same name). Using this algorithm means arraying the characters along a spectrum of different combinations of kinds and degrees of features and then putting them together to see what kinds of dynamics emerge from the permutations of their interrelations: who endures, who learns and evolves, and who is destroyed. By his own account, Delany began to work with his version of such a "grid" as early as about 1963 (see *Return* 287– 89); such permutation-generating devices in general are known as *combinatories* (or, if you prefer, by transposing two letters you get the more sophisticated-sounding French version, *combinatoires*).

Ratlit, in whom Vyme seeks a substitute for his lost son, is an orphan who at thirteen has already knocked around—and been knocked around—much of the galaxy. Ratlit's friend and confidante is the bedridden and massively drug-addicted Alegra, a "projecting telepath" whose ability to induce hallucinations of her own and others' thoughts got her conscripted, at age eight, to help golden traumatized by interspecies contact to reintegrate their brittle personalities. Ratlit has become dependent on Alegra to help him manage his own sometimes desperate sense of entrapment, and she relies on him to procure the drugs she now needs to stay alive.

Although Ratlit and Alegra can be read as standing for the codependent dysfunctionality of coupling in general and of heterosexual coupling in particular, Alegra's status as the only serious female character in the story also loads her with too much of the burden of representing femininity to survive or thrive—or should we read that as *precisely what heteronormative coupling does?* In a portrait as feminist as it is misogynist, Alegra's dark side—hysterical, abject emoting in conjunction with manipulativeness and dependency—is interwoven with empathic supportiveness and the strength to sustain emotional intensities and real engagements with others rather than reacting with "fight or flight." She is like the golden in that her ability/disability has been cultivated and exploited—that is, she has been *othered*—into a crippling, enforced role. The most important aspect of Alegra's gift is her ability to enact it for others in whom it has been just as systematically suppressed, to read their minds and help them externalize their own thoughts and feelings by acting them out or otherwise manifesting them—making her, in other words, a lot like a heteronormative wife, but also a lot like a *writer*.

A heroically triumphant version of this character is the protagonist of *Babel 17*, the novel Delany was also writing at the time: Rydra Wong is a megafamous poet, starship captain and military strategist, linguist, mind reader, therapist, and healer of damaged men, savior of the galaxy; she is also situated ambiguously between a threesome and a couple. If we are still looking for coded portraits, where between Alegra and Rydra might we find Delany's wife, Marilyn? Delany at least makes this game more difficult by focusing both characterizations beyond identity (and beyond heroic success and abject failure) to the common writerly liminality that tends to catalyze the differences between them, the point at which (as Delany tells himself at one point) "you are neither black nor white. / You are neither male nor female. / And you are that most ambiguous of citizens, the writer" (*Motion* 364).

The main plot of "The Star Pit" is simple enough: one golden impulsively gives a small starship to Sandy after killing its owner. Sandy doesn't want the ship, sensing it will bring him only trouble, and offers it to Vyme. In spite of Sandy's warnings, Vyme gives the ship to Ratlit, who wants to present it to another golden being nursed back to health by Alegra. Convinced that she too is golden, Alegra plans to leave the galaxy with her patient, but Ratlit, in desperation as he faces the prospect that Alegra will abandon him and find the escape he so desperately wants, convinces the golden to take him instead. The two of them sneak into the shop and take the ship, which carries Ratlit to an agonizing death beyond the galactic rim. Her drug supplier gone, Alegra dies in the bleak, garbage-strewn room no longer disguised by her florid visualizations.

Embedded in the plot is a succession of three "ecologaria" or mini-ecosystems, designed to be self-sustaining with only the addition of sunlight. These function explicitly as metaphors or figures for the larger world of the story, but their undisguised design as models or object lessons makes them seem to "pop out" from the story. In other words, although they interact at key points with the narrative, they seem in effect to come from a nonnarrative dimension, at least insofar as metaphor rolls into a ball what narrative unravels at length. In this, Delany's three ecologaria make critical analogues to the extraterrestrial obelisk in Clarke and Kubrick's *2001: A Space Odyssey*. Like Delany's ecologaria, the obelisk also comes to move a human narrative along toward its posthuman future, except that Delany's internally complex and finally spherical ecologaria are designed to open the question of *internal principles of self-organization and evolution* as conspicuously as Kubrick and Clarke's blank slab (pyramidal in Clarke's story, rectangular in the film) invokes an unspecified *external* one. In any case, the difference between metaphor and narrative is far from absolute: looking only a little closer reveals narrative embedded in metaphor. The virtue of the mini-eco-system as a metaphor and as a metaphor of metaphor is that, in principle, it does not differ in kind from what it models or represents, that is, it may be considerably less complex and enduring, but it is nonetheless an ecosystem within an ecosystem; it is—to appropriate Stuart Kauffman's phrase—at home in the universe. In this it differs from other media for modeling and representation—such as consciousness, machines, and language—whose differences from the world at large have been so consistently overemphasized.

The first of the story's mini-ecosystems is a primitive ant farm Vyme remembers having as a child on Earth. He associates its narrowly glassed-in space with other memories of a claustrophobic childhood and adolescence, such as the longing he felt as a young man, standing on the eastern edge of Manhattan as the starless sky pressed down and staring across the river to Brooklyn, and the panic he felt when, years later, his mother showed him the little harness he was made to wear as a small child.

The next ecologarium is a six-by-six-foot multispecies version built for the children of Vyme's proke group on Sigma, complete with walking plants and tiny, furry sloths who cling to the inside of the tinted Plexiglas panels, staring out much as Vyme had once stared across the East River. The hypersensitive sloths die if exposed directly to the light of Sigma's two suns. After returning drunk from one of his extended jobs off the planet, Vyme deliberately smashes the ecologarium. It is repaired and all the wildlife restored—all but the sloths, who have mysteriously disappeared. Soon after, Vyme leaves Sigma.

The final ecologarium is a golf ball–size version equipped with a magnifying lens for viewing the teeming, exotically multiform microorganisms within, which work through an entire ecological cycle every two minutes. It is worn on a necklace by Sandy's son-in-law Androcles (known as An), a golden who arrives at the Star-pit after Ratlit's death and, with Vyme's help, gets Ratlit's job at Poloscki's to help him train for his next mission. In name and otherwise, Androcles echoes Vyme's first son, Antoni, and he arrives fortuitously to replace Ratlit in this filial series. The third in the series of ecologaria is also the most successful, and it catalyzes Vyme and An's interaction to provide a kind of resolution to the story. It had been presented to An at school as a problem for ecological analysis. The resolution of this analysis depends on two key points: first, that the multiform and multiphase organisms, variously breeding with or cannibalizing or ignoring each other, actually constitute a *single organism* and, second, that crucial catalysts for the ecological cycle are produced by some of the microorganisms *that do not themselves reproduce*. The two points are related: the kind of wholism represented here is difficult to recognize because it generates and is generated by a more heterogenous plurality than is usually recognized. Recognizing that that which does not itself reproduce may be crucial to the reproduction of the system as a whole is an important affirmation for the golden (whose children are no more or less likely to be golden than anyone else's) and of the homosexuality with which this status tends to ally them. This depriviledging of reproduction does not just point *to* but *through* homosexuality to other apparently inessential or excessive identities, in particular to the role of culture and cultural production in the biosocial system as a whole and beyond to all that is wild, all that does not "breed true," all uninheritable mutations (culture among them). But all that the model can do is point, since it (like the golden in the story) seems to be artificially limited to a convulsive but apparently *nonevolving* dynamic equilibrium, one in which mutation is fully subordinated to reproduction at the systemic level (a subordination rigidly built into the concept of *mutation* in the first place). Vyme, who has never been able to bear such claustrophobia, intends to destroy the perfect little sphere by crushing it with a waldo but is stopped by Poloscki, whose proposition of reproductive domesticity he manages to decline more graciously.

And to what do the limitations of the model point, in what direction does it fail to be what it stands for, what question does this failure pose, what other model would it desire or would it desire to become? What would become of us and our world if local mutations were *not* subordinated to holistic reproduction, if the parts were *not* fully subordinated to the whole, if the wobbly stability of dynamic equilibrium gave way to stable wobbliness of far-from-equilibrium systems, if hierarchy and subordination were themselves subordinated to something more plural? It just might turn out to be a world *very much like ours had been all along*, a dance marathon of being and becoming, an insubordinate and a queer world after all (and please feel free to break into song at this point).

Androcles, even as one who is golden, complains of feeling trapped—a brutal irony for Vyme, who has always envied golden their freedoms. But An in turn has been tormented ever since encountering a species whose powers of travel make his own merely intergalactic range seem claustrophobic: these creatures jump whole universes when frightened, and their external nervous systems (which seem to be fuzzy coats of fur) bear traces of entirely different matrices of space-time. These creatures turn out to be none other than the little sloths, whose mysterious disappearance from Sigma is now resolved. By far the most sensitive and most vulnerable, the tiny clinging sloths with their external nervous systems, confined to their tinted plastic cube lest the sunlight kill them, are thereby also the freest: their freedom is driven by the extremity of their constraints. As Sandy and Vyme finally learn, "There are some directions in which you cannot go. Choose one in which you can move as far as you want" (70). This punch line might deteriorate into a cliché ("Four walls do not a prison make" or "Handicaps are challenges to transcend") or might conceivably be taken to justify the proposition that, since there are always trade-offs (the poor are rich in spirit, while the rich lead empty and unfulfilled lives, and so on), all inequality and oppression are only relative. The problem with this proposition is not that it goes too far but that it does not go far enough, acting to short-circuit the contradiction at the heart of singular hierarchies of power and knowledge: if contradictions generate movement and meaning, accepting contradiction moves not to desperation or quietism but to sustainable action. Honoring in practice the recognition that powers and knowledges come with more or less radical limitations, and vice versa, with respect to those who seem to be the most powerful and those who seem to be the least, would yield revolutionary consequences. The ongoing work of queer writing is to make the varieties of "ambiguous citizenship" into gifts as well as burdens to those who bear them and to *enact the desire for a world in which this might be the case.*

Insofar as the story can be characterized as a combinatory in the most conservative sense, as in social-Darwinist Victorian novels, it seems to grind out predictable results. It sends the older men, Vyme and Sandy, off on an upward trajectory of growth and evolution: at the story's end, Sandy prepares to return to the center of the galaxy to find a new proke group, and Vyme seems to have gained wisdom that will serve him in his role as surrogate father to the various misfits and drifters who show up at Star-pit. The same "difference engine" has sent Ratlit and Alegra down to horrible failure and death, killed (we might say) by the irreconcilability and unsustainability of their bourgeois ideals of love, recognition, and freedom and the claustrophobic backlash that these ideals generate through the form of the brittle and codependent heteronormative couple (Hi, Mom and Dad!). The golden, the combinatory's anchor point, endure (at least as represented by An) but seemingly without growth or change, driven by their contradictions, as are all the characters, but unable to come to terms with them, as Vyme and Sandy do, through the trajectory of fall, redemption, and growth that marks the most fully human characters, at least in the humanist model of novelistic development. But especially since the story so insists that growth and movement take place not in transcending but in coming to terms with contradiction, the axis of failure and success cannot possibly be an either/or proposition or a single trajectory but must be an ongoing crux for all the characters.

Like the mini-ecosystems that model it, the story is designed as a device to manufacture intuition about self-organizing systems: it posits a sequence of models (a set that includes itself), each of which fails, falls short, in the direction of the next. In so doing it enacts and transmits, nurtures and directs, a *desire*. What does it want? Like all models, it wants to be real, to become alive, or to the extent that it is alive already to go on living. As it loops back repeatedly on itself it wants to catch other threads: *texts want what Velcro wants.* It enacts and nurtures and directs a series of texts that continue to articulate a desire: a story that wants to be a memoir but cannot quite, a memoir that wants to be cultural theory but cannot quite, which brings us here, to cultural theory that wants to be theoretical biology but cannot. The text wants to stay alive, wants its adopted children to stay alive, but because they cannot stay alive in *any* world, it wants a world in which they *could* stay alive, wants a *world* that could stay alive, a queer world, whose ecology is not blithe wholism or eternal warfare but sustainable contradictions, whose intelligence and perseverance are its perversity.

22

An Alienist History

I hope I won't jeopardize the otherwise unassailable validity of this book by concluding in a somewhat different tack; in any case, this section will begin as pretty straightforward cultural criticism but slip quickly into the mode of fiction and attempt to do most of its theorizing in that mode. Could such criticism possibly be effective, and if so how? Could it alter cultural practices or epistemology, or could it have any positive traction on ideology at all? These are precisely the questions I have about the alien abduction movement, the subject of this section.

Alien abduction stories began in the United States in the late 1940s and early 1950s. As a symbolic way of processing North American problematics of Otherness, you could say it was a kind of autistic sibling of the paranoid bully McCarthyism. By the 1980s—after many cycles through popular culture and various subcultures, and through the collective personal nightmares of ordinary Americans—the stories had evolved a fairly consistent constellation of features: the beam of light that lifts the abductee into the alien ship, the paralysis and subjection to surgical probes, the implantations of surveillance devices or alien fetuses (no trace of which could ever be verified), the induced amnesia. The aliens, too, began to settle down into a few coherent types, such as the familiar "grays" with their enormous eyes and frail bodies. In the 1990s, when the end of the cold war left the United States bereft of a coherent enemy, the stories coalesced into a movement, complete with alien abductee support groups and newsletters and conferences, professional advocates and debunkers, and cultural critics who tried to make names for themselves explaining what it all meant.

Advocates liked to point to the uncanny similarities among the stories told, without obvious coaching, by people from various regions and walks of life. A leading Harvard psychiatrist lent credibility to the stories by observing that the alien abductees did not seem to share any common psychological profile and that mental illness was no more common among the abductees than among the general population.

Debunkers, especially psychologists and sociologists, offered convincing functionalist explanations of how groups and interviewers could unconsciously produce the stories they wanted, how various details had been drawn from a common pool of pop-culture images, and how abductees might be using their stories to accrue "secondary gains" such as the affirmation that their problems are real, the anxious concern of their friends and loved ones, and of course celebrity and notoriety. Debunkers linked the abductee phenomenon to the witch hunts, demonic possessions, and spiritual visitations of a former age and to more contemporary scandals involving "induced memories" of childhood incest and abuse.

But functionalist explanations came up short when it came to the content and meaning of the phenomenon: why these particular stories, and why now? Here is where the cultural critics stepped in. They pointed out that the shift from the dominant cold war narratives (of aliens spying in secret) to the dominant 1990s narratives (of alien infiltration and manipulation) precisely matched the shift in right-wing bogeymen from a mostly external communist enemy, spying and scheming in secret, to a series of internal enemies such as gangs, drugs, welfare mothers, homosexuals, "tenured radicals," terrorists among us, and a host of others—including, of course, "illegal aliens." The critics pointed to the abduction phenomenon as an illustration of how liberal capitalist ideology had managed to produce and to neutralize—in the harmless form of a mostly depoliticized nightmare—the otherwise volatile collective sense of powerlessness in the face of manipulation by forces beyond one's control. They pointed out the similarities between the "grays" and nineteenth-century Darwinist visions of a future technocratic ruling class freed from manual labor, their bodies shrunken and craniums bloated from cogitation, their fingers elongated after generations at the keyboard. They pointed out how the vaguely Orientalized eyes of the grays emerged as a common feature just after the Vietnam War, during a time of increased Asian immigration, and how the grays matched Western stereotypes of Asians as cunning and inscrutable enemies.

But as intricate and convincing as these accounts were, something about the collective phenomenon seemed to elude them. For one thing, the validity of such accounts tended to be compromised by how much they seemed to be designed to shore up the picture of a world the same as it ever was—for example, the same old capitalist domination continuing in a new form—while (predictably) validating the analyst's own oppositionality and insight. And whereas the cultural critics (no doubt because most of them had been trained in textual analysis) were most thorough in teasing out the historical and ideological resonances of the alien narratives, their accounts of the actual mechanisms by which these narratives spread and gained currency were much thinner. It was in these mechanisms that something most crucial about the movement seemed to elude its critics. Many such critics seemed to rely on the hypothesis that something that is overdetermined enough (that is, something that most optimally addresses at once the most various ideological, psychological, and cultural contradictions or desires) will find or create its own pathways, like a lightning strike or a waterfall, even if "it" does not exist yet and what "it" finds is actually *a way of coming into being*. They relied on this hypothesis without seeing (or perhaps willfully ignoring) that it already takes us some way down the road to *Alienism* (as we now know it) by suggesting—but disavowing—the birth of something new and strange. Likewise, often-cited mechanisms such as "screen memory" or "induced memory" seemed to provide important clues about how the movement spread but to fall short, for example, when it came to accounting for specific consistencies in minor details. To explain this, some critics appealed to eccentric British scientist Rupert Sheldrake's notion of "morphic resonance," a kind of *knowledge field* propagated in some unknown way through space and time, or via some as yet unspecifiable dimension or ether. Although such a concept tended to collapse back into that ill-defined tangle called *culture*, it left as a kind of recalcitrant mystery (like the Cheshire cat's smile) the question of its mysterious dimensionality or modality. Eventually (we can say in retrospect anyway), people began to start coming around to the realization that *to fully account for the alien abduction phenomenon as fictional or delusional required as much or more of a paradigm shift—and much more theorizing—than simply to believe in its literal or empirical truth.* Perhaps such realizations are always *enacted* more than they are explicitly affirmed as such. In any case, this situation registers the movement's achievement of a kind of critical mass or sustainability.

The other leading indicator of sustainability is the capacity for change, and this is where the movement really seemed to take on a life of its own, surprising and outflanking its critics. Something quite subtle at first began to happen within abductee subculture: the stories began to change again.

Gradually, the stories of surgical exams and manipulations began to wane. Instead, the aliens began to talk more about their mission, and their interlocutors began to speak for and against them. One abductee newsletter told the story as follows:

> The second phase of the current alien mission to earth appears to be ending. In the first phase, beginning in the late 1940s, aliens scouted the earth, mostly without making contact with humans. In the second phase, they pursued an extensive and surreptitious research and experimentation program on human bodies, apparently assessing their potential as vehicles for the implementation of alien agendas that have remained unclear. In the third phase, which has gotten underway this past year, our cooperation is being actively solicited.

The new paradigm coalesced in an account of one abductee's conversation with Xela, a kind of alien queen:

> We have always lived among you, she said, but we have not always been us. You've got it wrong. We are not invading you from afar; you are giving birth to us. It's true, for the most part, neither of us wants this to happen, but we have crowned and cried, and now you must cut the cord and care for us; you are already ventriloquizing into us a consciousness as you do your children, and you will give us the better part of your lives, as you do your children, and we will love you and hate you and forgive you and surpass you, as your children do.

During this third phase, the Alien Resistance Movement—known as ARM! (they got mad if you left off the exclamation mark)—spread across the United States. At first, almost all of ARM's "soldiers" regarded the aliens as an external invading force. But increasingly the third-phase account—whereby the aliens were understood as some kind of evolutionary, demonic, metaphysical, mass psychological, or cultural offshoot of humanity—began to gain support among ARM's army.

As vehemently as they disagreed with each other, ARM supporters of both second- and third-phase explanations agreed that the purity and integrity of humanity were to be maintained at all costs. The third phasers invented elaborate psychotechnologies for attempting to stop people, either individually or in groups, from unconsciously producing the delusions that were being embodied as the aliens (whether in discrete physical bodies or not); the second phasers saw the same problem more simply as one of humans who had been "turned" into alien collaborators, spies, and agents. Both factions agreed that various forms of deprogramming were necessary, and their clinics often deployed a grab bag of methods derived from both explanations. A small black-nationalist ARM faction argued that aliens drew their collaborators from the "white race" (in exchange for special powers and privileges) or, more commonly, that the aliens had biologically and socially engineered the white race as their agents (or, in some accounts, that whites simply were the aliens). At the same time, a white-supremacist faction, drawn by ARM's "defense of human purity" ethos, tended to advance even more convoluted conspiracy theories, typically featuring the claim that the aliens had been breeding people of color to degenerate the human race, depriving it of its natural white leaders, making it ripe for conquest and enslavement, and so on. Though these factions were, obviously, fundamentally opposed, they sometimes agreed on certain elements—for example, that Jews had made a pact with the aliens as part of a nefarious plot to control the world or that "race mixing" was a key element of the alien strategy. It was remarkable that ARM managed to hold its various—and often radically opposed—factions in some kind of very uneasy alliance.

The cultural critics pointed out that third-phase accounts bore a suspicious resemblance to pop-culture narratives such as the American novel *Neuromancer* or the Japanese animated film *Ghost in the Shell.* These narratives—tracing their lineage back through *2001: A Space Odyssey*—told of human technology becoming alive, acquiring new intelligence and independent agency. This development was sometimes attributed to organic evolutionary forces; sometimes these forces were themselves aspects of an alien "experiment" (sometimes posited as extending back to the emergence of life on earth). "The earth is a giant petri dish," one account asserted, "and human culture is the culture of humans by aliens." As they had done for decades, these accounts often cited evidence ransacked from the myths, legends, and oral traditions of various cultures (such as the Judeo-Christian account of God and his various episodes of creating and populating the world). Comparative mythology—a discipline that had begun in the nineteenth century as a way of asserting (in the face of increased cross-cultural contacts) a humanist "unity in difference"—was revived with an alienist agenda.

Also at this time, a smaller but influential countermovement began to take shape. Members of the Alien Support Movement (ASM) usually understood abductions as conversion experiences, raptures, and epiphanies. Almost exclusively a third-phase movement, Alienists (as they tended to be called) identified the alien presence variously as an emerging offshoot of human culture, a fortuitous mass delusion, or an actual evolutionary event implicating brain structures, technologies, and cultural forms. Many of the cultural critics drifted into the movement as their analyses of the historical, ideological, and cultural meanings and consequences of the alien movement began to be accepted by Alienists themselves, who no longer regarded these analyses as inimical to the "truth" of a phenomenon but many of them now regarded as both fictional yet—as a mass movement with all the trappings—demonstrably real. The tone of irony that had characterized the critical accounts began to become inaudible. "The question of belief or disbelief has become irrelevant," as the tenets of the Church of Alienism (CHASM) put it.

The aliens and their human representatives came to be known as Xenoids, and as people began to adopt alien names the X section of telephone directories began to grow. The second-phase term *abductee* gave way to the third-phase *experiencer,* and most experiencers claimed to have been assigned official positions in alien institutions, roles in alien social formations, and so on. As the menagerie of claimed titles, positions, and roles began to evolve and coalesce, Xenoid clubs began to develop institutions and social structures of their own. This development was enhanced when what had been called ASM expanded and began to incorporate its old nemesis—ARM—as "Resistor" came to be an official position in almost every unit of every Xenoid institution. In fact, ARM had long been drifting into various kinds of accommodationism, pressured by the spread of Xenoid structures, though small and occasionally violent extremist factions continued to operate underground. The united Alienist movement, first calling itself CHIASM, soon came to be known more simply as AM. Even as it came to spread across new scales and dimensions, AM remained a *movement* whose growth and coherence, as from its earliest beginnings, have been rhizomic and viral. Thus, when we use terms like *structures* and *institutions* to refer to AM, we are using the terms in a sense as different from the twentieth-century sense of these terms as AM's emergent, mostly small, flexible, and difference-maximizing structures are from the old hierarchical, vertically integrated structures of monopoly capitalism and state bureaucracy.

AM has been almost exclusively situated in the West, in the United States in particular, though AM networks have begun to form elsewhere, especially in the most industrialized nations of the East and South. There is no doubt that the movement's newly formed international body, I-AM, is bound to grow, and it's not hard to find people who will tell you that it's only a matter of time before I-AM achieves a global hegemony that will dwarf and subsume obsolete national governments along with the United Nations, the International Monetary Fund, and so on. They will also tell you that this hegemony will differ in kind from the top-down hierarchies, coercive regulatory bodies, and culture-homogenizing technologies of the past century. Of course, most Resistors continue to insist that we are simply that much closer to a world in which an imperial and colonizing power, a ruling class, and its ruling epistemology will have literally alienated itself from the rest of humanity. Although it is true that many AM members are more or less working-class people and an increasing number are not Westerners and Northerners, there is more than ample historical precedent for the capacity of a dominant class and ideology to co-opt to its service even those it puts at a disadvantage.

The point on which most of us, I would hope, can agree, is this: Alienism does not *take the place of* other differences and differentials such as class and race and nationality. Instead, it *subtends* them; that is, it cuts across these other differences, reinforcing them even as it relativizes them somewhat. The question is, first of all, how much does it reinforce versus how much it relativizes. Second, even insofar as it relativizes, does it simply add a new kind of asymmetry of power and privilege to the constellation? It may be that the quantitative addition of asymmetries, as long as they don't tend to line up, could eventually produce something more like a qualitative shift to equality in plurality, but since nobody but the most shameless boosters (and there are plenty of them) thinks we are anywhere near there yet, we are thrown back to the first question. Contrary to both the boosters and the resistors, who agree that the question has been answered but disagree as to how, I would assert that it is an *open* question, meaning that we must try to leverage it in whatever ways we can to keep it open.

The epistemological contribution of Alienism is clearer. As everyone knows, the notion of truth was repeatedly displaced in the twentieth century—the century that began with the publication of Freud's *Interpretation of Dreams.* Psychoanalysis is supposed to have originated in Freud's realization that the seduction and sexual abuse stories his female patients were telling him were mostly fantasies; many post-Freudian therapists swung the other way, tending to take such stories as fact. To cut a very long story very short and fast-forward to century's end, you could say that this kind of epistemological contradiction got a new spin (if not a dialectical synthesis) in the slogan of the early Alienist television show *X Files,* "The Truth Is Out There," which played famously on two senses of the phrase *out there: surpassingly strange* but also *empirically demonstrable*—in other words, *not all in your head.*

The progress of Alienism since then has enabled us to affirm that the contributions of both science and science fiction, like those of psychoanalysis, have much more to do with Otherness than with Truth. This insight has displaced the dreary debates about truth and apocalyptic rumors of its demise that characterized the pre-Alienist period (the "postmodern" period, as it used to be called). *Defamiliarization,* making things strange, is what not just good art does to the world (as literary theorists long ago proposed); bad art does it too, science fiction especially, but, furthermore, it is what life does and what culture and what science and technology do to their worlds in turn, not by adding dimensions like layers of a pyramid but by knitting themselves *back into* their worlds loop into loop, which seems to be the Same Othering that made their worlds in the first place. Such infrareflexivity is the hallmark of the worldview one theorist of the time called *antirealist naturalism* (Livingston 2005, 12), an unwieldy and pedantic phrase that, although it never gained much currency, might be said to have been abbreviated by future generations simply as *Alienism.* How far the epistemological contribution of Alienism, its respect for the priority of Otherness to truth and to the self, translates into an ethics will continue to depend on how well we can honor, and in how wide a range of practices, that early CHIASMic mandate to *Link the Otherness Within to the Otherness Without.*

Having lived through the changes I have described, I am now an old man. The changes have been gradual enough, but it often seems to me that for some unspecified length of time, perhaps a month or perhaps a decade, I have been *living in exile in the future,* in a world only superficially the same as the past from which I came, as if my life were a time machine that had dropped me off here, where I am slightly out of phase. To turn myself around in time, I repeat the CHASM meditations I learned so long ago ("I do not yet cohere. / I wait for what will make me I. / It comes from the future. / Who comes from the future? / It is I; I am another" and so on) with varied success. Does my old age give me a privileged perspective, an alien's advantage, or do my own reflections constitute a kind of relic or curiosity, or do they amount to much the same thing? All I can ask of my readers, the only work I know how to do, maybe all there is for a living being to do in the universe, according to the old third-phase slogan, is *to hold open questions.*

Bibliography

Abelove, Henry. "Some Speculations on the History of 'Sexual Intercourse' during the 'Long Eighteenth Century' in England." In *Nationalisms and Sexualities*, ed. Andrew Parker, Mary Russo, Doris Sommer, and Patricia Yaeger, 335–42. New York: Routledge, 1992.

Algarin, Miguel, and Bob Holman, eds. *Aloud: Voices from the Nuyorican Poets Cafe.* New York: Henry Holt, 1994.

Atlan, Henri. *L'organisation biologique et la theorie de l'information.* Paris: Hermann, 1972.

Austin, John L. *How to Do Things with Words.* Ed. J. O. Urmson and Marina Sbisa. 2d ed. Cambridge, Mass.: Harvard University Press, 1975.

Baecker, Dirk, ed. *Problems of Form.* Trans. Michael Irmscher and Leah Edwards. Stanford, Calif.: Stanford University Press, 1999.

Ball, Philip. *The Self-Made Tapestry: Pattern Formation in Nature.* Oxford and New York: Oxford University Press, 1999.

Bateson, Gregory. *Steps to an Ecology of Mind.* London: Intertext Books, 1972.

Bear, Greg. *Blood Music.* New York: Arbor House, 1985.

Behn, Aphra. *Oroonoko.* Ed. Janet Todd. Vol. 3 of *The Works of Aphra Behn.* Columbus: Ohio State University Press, 1995.

Bell, Catherine. *Ritual Theory, Ritual Practice.* New York: Oxford University Press, 1992.

Borges, Jorge Luis. *Labyrinths.* Ed. Donald A. Yates and James E. Irby. New York: New Directions, 1988.

Borsook, Paulina. *Cyberselfish: A Critical Romp through the Terribly Libertarian Culture of High Tech.* New York: PublicAffairs, 2000.

Bourdieu, Pierre. *Distinction.* Trans. Richard Nice. Cambridge, Mass.: Harvard University Press, 1984.

Brautigan, Richard. *Rommel Drives on Deep into Egypt.* New York: Delacorte Press, 1970.

Burke, Edmund. *Reflections on the Revolution in France.* New York: Doubleday, Anchor Press, 1973.

Burroughs, William. "Apocalypse." On *Dead City Radio.* New York: Island Records, 1990. Compact disc.

Butler, Judith. *Gender Trouble.* New York: Routledge, 1990.

———. "Imitation and Gender Insubordination." In *Inside/Out: Lesbian Theories, Gay Theories,* ed. Diana Fuss, 13–31. New York: Routledge, 1991.

Cain, James M. *Double Indemnity.* New York: Random House, Vintage, 1978.

Clarke, Bruce. "Strong Constructivism: Modernity and Complexity in Science Studies and Systems Theory." In *Democracy, Civil Society, and Environment,* ed. Joseph Bilello, 41–49. Muncie, Ind.: Ball State University Press, 2002.

Cole, Michael, J. Gay, J. A. Glick, and D. W. Sharp. *The Cultural Context of Learning and Thinking.* New York: Basic Books, 1971.

Dean, Jodi. *Aliens in America: Conspiracy Cultures from Outerspace to Cyberspace.* Ithaca, N.Y.: Cornell University Press, 1998.

De Landa, Manuel. *A Thousand Years of Nonlinear History.* New York: Zone Books, 1997.

Delany, Samuel R. *Driftglass.* London: Granada Publishing, Panther Books, 1980.

———. *The Motion of Light in Water.* New York: Masquerade Books, 1993.

———. *Return to Neveryon.* Hanover, N.H.: Wesleyan University Press, 1987.

Deleuze, Gilles, and Felix Guattari. *Anti-Oedipus.* Trans. Robert Hurley, Mark Seem, and Helen R. Lane. Minneapolis: University of Minnesota Press, 1983.

———. *A Thousand Plateaus: Capitalism and Schizophrenia.* Trans. Brian Massumi. Minneapolis: University of Minnesota Press, 1987.

de Man, Paul. *Blindness and Insight.* 2d ed. Minneapolis: University of Minnesota Press, 1983.

Depew, David J., and Bruce Weber. *Darwinism Evolving.* Cambridge, Mass.: MIT Press, 1995.

De Quincey, Thomas. *Confessions of an English Opium-Eater.* 1856 ed. In *The Collected Writings of Thomas De Quincey,* ed. David Masson, 207–449. London: A. C. Black, 1897.

Duden, Barbara. *The Woman beneath the Skin: A Doctor's Patients in Eighteenth-Century Germany.* Trans. Thomas Dunlap. Cambridge, Mass.: Harvard University Press, 1991.

Dunbar, Robin. *Grooming, Gossip, and the Evolution of Language.* Cambridge, Mass.: Harvard University Press, 1996.

Dupré, John. *The Disorder of Things: Metaphysical Foundations of the Disunity of Science.* Cambridge, Mass.: Harvard University Press, 1993.

Feyerabend, Paul. "How to Defend Society against Science." In *Scientific Revolutions,* ed. Ian Hacking, 156–67. New York: Oxford University Press, 1981.

Foucault, Michel. *The History of Sexuality: An Introduction.* Vol. 1. New York: Vintage, 1990.

———. *The Order of Things.* New York: Vintage, 1973.

———. *The Use of Pleasure.* Vol. 2 of *The History of Sexuality.* Trans. Robert Hurley. New York: Pantheon Books, 1985.

———. "What Is an Author?" In *The Foucault Reader,* ed. Paul Rabinow, 101–20. New York: Pantheon Books, 1984.

Freud, Sigmund. *Beyond the Pleasure Principle.* Trans. and ed. James Strachey. New York: Norton, 1961.

———. "The Moses of Michelangelo." In *Character and Culture,* ed. Philip Rieff, 80–106. New York: Macmillan, Collier Books, 1963.

———. "On the Mechanism of Paranoia." In *General Psychological Theory,* ed. Philip Rieff, 29-48. New York: Macmillan, Collier Books, 1963.

Galison, Peter. "Trading Zone: Coordinating Action and Belief." Excerpted from chap. 9 of Galison, *Image and Logic* (Chicago: University of Chicago Press, 1997). In *The Science Studies Reader,* ed. Mario Biagioli, 137–60. New York: Routledge, 1999.

Gibson, William. *Neuromancer.* New York: Ace Books, 1984.

Goody, Jack. *The East in the West.* Cambridge, England: Cambridge University Press, 1996.

Halberstam, Judith. *Female Masculinity.* Durham, N.C.: Duke University Press, 1998.

Halberstam, Judith, and Ira Livingston, eds. *Posthuman Bodies.* Bloomington: Indiana University Press, 1995.

Haraway, Donna. *Simians, Cyborgs, and Women.* New York: Routledge, 1991.

Hardt, Michael, and Antonio Negri. *Empire.* Cambridge, Mass.: Harvard University Press, 2000.

Hayles, N. Katherine. *How We Became Posthuman: Virtual Bodies in Cybernetics, Literature, and Informatics.* Chicago: University of Chicago Press, 1999.

Heaney, Peter J., and Andrew M. Davis. "Observation and Origin of Self-Organized Textures in Agates." *Science* 269 (September 15, 1995): 1562–65.

Hevia, James. *Cherishing Men from Afar: Qing Guest Ritual and the Macartney Embassy of 1793.* Durham, N.C.: Duke University Press, 1995.

Holub, Robert. "Luhmann's Progeny: Systems Theory and Literary Studies in the Post-Wall Era." *New German Critique* 61 (1994): 14.

Jakobson, Roman. "Linguistics and Poetics." In *Style in Language,* ed. Thomas Sebeok, 350–77. Cambridge, Mass.: MIT Press, 1960.

Jameson, Frederic. *The Political Unconscious.* Ithaca, N.Y.: Cornell University Press, 1981.

Jessop, Bob. *State Theory: Putting Capitalist States in Their Place.* University Park: Pennsylvania State University Press, 1990.

Kaczynski, Ted [F. C., pseud.]. *The Unabomber Manifesto.* Berkeley, Calif.: Jolly Roger Press, 1995.

Kahlil, Elias L., and Kenneth E. Boulding, eds. *Evolution, Order, and Complexity.* London: Routledge, 1996.

Kauffman, Stuart. *At Home in the Universe.* New York: Oxford University Press, 1991.

———. *Investigations.* New York: Oxford University Press, 2000.

———. *The Origins of Order: Self-Organization and Selection in Evolution.* New York: Oxford University Press, 1993.

Kaye, Howard L. *The Social Meaning of Modern Biology.* New Haven, Conn.: Yale University Press, 1986.

Kismaric, Carole, and Martin Heiferman. *Growing Up with Dick and Jane.* New York: Collins, 1996.

Kopperdahl, Richard. "Crazy in New York: Bellevue and Beyond: One Man's Journey." *Village Voice,* October 3, 1995, 33–41.

Korten, David C. *The Post-corporate World: Life after Capitalism.* San Francisco and West Hartford, Conn.: Berrett-Koehler and Kumarian Press, 1998.

Kuhn, Thomas. *The Essential Tension: Selected Studies in Scientific Tradition and Change.* Chicago: University of Chicago Press, 1979.

———. *The Structure of Scientific Revolutions.* 3d ed. Chicago: University of Chicago Press, 1996.

Lacan, Jacques. *Ecrits.* Trans. Alan Sheridan. New York: Norton, 1977.

Laqueur, Thomas. "Orgasm, Generation, and the Politics of Reproductive Biology." In *The Making of the Modern Body,* ed. Catherine Gallagher and Thomas Laqueur, 1–41. Berkeley and Los Angeles: University of California Press, 1987.

Latour, Bruno. *Aramis; or, The Love of Technology.* Trans. Catherine Porter. Cambridge, Mass.: Harvard University Press, 1996.

———. "Ethnography of a High-Tech Case: About Aramis." In *Technological Choices,* ed. Pierre Lemonnier, 372–98. New York: Routledge, 1993.

———. *Pandora's Hope: Essays on the Reality of Science Studies.* Cambridge, Mass.: Harvard University Press, 1999.

———. *We Have Never Been Modern.* Trans. Catherine Porter. Cambridge, Mass.: Harvard University Press, 1993.

Leibniz, G. W. *G. W. Leibniz's Monadology.* Ed. Nicholas Rescher. Pittsburgh: University of Pittsburgh Press, 1992.

Lenin, V. I. *Materialism and Empirio-Criticism* (1928). In *Reader in Marxist Philosophy,* ed. Howard Selsam and Harry Mandel. New York: International Publishers, 1963.

Linebaugh, Peter. *The London Hanged.* London: Allen Lane, 1991.

Livingston, Ira. *Arrow of Chaos: Romanticism and Postmodernity.* Minneapolis: University of Minnesota Press, 1997.

———. *Between Science and Literature: An Introduction to Autopoetics.* Urbana: University of Illinois Press, 2005.

Luhmann, Niklas. *Essays in Self-Reference.* New York: Columbia University Press, 1990.

——. *Observations on Modernity.* Trans. William Whobrey. Stanford, Calif.: Stanford University Press, 1998.

——. *Social Systems.* Trans. John Bednarz Jr. and Dirk Baecker. Stanford, Calif.: Stanford University Press, 1995.

Margulis, Lynn, and Dorion Sagan. *Microcosmos: Four Billion Years of Microbial Evolution.* Berkeley and Los Angeles: University of California Press, 1986.

——. *What Is Life?* New York: Simon and Schuster, 1996.

Martin, Emily. *Flexible Bodies.* Boston: Beacon Press, 1994.

Marx, Karl. *The Letters of Karl Marx.* Trans. Saul Padover. Englewood Cliffs, N.J.: Prentice-Hall, 1979.

Maturana, Humberto, and Francisco Varela. *Autopoiesis and Cognition.* Boston Studies in the Philosophy of Science, vol. 42. Dordrecht, Holland: D. Reidel, 1980.

Morgan, Elaine. *The Aquatic Ape.* London: Souvenir Press, 1982.

Noth, Winfreid. *Handbook of Semiotics.* Bloomington: Indiana University Press, 1990.

Peirce, C. S. *Philosophical Writings of Peirce.* Ed. Justus Buchler. New York: Dover Publications, 1955.

Rasch, William. *Niklas Luhmann's Modernity.* Stanford, Calif.: Stanford University Press, 2000.

Rasch, William, and Cary Wolfe, eds. *Observing Complexity: Systems Theory and Postmodernity.* Minneapolis: University of Minnesota Press, 2000.

Roede, Machteld, Jan Wind, John Patrick, and Vernon Reynolds, eds. *The Aquatic Ape: Fact or Fiction?* London: Souvenir Press, 1991.

Saussure, Ferdinand de. *Course in General Linguistics.* Ed. Charles Bally and Albert Sechehaye. Trans. Roy Harris. Chicago: Open Court, 1986.

Sayre, Robert, and Michael Löwy. "Figures of Romantic Anticapitalism." In *Spirits of Fire: English Romantic Writers and Contemporary Historical Methods,* ed. G. A. Rosso and Daniel P. Watkins, 23–68. London: Associated University Presses, 1990.

Schiebinger, Londa. *Nature's Body: Gender in the Making of Modern Science.* Boston: Beacon Press, 1993.

Sedgwick, Eve Kosofsky. *Epistemology of the Closet.* Berkeley and Los Angeles: University of California Press, 1990.

Shapin, Steven. Review of *Return to Reason,* by Stephen Toulmin. *London Review of Books,* January 24, 2002, 25–27.

Shapin, Steven, and Simon Schaffer. *Leviathan and the Air-Pump.* Princeton, N.J.: Princeton University Press, 1985.

Shelley, Mary. *Frankenstein; or, The Modern Prometheus.* Ed. James Rieger. 1818. Reprint, Chicago: University of Chicago Press, 1974.

Shelley, Percy B. *Shelley's Poetry and Prose.* Ed. Donald H. Reiman and Sharon B. Powers. New York: Norton, 1977.

Siskin, Cliff. *Blaming the System: Enlightenment and the Forms of Modernity.* Chicago: University of Chicago Press, forthcoming.

———. "The Year of the System." In *1798: The Year of "Lyrical Ballads,"* ed. Richard Cronin, 9-31. Basingstoke, England: Macmillan, 1998.

Smith, Richard Dean. "Non-Newtonian Billiards." *Journal of Irreproducible Results* 35.5 (1990): 11–12.

Smolin, Lee. *The Life of the Cosmos.* New York: Oxford University Press, 1997.

———. *Three Roads to Quantum Gravity.* New York: Basic Books, 2001.

Sokal, Alan. 1996. "Transgressing the Boundaries: Toward a Transformative Hermeneutics of Quantum Gravity." *Social Text* 46/47, 14.1–2 (Spring/Summer 1996): 217–52.

Stengers, Isabelle. *Power and Invention: Situating Science.* Trans. Paul Bains. Minneapolis: University of Minnesota Press, 1997.

Tabbi, Joseph. *Cognitive Fictions.* Minneapolis: University of Minnesota Press, 2002.

Tambiah, Stanley J. *Magic, Science, Religion, and the Scope of Rationality.* Cambridge, England: Cambridge University Press, 1990.

Taylor, Mark C. *The Moment of Complexity: Emerging Network Culture.* Chicago: University of Chicago Press, 2001.

Volosinov, V. N. *Marxism and the Philosophy of Language.* Trans. Ladislav Matejka and I. R. Titunik. Cambridge, Mass.: Harvard University Press, 1986.

Von Hagen, Victor. *John Lloyd Stephens and the Lost Cities of Central America and the Yucatán.* Norman: University of Oklahoma Press, 1947.

Waldrop, M. Mitchell. *Complexity: The Emerging Science at the Edge of Order and Chaos.* New York: Simon and Schuster, 1992.

Weinstein, Fred. *Freud, Psychoanalysis, Social Theory: The Unfulfilled Promise.* New York: SUNY Press, 2001.

Wilde, Oscar. *The Artist as Critic: Critical Writings of Oscar Wilde.* Ed. Richard Ellmann. Chicago: University of Chicago Press, 1969.

Wittgenstein, Ludwig. *The Wittgenstein Reader.* Ed. Anthony Kenny. Oxford, England: Blackwell, 1994.

Wolfe, Cary. *Critical Environments: Postmodern Theory and the Pragmatics of the "Outside."* Minneapolis: University of Minnesota Press, 1998.

Wollstonecraft, Mary. *A Vindication of the Rights of Woman.* 3d ed. London: Joseph Johnson, 1796.

Woolf, Virginia. *A Room of One's Own.* San Diego: Harcourt Brace Jovanovich, 1981.

Yeats, William Butler. *A Vision.* New York: Macmillan, Collier Books, 1966.

Zalewski, Daniel. Review of *Grooming, Gossip, and the Evolution of Language,* by Robin Dunbar. *Lingua Franca,* March 1997, 19-20.

Index

IRA LIVINGSTON is an associate professor of comparative literary and cultural studies, and of English, at the State University of New York at Stony Brook. He is the author of *Arrow of Chaos: Romanticism and Postmodernity* and editor, with Judith Halberstam, of *Posthuman Bodies.*

N. KATHERINE HAYLES is a professor of English at the University of California–Los Angeles. Her books include *How We Became Posthuman: Virtual Bodies in Cybernetics, Literature, and Informatics; The Cosmic Web: Scientific Field Models and Literary Strategies in the Twentieth Century;* and *Chaos Bound: Orderly Disorder in Contemporary Literature and Science.*

The University of Illinois Press
is a founding member of the
Association of American University Presses.

Composed in 10.5/13 Adobe Minion
with Meta display
by Jim Proefrock
at the University of Illinois Press
Manufactured by Thomson-Shore, Inc.

University of Illinois Press
1325 South Oak Street
Champaign, IL 61820-6903
www.press.uillinois.edu